The Business Environment

Related titles in the series

Advertising
Book-keeping
Business and Commercial Law
Business and the European Community
Business Studies
Business French (book/cassette pack)
Business German (book/cassette pack)
Business Italian (book/cassette pack)
Commerce
Economics
English for Business
Financial Management
Information Technology
Management Theory and Practice
Marketing
Office Procedures
Organizations and Management
Spreadsheet Skills (including free disk)
Statistics for Business
Teeline Shorthand
Typing
Wordprocessing Skills (including free disk)

Books by the same author

Answer the Question: Get the Job!
The Barclays Guide to Managing Staff for the Small Business
The Business Organisation
The Business Planner: A Complete Guide to Raising Finance
Correct Letters
Franchising: A Practical Guide for Franchisors and Franchisees
Getting a Result
How to Buy and Run a Shop
How to Organise a Conference
How to Recruit
How to Win at Interviews
How to Win at Job Hunting
The Perfect Conference
Running a Successful Advertising Campaign
Using Direct Mail
Using Exhibitions
Using Press Advertising
Using Radio Advertising

The Business Environment

Iain Maitland

MADE SIMPLE
B O O K S

To Tracey, Michael and Sophie

Made Simple
An imprint of Butterworth-Heinemann Ltd
Linacre House, Jordan Hill, Oxford OX2 8DP

A member of the Reed Elsevier plc group

OXFORD LONDON BOSTON
MUNICH NEW DELHI SINGAPORE SYDNEY
TOKYO TORONTO WELLINGTON

First published 1994

British Library Cataloguing in Publication Data
Maitland, Iain
  The Business Environment
  I. Title
  658

ISBN 0 7506 0954 0

Printed and bound in Great Britain by Clays, St Ives plc

Contents

Preface

The Business Environment is written for you – the student studying a business-orientated course at GCSE, A, GNVQ2, GNVQ3 or GNVQ4 level, or for a degree or professional examination. It is a clear and straightforward guide which looks at the key topics and themes relating to businesses and their relationships with their environment. Individual courses and examinations are forever changing in terms of names, contents and approaches, but this book deals with subjects of perennial and universal interest, giving you a broad, all purpose understanding of the business environment which can be applied to any relevant course, whatever its status.

Part One: Business Organizations takes an overview of the businesses which operate within the business environment. Types of Business considers sole traders, partnerships, private and public limited companies, cooperatives and other organizations. Business Structures explains the different types of structure that exist as well as who's who in a business, principles, practices and relationships and the use of organization charts. Business Activities contemplates business objectives, how to trade successfully, business responsibilities and the decline of a business.

Part Two: Business Resources studies those essential resources which firms must use if they are to succeed. Financial Resources details calculating financial needs, types and sources of finance and raising, using and accounting for finance. Physical Resources discusses locating a business, choosing a property, selecting equipment, rights, duties and restrictions and disposing of physical resources. Human Resources examines recruiting staff, managing employees, ending employment, and employment laws.

Part Three: Business Markets moves into the marketplace where businesses use their resources and conduct their activities. Market Principles views demand, supply and the ways in which they interact to determine price. Forms of Market sets out the main markets in which businesses trade, namely perfectly competitive, monopolistically competitive, oligopoly and monopoly markets. Market Practices looks at the realities of business transactions along with consumer protection laws, competition policies and laws and regulatory bodies and their activities.

Part Four: The Local and National Environment takes a wider perspective of the business environment, with particular reference to the UK. The State considers the framework of the legislature, the executive and the judiciary and how they fit together. The Economy studies the UK's national income, the economic objectives of the government, the problems it faces and the policies it may pursue. The Population contemplates the size and structure of the UK population, along with its occupational and geographical distribution across the country.

Part Five: The International Environment broadens the scope of the book even further, to look out to Europe and beyond. The United Kingdom examines this country's role as a trading nation, detailing its exports, imports and balance of payments. Europe discusses the European Union, the Single Market, the European Monetary System, the European Free Trade Association, the European Economic Area Agreement and other international organizations and agreements. Trading Overseas ponders the do's and don't's for UK businesses venturing abroad – seeking information, selling overseas, signing contracts, handling documents and getting paid.

Supported by a wide and varied mix of relevant figures, charts and illustrations, backed up with useful rapid revision questions and answers and complete with further reading and useful addresses sections and a comprehensive glossary and index, this short and simple guide to the business environment provides you with a solid grounding in the subject for lower level courses, and a good introduction for higher level courses. Whatever your course, this book is right for you.

Iain Maitland

Acknowledgements

I wish to thank the following for their assistance during the compilation of this text:

Association of County Councils
Association of Exhibition Organisers
Barclays Bank plc
The Central Office of the Industrial Tribunals
The Commission for Racial Equality
The Cooperative Development Agency
The Department of Employment
The Department of Trade and Industry (Overseas Trade Division)
The Equal Opportunities Commission
The Health and Safety Executive
The Institute of Management
The Institute of Personnel and Development
The Law Society
The Office of Fair Trading
Suffolk Coastal District Council
Suffolk County Council

Part One
Business Organizations

1
Types of business

1.1 What is a business?

A business may be defined as 'an organization which produces and/
or distributes goods and/or services for profit'. Within this rather
broad and all purpose description, businesses can be classified in
various ways.

Legal status

Businesses can take one of several legal forms – a *sole trader* where
one person owns and runs the firm, a *partnership* in which two or
more people share ownership and control, a *private* or *public limited
company* where shareholders own the concern and a board of directors manages it and a *cooperative* which workers own and run on a
democratic basis.

Economic form

Alternatively, businesses can be grouped according to their economic
form. A *horizontal* business specializes in a single activity within the
production and distribution sequence, perhaps producing cakes. A
vertical firm combines two or more related activities within the chain,
such as milling flour and baking cakes. A *conglomerate* concern mixes
wholly unrelated activities, like producing cakes and providing insurance services!

Economic activity

Similarly, businesses may be classified with regard to their economic
activities. *Primary* firms are involved in the extraction of raw materials from above or below the ground, as in fishing, farming and mining.

Secondary concerns manufacture and process products, as in car and truck manufacturing and food processing. *Tertiary* firms supply services such as banking and retailing.

Other classifications

In addition to these three key areas, business can be classified in many other forms – by sales, profits, number of employees, share of the market, whether they trade locally, regionally, nationally or inter-nationally, and so on. There is really no limit to the ways in which firms can be compared and contrasted, grouped together here, separated there and so forth.

It is sensible to take an initial look at businesses according to their legal status – sole traders, partnerships and the like – before considering different aspects such as economic form, economic activity and other classifications. Then, other comparisons can be made between the various concerns, as summarized in Figure 1.1.

1.2   Sole traders

A sole trader, or sole proprietor, is a self-employed person who owns and controls his or her own business. Typically, you will think of a window cleaner, a plumber or an electrician but a sole trader could also own a chain of shops, offices or factories, employing managers and staff to run them on a day-to-day basis. The sole trader makes all of the key decisions though, deciding what they want to do, and achieve. They finance the business, either from their own resources such as savings or ploughed back profits once they have started trading, or from elsewhere such as a loan from a bank or even Great Aunt Queenie! Their business may be run from home, a van or from other premises such as a shop or warehouse, with employees taken on, as necessary. If successful, the sole trader takes all of the profits. Unsuccessful, and they must deal with the losses.

Imagine that you are a sole trader – a freelance writer working from home and selling articles to newspapers and magazines, a mechanic operating a car repair business from the back of a van, a retailer running your own bookshop, or whatever you would most like to do. You can probably list the main benefits of being your own boss:

1   It is relatively easy to start trading – you might be able to begin today if you wanted to! There are few legal requirements – you may need a licence to run certain businesses such as a turf accountants or to sell particular goods such as alcohol. You could

	Sole trader	Partnership	Private limited company	Public limited company
Legal status				
Economic form	Horizontal/vertical/ conglomerate	Horizontal/vertical/ conglomerate	Horizontal/vertical/ conglomerate	Horizontal/vertical/ conglomerate
Economic activity	Primary/secondary/ tertiary	Primary/secondary/ tertiary	Primary/secondary/ tertiary	Primary/secondary/ tertiary
Sales	Limited, often to what one person can achieve on their own. Probably a five figure annual turnover	Difficult to quote an average – typically, a six figure sum for annual sales	Hard to assess, probably six figure sales each year	Extensive – hundreds of thousands or even millions of pounds a year
Profits	Slim, probably a bare living but no more. Less than an employee's wage sometimes!	Probably enough for a decent living for each partner, plus enough for growth	Hopefully enough to pay a good dividend on shares, with a balance for re-investment	Substantial – hundreds of thousands or even millions of pounds per annum
Number of owners	One only	2–20, often 2–6 to be at its best	2+, typically 6–12 in a family firm	2+, typically hundreds or more, even thousands
Number of employees	Some work alone. Others may employ a handful of staff	May employ a handful of people, sometimes more	Probably employs many, perhaps up to 100 or more	Will employ hundreds or more in most cases
Market share	Very small, with little influence	Small, but may have some influence	Small, but with some influence	Large – may well dominate
Trading area	Usually local, or regional at best	Local or regional	May be local, regional or national	National or international
Key advantage	Absolute control	Shared skills and responsibility	Limited liability	Limited liability
Key disadvantage	Unlimited liability	Unlimited liability	Separation of ownership and control	Separation of ownership and control

Figure 1.1 Forms of business: a quick comparison

require permission from the local authority if you wish to work from home, perhaps manufacturing items which might disturb your neighbours. If you intend to trade under a name other than your own, you will have to display a notice on your premises stating your full name and address and also provide this information on all correspondence and documents, so suppliers and customers know whom they are dealing with.

2   You have absolute control over every aspect of the concern, and do not have to share power or decision making with colleagues. As examples, you can choose where the business is based (town or country, high street or back street), when you trade (nine to five, eight 'til late), what you make, buy and sell (clothes, toys, books) and so on. It is up to you. Nevertheless, do be aware that other organizations and individuals will influence your decisions, sometimes quite strongly. Competitors may affect your choice of location, the local council could try to stop you opening on Sundays and customers will have a say in your stock selection – offer goods that they dislike, and they will not buy them!

3   You can operate a flexible business, which adapts quickly and easily to developing circumstances. Closely involved with all areas of the operation, you should be able to spot opportunities and problems at an early stage, making speedy decisions on your own and implementing changes to take advantage of or to resolve them, as appropriate. For example, if a new customer moves into the area, you can approach them personally to drum up business. Alternatively, the quality of goods supplied to you by a manufacturer may worsen suddenly, and you can switch rapidly to another supplier for future deliveries.

4   You can develop a leaner and more efficient concern, because of that hands on, day-to-day involvement with all aspects of it. You should be able to spot waste and inefficiency around you, whether that involves baking 100 pies when only 50 are sold, employing two part-time employees when only one of them is constantly busy, or whatever. You can remedy matters immediately to save money – your money – and to improve the business so far as you possibly can. The larger the business is, the harder it is to cut costs effectively, and have the business running at its most effective.

5   It is possible to keep your financial affairs private and confidential. Apart from your legal obligation to provide statements to the Inland Revenue for income tax purposes and to Customs and Excise for value added tax, your finances are your concern, and no-one else's. Only you know if you have made a profit, earned £5000 or £50 000 over the year, or have suffered a loss. Larger firms have a legal responsibility to publish their accounts for all to see. Thus, everyone can tell if they are doing well or badly and,

if they seem unsuccessful, suppliers and customers may be reluctant to deal with them in case they cease trading, leaving bills unpaid and goods undelivered.

6   You receive all of the profits of the firm, without having to share them with anyone. Clearly, this is a great incentive to work even harder and make more money, as you know that the skills, knowledge and endeavours that you put into the concern, will benefit you, and you alone. Of course, it is also entirely up to you how you spend the profits and you may choose to re-invest (some of) them in the business perhaps on new or better equipment and machinery or to withdraw them to spend on yourself and your family. That can be a tough decision to make.

Despite these benefits, there are also drawbacks involved in working on your own as a sole trader. Here are some of the most significant ones, which many people do not know about or think of until they begin trading:

1   You have limited skills, knowledge and experience as an individual which can make it difficult to start and run a successful business. You may be a brilliant window cleaner, electrician or writer but there is so much more to do than wiping windows, wiring plugs or stringing words and sentences together. You could also have to raise finance, select suitable premises, recruit quality staff, keep books and records, find good suppliers, sell to customers and so on. To succeed you have to be a Jack or Jacquie of all trades – and master or mistress of them all. There are so many tasks that take skills and expertise which you may not possess, and employing others to do them for you costs money which you might not be able to afford.

2   It is very hard work and far harder than being an employee. The hours will be long – you may have to deal with correspondence before starting work, labour all day through tea and lunch breaks to get the job done, and cash up and complete books and records in the evenings. Stock may have to be collected at weekends. It can be physically demanding. Making products can be painstaking and backbreaking work. Heavy goods may need to be loaded and unloaded regularly. Items might have to be maintained and repaired. It may be mentally demanding too – there is always something else to do, and so little time to do it, and it falls to you, and you alone, to sort it out.

3   It is difficult to expand a small, owner-operated business because you have limited resources at your disposal. As examples, you will probably have a modest sum of money to invest, and will be restricted in the additional amount that can be raised to fund growth. You can only do so many tasks yourself and one job at

a time, whether painting this house or that one, repairing this car or another one. You have limited skills and expertise too which can hinder expansion into other, potentially profitable activities. A sole trader who does manage to expand – opening another shop, office or whatever – will find that some tasks and responsibilities have to be handed over to other people and many of the advantages of sole trading such as absolute control, flexibility and efficiency will then be lost.

4   The business is almost inevitably dependent on you – if you are a plumber or a builder and take time off or fall sick then the business invariably grinds to a halt until you return from holiday or recover from your illness. If you die, it ceases to exist, perhaps with dire consequences for your dependents, who rely on you for financial support. Even if you operate a shop, office or factory and employ people, your absences will probably affect the smooth running of the operation and its activities. It may need to be sold if you die, unless someone is ready and able to step in and take over from you.

5   You are personally and fully responsible for the debts of your business. More formally known as *unlimited liability*, this means that if your venture fails and you cannot pay the bills, you may not only have to sell your business and all of its assets such as equipment and machinery but could also have to sell your home and other personal possessions such as your car, in order to settle the debts. Not surprisingly, knowing that you might lose everything – business *and* personal belongings – is enormously stressful. Many sole proprietors crack up under the strain.

1.3   Partnerships

The Partnership Act 1890 – still the most relevant legislation in the 1990s – defines a partnership as 'the relation which subsists between persons carrying on a business in common with a view of profit'. Thus, a partnership may comprise two people running a market stall in a car park or a large firm of solicitors in the high street – so long as it is a business (not a charity) and is trying to make a profit (even if it actually makes a loss!). The Act limits the number of people entering into partnership with each other to between two and 20, although there are exceptions in certain circumstances. Partners put in finance, share ownership and control and apportion the profits and losses between themselves, as appropriate.

Think what it would be like to go into partnership with other people – family, friends or business colleagues – in order to open a second shop, office, factory, or whatever. Work out what the advantages may be. These could include the following:

- The partners' names and addresses
- The partnership's name and address
- Its trade or profession
- The partners' capital investments
- Their responsibilities for investing further funds
- The ratio and method of sharing profits and losses
- The partners' management and work responsibilities
- Their salaries and other drawings
- Holiday and sickness arrangements
- The partnership's length
- The terms and conditions of withdrawing from the partnership
- The terms and conditions of selling shares of the partnership
- The grounds for dissolving the partnership
- The procedures following the permanent illness, retirement or death of any of the partners

Figure 1.2 Partnership agreement checklist

1 Like a sole trader, it is simple to commence trading as there are few legal formalities to comply with. However, it is sensible for anyone entering into a partnership to insist that a partnership agreement, or 'deed of partnership', is drawn up by a solicitor which sets out the exact rules and regulations of the partnership so that all of the partners know what they can and cannot do. A checklist of areas which need to be covered in this legally binding document is given in Figure 1.2.

2 Similarly, a partnership is usually a flexible concern as the partners' day-to-day dealings with all aspects of the firm's operation and activities enable them to recognize and adjust quickly to meet changing scenarios. Accordingly, it should also become a lean and efficient business, with the partners tackling any waste and inefficiency that they can see around them. It is in their interests to do so – it will cost them money if they do not, and might even undermine the financial stability of the concern.

3 Increased skills, knowledge and experience are made available to the business, making it more likely to succeed than a firm run by a sole proprietor with limited expertise. Partners can also concentrate on what they do best, whether bargaining with the bank manager or suppliers, selling to customers, keeping the books or

whatever. One partner's strengths may be complemented by another, their weaknesses covered by a third partner and so on – all to the overall advantage of the partnership.

4   The workload and responsibilities of the business can be shared out between the partners. The number of hours worked per partner should be less than for a sole trader, and days off and holidays can be taken, with the remaining partners covering for that person's absence so that the business continues without interruption. The stress and worry of self employment – will the bills be paid this month?, will sales pick up soon? and so forth – are also spread out between several people, all of whom can help to resolve these worries.

5   A partnership should find it easier to expand the business and its range of activities – more people means a greater breadth and depth of resources are available. For example, six partners should have more money between them to fund growth than a sole trader has, and ought to be capable of raising extra, additional sums if necessary. Some partners may have expertise in other regions, trades or industries should the partnership wish to open another outlet elsewhere, sell its goods into a different market or manufacture alternative products. A sole proprietor probably will not. If other outlets are opened, the partners can retain control, without having to hand over responsibility to managers and employees which they may prefer not to do.

6   As with a sole trader, a partnership is also able to conduct its financial affairs in a private and confidential manner, only sharing this information with Customs and Excise and the Inland Revenue – no-one else knows if the partnership is trading successfully or not. Thus, if the business is doing badly, it has a chance to improve its fortunes without suppliers and customers being aware of any difficulties, and possibly adding to them by tightening up on the terms of supplying goods, or by taking away their valuable custom, as appropriate.

Naturally, a partnership also has some disadvantages that need to be considered carefully. These are a few of the major ones that any prospective partner ought to mull over before going any further with their plans:

1   Partners have to share control of all aspects of the business with each other. Everyone has to have a say in where the firm is to be located, when it will open, what goods will be made, bought and sold, and so on. It can be very difficult to reach agreement on everything with any disagreements and ill feeling affecting the smooth running of the business. Differences can worsen over the years as partners want the firm to go in alternative directions –

one wishes to open more outlets, another wants to sell new products, a third prefers to stay the same, and so forth.

2   Profits must be shared out between the partners, either equally or in the proportions agreed in the deed of partnership which was (or should have been) signed before the business began operating. Problems can arise if one partner feels that another is not contributing as much to the business as they should be, while still obtaining a substantial share of the financial rewards. Also, partners may dispute what to do with any profits generated – one might want to buy or rent better premises, while others could wish to take out any surplus for their own private use.

3   Like a sole trader, a partnership has unlimited liability whereby partners are held personally responsible for all debts, and may be forced to sell their own personal belongings to meet any outstanding financial obligations which the business has been unable to settle in full. It is possible to set up and run a *limited partnership* where some partners have limited liability so that their responsibility for debts is limited to the amount of money they have invested in the partnership. If they put in £5000, they lose this, but no more. However, at least one partner has to have unlimited liability, and could therefore lose everything. It can be a huge worry, especially if you are that partner.

4   Partners are 'jointly and severally responsible' for each other's actions – whatever one partner does on behalf of the business is binding upon the other ones. This means that if a foolish or untrustworthy partner places a big order for raw materials that cannot be paid for or promises to supply a substantial quantity of finished goods at a ridiculously low price, his or her partners are tied to it, for better or for worse. Accordingly, if the partnership is unable to pay the bill or deliver the products, all of the partners must suffer the consequences. You could lose your home because of a partner's stupidity.

1.4   Private limited companies

A private limited company – identified by the word *limited* or the abbreviation *ltd* which must by law follow its name – is considered to be a separate, legal entity, distinct from its owners and able to trade in its own right. It is formed when at least two people put in money in exchange for shares in the company, which entitle them to a proportion of any profits that may be generated. These owners are known as *shareholders*, and they enjoy limited liability. They appoint a board of directors to administer the company for them and can vote to remove and replace any or all of the directors at an annual general meeting (AGM) when the board has to make a progress report to

- The name of the company – which must end with *limited* or *ltd* so that everyone is aware that the owners' liability is limited
- The address of the company's registered office – so that everyone knows where to send documents
- The objectives of the company – so that any prospective shareholders know what it can and cannot do
- The amount and type of shares to be issued
- The names of the first company director and secretary
- A statement that shareholders have limited liability
- An undertaking that the signatories wish to form the company and purchase shares

Figure 1.3   Memorandum of association checklist

- The procedures for calling meetings
- The rules and regulations of conducting meetings, and voting
- The methods of electing directors
- The rights and responsibilities of directors
- The rules and regulations regarding the transfer of shares – which must be conducted in private and with the consent of all shareholders of a private limited company
- The borrowing powers of the company

Figure 1.4   Articles of association checklist

them. In turn, the board appoints managers to carry out its policies on a daily basis.

To form a private limited company, the shareholders must register it with the Registrar of Companies which is the official body responsible to the government for maintaining a record of all companies operating in the UK. To do this, they must prepare various documents, the two most important of which are the *Memorandum of Association* and the *Articles of Association*. The Memorandum governs the relationship between the company and its environment, while the Articles set out the relationship between the company and its shareholders, and provides a framework for its internal affairs. Figures 1.3 and 1.4 detail the main contents of these important documents.

Once compiled, the Memorandum and Articles of Association are submitted to the Registrar along with a statutory declaration that various Companies Acts have been complied with plus a statement of the company's authorized share capital outlining the amount of finance that can be raised by issuing shares. If all is in order, the Registrar grants a *Certificate of Incorporation* which is best described as the company's birth certificate. The private limited company now exists as that separate legal entity, and can begin to trade!

A private limited company holds many attractions for its owners, including:

1   Shareholders have limited liability, so they can only lose the money that they invested in the company rather than their homes, cars and everything else that they possess. Removing the risk of personal catastrophe that is ever present for sole traders and partnerships should mean that it is easier to raise finance from eager, would-be shareholders, and to expand more rapidly than its smaller counterparts are able to do.

2   It is possible for shareholders to appoint directors who have skills, knowledge and expertise in very specific areas, perhaps in pro- duction, marketing or finance. Such specialization should mean that a private limited company has a far greater chance of becom- ing a lean, efficient and successful business than those owned and run by sole proprietors and partners with limited, across the board experience. Ignorance and the mistakes made by uninformed owner-managers are the main causes of failure among small businesses.

3   A private limited company has its own legal identity which means that it will continue to exist after the death of one or more of its shareholders, unlike many sole traders' and partnerships' firms which will cease trading. Although the law regards a company as a separate body, it is more realistic to view it as a puppet, with the shareholders and directors holding (or perhaps fighting over) its strings.

As with other types of business, there are drawbacks involved with a private limited company.

1   Almost certainly the biggest disadvantage is that ownership and control are separated between shareholding owners and control- ling directors. This may not be a problem in smaller, family-run companies where shareholders and directors are one and the same, but it often is when they differ which will happen as the company grows. Shareholders are usually entitled to see the company's annual report and accounts, attend, speak and vote at the annual general meeting and hire and fire the board – but it is that board which controls the business and its activities on a day-to-day basis.

2   Shares in a private limited company have to be sold privately – they cannot be advertised to the general public. Also, they can only be sold with the agreement of the other shareholders who

may veto a sale to an individual or organization that they do not wish to become involved in the company. Obviously, this is a disadvantage for shareholders who wish to sell shares, and a deterrent to would-be purchasers who might want to resell them in the future – and it can sometimes act as a barrier to raising finance for growth. (Of course, *some* shareholders will consider this as a plus, as it allows them to retain control of the company!)

3   Starting and running a private limited company involves considerable red tape and bureaucracy which all small businesses wish to avoid. Many forms such as the Memorandum and Articles of Association need to be completed, submitted and approved, annual general meetings have to be held, annual returns need to be sent to the Registrar of Companies and so on. Paperwork and officialdom do play a useful role in acting as checks and constraints on sloppy and dishonest business people but with time consuming and financial costs for everyone else.

1.5   Public limited companies

A public limited company – recognizable by the initials *plc* after the name – has many similarities with a private limited company. Indeed, the two are often confused. Both are separate legal entities, may be formed by two or more people, offer limited liability to shareholders, and so on. However, there are some key differences between the two types of company. In particular, the founders of a plc must raise minimum capital of £50 000 via shares and provide proof of this to the Registrar after the Certificate of Incorporation is issued but before a Certificate of Trading is granted, and the company can begin to trade. Also, shares in a plc can be advertised and sold publicly to anyone, and permission does not need to be given by the other shareholders.

A public limited company offers several benefits to its owners. Some are the same as for a private limited company, while others are different:

1   Limited liability means that investors are protected if the company fails and creditors demand payment of the debts. They will lose their investment but no more. Combining this advantage with the free and easy transfer of shares ensures that a public limited company usually finds it that much simpler to raise large sums of money and grow at a faster rate than private limited companies which are restricted by the controls on share ownership and sales.

2   Separating ownership and control can be a blessing, as it means that shareholders may own the company while better qualified directors can manage it on their behalf. These directors should know about the ins and outs of business, and can therefore avoid

many if not all of the mistakes that are made by owners who think they know what they are doing, but do not.

3   Having a separate legal identity from its owners and managers allows a public limited company to continue to trade after the death of any of these individuals. Clearly, this is an appealing prospect to would-be shareholders, potential lenders and everyone else in the business environment as they know that it will remain largely unscathed by personal problems and setbacks which can severely harm or even destroy smaller firms.

As expected, a public limited company also has its disadvantages which need to be contemplated, including:

1   The separation of ownership and control can be a major drawback in a plc – far more so than in a private limited company where both rest in the hands of just a few people who may be members of the same family. In theory, shareholders exercise the ultimate control of being able to sack the board assuming that the majority wish to do so. In practice, there may be hundreds or thousands of scattered shareholders unable to exert real influence on a board's day-to-day activities, and who are unlikely to pull together in sufficient numbers to take such extreme action.

2   Setting up and operating a plc involves red tape and form filling as with private limited companies. This can be time consuming and costly. Being obliged to submit annual accounts to the Registrar of Companies for all to see can be especially worrying. If the plc is doing badly, it has to (try to) work through its difficulties in public, rather than in private. Seeing it is in trouble, suppliers and customers may be increasingly reluctant to deal with it, turning a problem into a crisis.

3   As well as being an advantage in some respects, the free and easy transfer of shares can make a public limited company susceptible to being taken over, possibly by a competing firm. As an example of what can happen, a plc may be seen to be doing poorly, and some of its shareholders decide to sell their shares. A rival buys 51% of all of the company's shares and effectively becomes its owner. It then breaks up the company selling off the assets to cover the costs of buying the shares, and seizing that share of the market for itself.

1.6   Cooperatives and other organizations

Of course, sole traders, partnerships, private and public limited companies are not the only firms which operate within the business environment, although they are without doubt the leading ones. There are others that are owned and run along business-like lines too.

Workers' cooperatives

These cooperatives are owned and controlled by those people who work within them and in many respects can be compared to partnerships and their particular advantages and disadvantages. Distinguishing features of workers' coops are that they are funded by their members who receive equal shares of any profits. If more money is required, additional members may be taken in. They tend to be run democratically, in theory if not always in practice, with each member having one vote on decisions regardless of the money they have put in or the work that they do. They must register with the Registrar of Friendly Societies, who is the official responsible to the Government for maintaining a record of and supervising friendly societies such as these in the UK.

Retail cooperatives

These organizations tend to be grouped together under the same cooperative umbrella heading as workers' cooperatives, but are quite distinct from them. Indeed, they have more in common with private limited companies and their pluses and minuses. The key differences of retail coops are that they are owned by members who buy shares in them, from £1 up to a maximum of £10 000. These shareholders appoint a board to run the firm, and each have one vote on decisions, however many shares they own. Shares offer limited liability, do not increase in value, and can only be sold back to the cooperative. Members share in the coop's profits either as a rate of interest based on their shares or in the form of reduced prices in the shops.

Other organizations

Not surprisingly, a whole host of other organizations which might not automatically be classed as businesses could be referred to as being business-like in their approach to their operations and activities. These may include charities, clubs, societies and pressure groups. Taking a wider perspective, local authorities, the government and the civil service could be regarded in this way as well, although they are better viewed as the State, and part of the business environment itself.

1.7   Rapid revision

You will find a rapid revision test at the end of each chapter with questions on the right and answers below them on the left. Cover the answers with a sheet of paper so that only the first question is exposed. Answer it in your own words before looking at the suggested answer and going on to the next question. Once you are able to answer every question correctly, you should feel confident enough to move on to the following chapter.

Answers	Questions
–	1 What is a business?
1 It is an organization which produces and/or distributes goods and/or services for profit.	2 What is a sole trader?
2 He or she is a self-employed person who owns and controls his or her own business.	3 What are the main benefits of being a sole trader?
3 In brief: (a) easy to start trading; (b) absolute control; (c) flexibility; (d) increased efficiency; (e) private financial affairs; (f) all profits.	4 What are the major drawbacks of being a sole trader?
4 In short: (a) limited expertise; (b) hard work; (c) difficult to expand; (d) owner-dependent; (e) unlimited liability.	5 What does unlimited liability mean?
5 It means the sole trader's liability to debts cannot be limited just to his or her business assets. Personal belongings may have to be sold too, in order to settle debts.	6 What is a partnership?
6 It is the relation which subsists between persons carrying on a business in common with a view of profit.	7 What are the advantages of being in a partnership?
7 In summary: (a) easy to commence trading; (b) flexibility; (c) increased expertise; (d) shared workload and responsibility; (e) easier to expand; (f) private financial affairs.	8 What are the disadvantages of being in a partnership?
8 In essence: (a) shared control; (b) shared profits; (c) unlimited liability; (c) responsibility for other partners' actions.	9 What is a private limited company?

9   It is a separate legal entity, distinct from its owners and able to trade in its own right.

10   What is a Memorandum of Association?

---

10   It is a document which governs the relationship between a company and its environment.

11   What are the Articles of Association?

---

11   They are a document which sets out the relationship between a company and its shareholders.

12   What are the attractions of a private limited company?

---

12   Briefly: (a) limited liability; (b) appointment of skilled directors; (c) continuation of company after death of owners.

13   What are the drawbacks of a private limited company?

---

13   Quickly: (a) separation of ownership and control; (b) privately sold shares; (c) red tape and bureaucracy.

14   What is a public limited company?

---

14   Like a private limited company, it is a separate legal entity, detached from its owners and able to trade in its own right.

15   What are the key differences between a private and a public limited company?

---

15   The founders of a plc must raise minimum capital of £50 000 via shares. Shares in a public limited company can be sold publicly.

16   What are the benefits of investing in a public limited company?

---

16   Summarized: (a) limited liability; (b) easy transfer of shares; (c) employment of skilled directors; (d) continuation of company after death of owners.

17   What are the disadvantages of investing in a public limited company?

---

17   In short: (a) separation of ownership and control; (b) red tape and form filling; (c) public accounts; (d) susceptibility to being taken over.

18   What other organizations are run along business-like lines?

---

18   There are many. They include workers' and retail cooperatives, charities, clubs, societies and pressure groups.

19   Go over the questions again until you know all of the answers. Then move on to the next section.

2
Business structures

2.1 How is a business organized?

Clearly, each and every business is distinct in some way from its fellow concerns. Sometimes, the differences seem to be quite striking – the market trader who owns and runs his or her stall on a street corner is noticeably different from the large public limited company with national or international interests, in terms of legal status, economic form, activities, sales and profit levels, and so on. In other instances, the differences are less pronounced but can still be seen – one market stall is run by a sole trader, another by a partnership. One sells fruit and vegetables, the next offers bric-à-brac, and so forth.

Nevertheless, most businesses have similarities too, particularly with regard to the ways in which they are structured and run. After all, the vast majority of firms have to buy products of one kind or another, must manage staff, need to control their money, have to promote themselves, sell goods and services and carry out 101 comparable activities. Thus, they tend to be organized along similar lines in order to carry out all these tasks properly. It is possible to look at various small and large firms and recognize certain types of structure, identify who's who in the business and see specific principles, practices and relationships that are common to all. Many similarities can be highlighted by composing organization charts which show how businesses are structured.

2.2 Types of structure

The structure of a business organization largely depends upon its size and the complexity of its operations and activities. Smaller businesses – sole traders, partnerships and even some private limited companies – are often run in an informal manner. The sole proprietor does a bit of everything from investigating the market, through raising finance to dealing with paperwork. Partners and directors of small firms may divide duties among themselves according to their particular skills, knowledge and experiences but will still 'muck in' as and when necessary.

However, as a business expands – either internally or externally into new product, service or geographical markets – it will have to adopt a more formal structure so that everyone knows who does what. The sheer size of the concern and range of its interests make it impossible for it to continue to be run along informal, some might say amateurish and slapdash, lines any more. Three main types of formal structure can be readily identified, and are most commonly known as 'functional', 'divisional' and 'matrix' structures.

Functional structures

A growing business is usually organized into departments by function, such as purchasing, production, marketing, finance, personnel and administration in a smaller concern with the addition of perhaps research and development, sales and distribution in a larger one. With overall strategy set and coordinated by the owners or a board of directors as appropriate, each functional department has a clearly defined role and responsibilities. The purchasing department has to buy goods for the business, the production department has to turn them into finished products, and so on. All tasks are clearly grouped and divided up into relevant departments.

A functional structure has its advantages especially for a smaller firm selling one type or range of products or services in a single marketplace. It is relatively easy to administer and with everyone concentrating on what they do best, the firm will reap the rewards of such specialization. Nevertheless, some departments may put their own individual interests and goals before those of the concern which can cause difficulties. It is important that all of the departments and their employees pull together in the same direction and work as a unified whole, for the benefit of the business. A simple diagram of a functional structure is shown in Figure 2.1.

Divisional structures

As a growing business expands into other product, service and geographical markets, functional departments find it increasingly hard to control and link up all of the many different and sometimes conflicting operations and activities that are taking place inside of the concern. In effect, each department is having to handle several separate businesses selling various goods and services in scattered locations

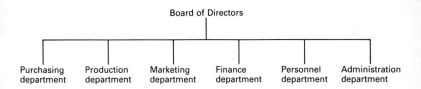

Figure 2.1 A functional structure

across the country, and all of them may be trying to go in different directions from the others. Thus, such a business will normally break up its original structure and regroup on the basis of product or geographical divisions. A central office headed by the board of directors determines overall group strategy and exercises control, with each division operating as a separate concern with its own functional structure, and responsibility for day-to-day decisions which should be compatible with the strategy laid down by head office.

A divisional structure frees directors to concentrate fully on long-term strategic planning and goals instead of becoming tied up with short-term, operational decision-making. Handing over day-to-day decision-making to the divisions should also improve the quality of the decisions that are being made because of the hands-on involvement of the decision makers at grass roots level. Furthermore, it will help to motivate those people who are given the responsibility to make decisions. If or when the business expands again, another division can be set up instead of trying to integrate it into a functional structure. An illustration of a divisional structure is given in Figure 2.2.

Matrix structures

A matrix structure might best be defined as a combination of functional and divisional structures. Typically, a business may be organized along functional lines with purchasing, production, marketing departments and so forth. Each department receives instructions from the board of directors, answers to it, and is expected to cooperate with the other departments for the common good of the firm. However, staff within these departments may also have to answer to and deal with product or geographical divisions or other teams involved with special projects. Perhaps the business is investigating the possibility of entering a new product or geographical market and sets up a team to investigate this. Everyone in purchasing, production and so on is expected to help.

The benefits of such a structure are that it increases flexibility and

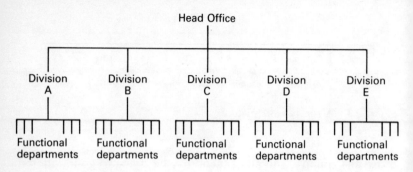

Figure 2.2   A divisional structure

coordination, although confusion over who answers to whom, who does what and the like can create ill feeling and even conflict. The loyalty of employees may be torn between their department heads and those in charge of project teams. To be successful it is important that each and every employee knows who is their immediate superior, and issues instructions to them. Figure 2.3 is an example of a matrix structure.

2.3   Who's who in a business

Whether businesses are organized and run via functional, divisional or matrix structures, various roles and responsibilities can still be identified in all of them. Taking a medium-sized company structured along functional lines as an average business, so far as one exists, the following can be recognized.

The board of directors

The board of directors which runs the company on behalf of its shareholders normally comprises a chairman, a deputy chairman, full time executive and part-time, non-executive directors. The chairman is in charge and can call meetings and set the agendas for discussion at them. During meetings, comments are addressed to 'the chair' and other directors are expected not to speak while these are being made – partly out of respect, but also because a secretary is taking notes of what is being said for the records. In the event of a tie when directors vote on a course of action, the chairman has the casting vote. The deputy chairman is usually an experienced fellow director who stands in when the chairman is absent. Both the chairman and deputy chairman are elected by the board members.

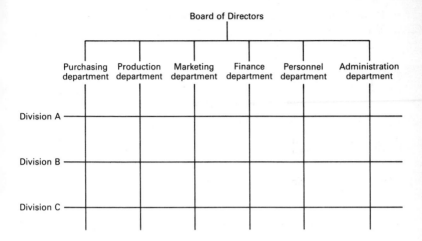

Figure 2.3   A matrix structure

The executive directors are senior people from within the company, most likely the heads of departments. The chief executive director is known as the managing director and it is his or her responsibility to implement the board's policies and to report on the results. The company secretary has the task of keeping the register of shareholders and noting changes of ownership. He or she is often the administration director and head of that department. Non-executive directors are on the board because of their specialist knowledge and expertise. They might be former executive directors or experts in their field. For example, an environmental specialist may be asked to join the board of an industrial company, conscious of its responsibilities to the environment and, more likely, its 'green' image in the marketplace.

The purchasing department

Businesses need to buy raw materials, component parts or finished products if they are to manufacture and/or sell goods to customers. Even if they offer services, certain items still have to be purchased, from office equipment, machinery and vehicles to pens, pencils and paper. The role of the purchasing, or buying, department is to negotiate deals with competitive and reliable suppliers, to obtain the necessary goods at the right prices and times, and on favourable terms and conditions. It is also expected to maintain satisfactory stock levels and to re-order goods as necessary. This department has to work closely with the production and marketing departments, to fulfil its responsibilities.

Although the number and type of employees within any department varies (very) considerably from one firm to another, purchasing staff probably consist of a purchasing director heading a team which handles the buying and stock control functions. The purchasing director is responsible for implementing the board's purchasing policies and is in overall control of such tasks as monitoring product and market trends and developments, researching sources of supply, agreeing appropriate deals, checking on the performance and quality of suppliers and goods, controlling stock levels and movements and ensuring stock security.

He or she is aided in the work by a chief buyer and a stock controller who share some of these various tasks. The chief buyer, purchasing officer or whatever other name is given to the post also coordinates a group of buyers for particular goods such as raw materials, component parts and finished products as well as numerous clerks who deal with the resulting paperwork. The stock controller may have stock and warehouse supervisors beneath him or her to administer the inflows and outflows of stock, with assorted storekeepers and clerks monitoring and recording the movements. (Figure 2.4).

The production department

This department is responsible for taking the raw materials and component parts bought by the purchasing department and turning them into finished, quality products, in the right quantities and at the right times. It needs to liaise regularly with the buying and marketing departments to keep up to date with stock levels and customer requirements, must allow for increasing and decreasing demand and should maintain accurate records for other departments such as finance and administration, or whatever they might be called in that particular firm.

A production director might lead a group comprising a designer, a production planner, a quality controller and a maintenance engineer and is in charge of controlling and coordinating them and their teams' activities. The designer and his or her draughtsmen produce the technical drawings and specifications of plant layout, products and component parts. The production planner takes an overall view of planning production, organizing materials, workers and machinery and scheduling a timetable. Working with him or her are a production engineer who calculates the mechanics of production, a production supervisor and operatives who turn theory into practice and a

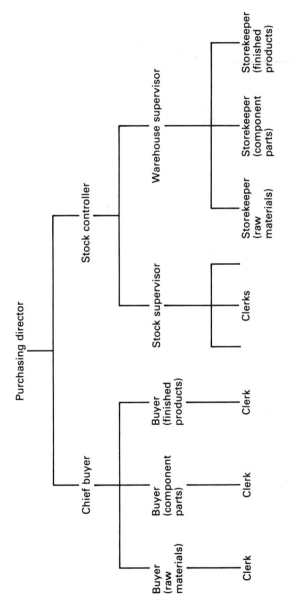

Figure 2.4 A purchasing department

production controller or progress chaser who ensures that the schedule is maintained.

A quality controller and his or her team of inspectors check and test production systems and finished goods to make certain that they are acceptable and adhere to the required standards expected by the firm and the law. Various clerks deal with the necessary documentation. A maintenance engineer along with numerous technicians work together to make certain that equipment and machinery used in the production processes are operating correctly and are safe. Clerks record the necessary information (Figure 2.5).

The marketing department

Marketing covers a range of activities which may be grouped together in one department, or could be separated out into several, smaller but closely associated ones. Market research has to discover who the firm's customers are, what they like and dislike, what type of goods and services they want, and at what prices. It does this by studying published data, conducting surveys and talking to existing and would-be customers. Advertising has to promote and publicize the company's products to persuade customers that these items are what they wish to buy. It does this by advertising on television, radio and other media such as the press, and by generating publicity at product launches, exhibitions and other staged events.

Sales has the task of actually obtaining orders for and selling goods to customers, whether by catalogue, over the telephone or via face-to-face dealings between customers and sales representatives. Distribution – sometimes known as despatch or transport – is responsible for physically moving the ordered and/or sold goods from the company's premises to the purchasers, distributing them by road, sea, air or rail as appropriate to wholesalers on industrial estates, retailers in high streets and shopping precincts or consumers in their own homes.

Hence, the marketing director heading this department has a broad, wide-ranging role and responsibilities, pulling together various functions in liaison with market research, advertising, sales and distribution managers. The market research manager will probably employ various researchers – desk researchers to study and report on existing, published research and field researchers to go out and actually interview people to generate fresh, up-to-date findings. Clerks will accumulate their findings. The advertising manager fronts a team of copywriters who draft copy such as scripts for television and radio advertisements and words for posters and press advertisements, plus artists who put together these words with pictures to produce eye-catching and appealing advertisements.

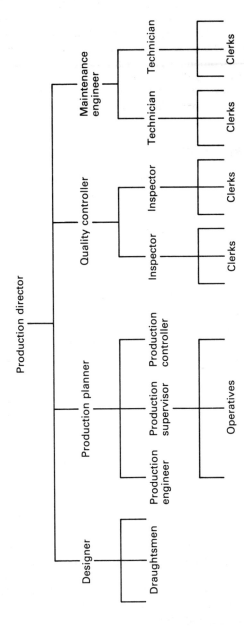

Figure 2.5 A production department

The sales manager is in charge of sales representatives each of whom has their own territory, perhaps London and the Home Counties, Anglia, the Midlands, or whatever. These reps, or agents if they work for the firm on a self-employed basis as often happens, go out on the road to make and maintain contact with existing and would-be customers, telling them about current and forthcoming products, and taking orders from them. A customer services assistant, or a whole team in bigger businesses, may be employed too, in order to inform customers of the concern's plans and product developments, and to handle complaints in a prompt and efficient manner. The distribution manager coordinates a team of drivers to deliver goods here, there and everywhere with mechanics on standby to service and repair vehicles, as required (Figure 2.6).

The finance department

Finance, or the accounts department, as it is equally likely to be referred to, handles all of the financial matters and transactions of a business. It issues and chases invoices, receives and pays bills, makes wages payments, keeps books and records, accounts for tax and value added tax to the Inland Revenue and Customs and Excise respectively, and so on. It also supervises the expenditure of its fellow departments to make certain that the individual and overall budgets of the firm are adhered to, and not exceeded as this might affect the smooth running and profitability of the concern.

Typically, the finance director may lead a team made up of a cost accountant, wages supervisor, financial accountant and a credit controller, below which are a host of clerks to attend to the various, associated clerical duties. A cost accountant investigates and details the firm's revenues and costs, breaking them down between different plants, departments and products to generate sufficient data for comparison between profitable and unprofitable areas and activities. A wages supervisor is responsible for paying wages and dealing with the concern's statutory obligations with regard to tax and national insurance contributions to the Inland Revenue and the Department of Social Security respectively.

A financial accountant maintains accurate and up-to-date financial records composing annual accounts to report to shareholders and to submit to the Inland Revenue and Customs and Excise. Below this accountant are purchase and sales ledger clerks who record the firm's daily financial dealings with other organizations and individuals. A credit controller assesses customers' creditworthiness, sets their credit limits and terms, monitors payments and chases and (hopefully) recovers debts that are overdue (Figure 2.7).

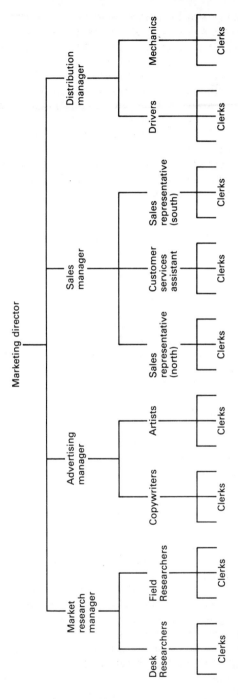

Figure 2.6 A marketing department

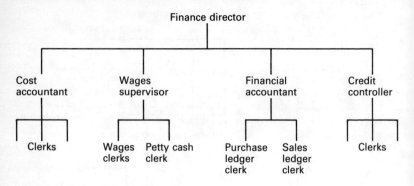

Figure 2.7   A finance department

The administration department

This department acts as a support for the other ones in the company, taking charge of all the routine and often overlooked matters which ensure the smooth running of the firm on a day-to-day basis. Typically, it controls and coordinates such behind the scenes activities as reception and secretarial duties, data processing, security and cleaning – mundane but essential services if the business is to operate in an efficient manner. 'Admin' is also likely to handle the firm's legal matters, such as share registration, insurance and various other duties.

Under the leadership and guidance of the administration director – who will invariably take personal responsibility for legal matters such as share registration – will be office, security and data processing managers. The office manager is in overall charge of the receptionists, secretaries and clerks, as appropriate. The security manager controls the guards and coordinates their activities. The data processing manager heads a team of computer programmers, systems analysts and clerks who organize and process information from within the business organization using computers (Figure 2.8).

The personnel department

As with the administration department, Personnel acts as a support for others within the firm. It drafts and continually updates a man-power plan which shows existing members and types of employees, anticipated internal and external changes and developments and the future numbers and types of employees required. It then administers this plan – recruiting, training, monitoring, transferring, promoting,

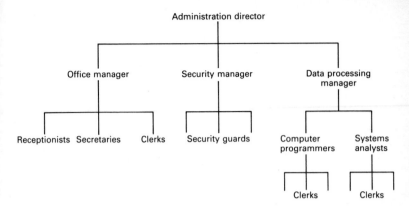

Figure 2.8   An administration department

dismissing and retiring staff, as appropriate. The department's responsibilities also include attending to contracts of employment, personnel records, health and safety, working conditions, industrial relations and innumerable other staff matters.

The personnel director may take sole charge of compiling and amending the manpower plan, along with selecting, transferring, promoting and dismissing staff, although these tasks are often shared with department heads in the majority of firms, with the personnel director perhaps taking an advisory role. There could be separate training, health and safety and welfare officers to take charge of these specific duties with an employment officer responsible for contracts of employment, personnel records and various other staff forms and formalities. These officers may be helped by clerks, inspectors, canteen staff, counsellors and nurses, as appropriate (Figure 2.9).

Naturally, it is important to bear in mind that every business is different. The so-called average firm falls somewhere between the two extremes of the sole trader who is in effect the purchasing department, production department and so on all rolled into one, and the huge public limited company with many departments, from research through to customer relations. Also, the names, roles and ranks of jobs vary from one concern to another. A chief buyer at one business might be a head purchasing officer elsewhere. A production controller and a quality controller may be one and the same in some firms. The person responsible for customer services may rank alongside directors in one concern, but could be a part-time assistant in another, with the same status as a cleaner. When looking at who's who in a business, the only certainty is that nothing is certain!

Figure 2.9   A personnel department

2.4   Principles, practices and relationships

No matter how a business is structured and who's who within it, all of the departments and employees need to work together well if the firm is to be successful. It is useful to be aware of some of the main principles, practices and relationships inside a business organization to gain a fuller understanding of how everyone fits in and relates to each other, for better or for worse.

Authority

Authority may be defined as the capacity to exercise power that is accepted by others. *De jure* authority is the formal right to exercise power. As an example, the purchasing director, stock controller and stock supervisor in the purchasing department all possess this authority over those employees below them. *De facto* authority is the informal capacity to exercise power – respect for a person means that his or her instructions (or suggestions) are followed. For example, the buyer of raw materials may exert some unofficial power over the purchasers of component parts and finished goods, perhaps because of his or her buying experience, standing in the firm or even due to his or her good nature. In a business organization, everyone should know who has formal authority and for what purpose, although this does not always occur especially in larger concerns, possibly with a complicated matrix structure.

Responsibility

It is possible to describe responsibility as an obligation to complete specific tasks or duties. As an example, one of the production supervisor's responsibilities may be to identify and then verbally report any problems on the production line and to follow this with a written report. Similarly, if someone is in charge of other employees, he or she is said to have responsibility for them and their actions. For example, a production supervisor is responsible for the operatives below him or her on the shop floor. It is important that responsibility is well defined and recognized so that everyone knows who is responsible for doing this, that and the other.

Span of control

As the phrase suggests, this refers to the number of employees that one person is able to control effectively. Not surprisingly, it will vary according to circumstances. For example, the chief designer in the production department has to supervise closely the highly skilled work of the draughtsmen to ensure that it is satisfactory, so his or her span of control tends to be limited. The unskilled and repetitive work of the clerk in the administration department requires less supervision so the office manager's span of control is wider. If the span of control is too narrow with one person supervising perhaps only a few employees then those being controlled may lack motivation and initiative, with fresh ideas few and far between. Too wide, and ill-supervised staff can become overconfident, and slack and careless in their work.

Decision-making

Everyone in a business has to make decisions of one kind or another almost all of the time. The board of directors decides what objectives are to be pursued, and how they are to be achieved. Purchasing, production, marketing directors and managers and their colleagues have to choose exactly what to buy, how much to produce, how best to market products and services and so on. Technicians, clerks and other dogsbodies at the bottom of an organization have to make decisions too, even if it is only to decide which mundane task to do first, second and third. Quite obviously, decision-making is important – setting unrealistic objectives, purchasing shoddy goods by mistake, producing too much in error and even delaying the completion of a particular task can have a (potentially fatal) adverse affect on the concern.

Whatever the type or level of decision to be made, decision-making should follow certain key steps. First, the decision which has to be taken must be identified, whether it is to do this or that task, proceed with this action or that one, or whatever. All of the various options available need to be recognized so that these alternatives can be weighed up, and compared and contrasted with each other.

The decision-maker then has to make sure he or she has gathered together complete and accurate, up-to-date information in all areas. Next, he or she has to interpret these data, separating facts from opinions so that decisions are not based upon personal views or speculation, which may be inaccurate and misleading. The right decision can then be made.

Delegation

This involves transferring various decisions and/or tasks from a superior to a subordinate. As an example, the marketing director may ask the advertising manager to take over the wining and dining of major, existing and would-be advertisers. Having delegated, the superior is then free to concentrate on more important matters. The workload is distributed evenly and completed quicker and more efficiently too as the subordinate may have a better grass roots understanding of the issues. Also, the subordinate may feel inspired to work that much harder, and could achieve greater job satisfaction.

To be successful, a supervisor should only delegate to a subordinate who is able enough to do the work properly. Similarly, it is important that he or she is not overloaded, nor given tasks to do that are incompatible with his or her normal duties. Delegated work must be clearly understood by the subordinate so that he or she knows what should *and* should not be done. It is also wise to allow the subordinate to do the work without interference or constant checks which may weaken morale and generate ill feeling. Fellow employees ought to be told of the delegated workload so the subordinate can carry out decision-making and/or tasks with their cooperation.

Centralization

A centralized business organization is one in which a tight knit group of senior people exercise authority. Typically, all key decisions are taken by the board of directors, with instructions passed down through the firm which the board expects to be carried out without discussion or amendment. What they say goes, or else! A decentralized concern disperses authority down through the organization. For example, a board of directors makes overall strategic decisions, with operational decisions passed to senior managers in each department and so on down the line as appropriate so that a clerk in the lower reaches of the firm can make the minor decision to re-order stationery when stocks are low, instead of having to ask for permission from a higher authority.

Although many sole traders and partnerships tend to run highly centralized businesses with authority retained by only a handful of people at the very top, most firms decentralize as they grow – the increasing size and complexity of their operations and activities make it almost impossible not to do so. Decentralization offers many benefits – top management can focus on the key issues, staff further down the organization can make speedier and more relevant decisions and like to be given responsibilities too. Nevertheless, there are drawbacks – senior managers may become over-reliant on employees who are not qualified to make decisions and could find it harder to spot (potential) problems at an early stage. Also, standards may vary from one department to another, depending on the quality of its managers, and their decision-making.

Relationships

Many different types of relationship exist within a business organization. For example, the stock controller answers to the purchasing director, works alongside the chief buyer and must liaise and co-operate with production and marketing management and employees if everyone is to do their job properly. A *line relationship* is a simple and straightforward one between a superior who issues instructions and a subordinate who acts upon them. A nurse in the personnel department has a direct line relationship with the welfare officer immediately above him or her, and an indirect line relationship with the personnel director further up the organization.

A *staff relationship* exists when a director or senior manager has a personal assistant (p.a.) or secretary who answers to him or her alone and who has to deal with subordinates but does not have a line relationship with those other employees in the organization. Sometimes, a p.a. or secretary will exercise authority on behalf of his or her boss or may generate their own informal power over a period of time. Not surprisingly, there can be problems when staff and line relationships overlap. For example, the administration director's personal assistant may tell the office manager what to do. Although this instruction comes from the director above him or her in a line relationship, the office manager resents taking orders from a p.a. whom he or she considers to be below him or her in seniority.

Lateral relationships tend to be less problematic, with two employees working together at the same level, assisting each other in order to do their work properly. Bought and sales ledger clerks in the finance department could be said to have a lateral relationship as might mechanics and drivers in the marketing department. *Functional relationships* exist between a person in one department and someone else in another. Thus, the health and safety officer in the personnel department has a functional relationship with managers and employees in purchasing, production, marketing and so forth.

2.5 Organization charts

An organization chart is a diagram which illustrates the basic structure of an organization. It shows the lines of authority and responsibility and highlights the relationships between departments and employees, thus giving an overall view and impression of the organization. Such charts have several uses – they help to generate ideas for an improved structure, can indicate to employees where they are positioned within the organization and may be referred to when the business is being re-organized, perhaps from a functional to a divisional structure.

However, it is important to be aware of the shortcomings of organization charts. They tend to convey a rigid and limited image of status and authority and fail to take account of the levels of cooperation which exist between departments and employees, and to reflect the degree of flexibility within most successful organizations. Also, they can make employees feel pigeon-holed and reluctant to demonstrate any initiative. If they are not prepared with scrupulous accuracy – which is not as easy a task as it seems, especially in a large and sprawling organization – they can be confusing, with employees feeling uncertain who does what and who answers to whom.

Organization charts are most commonly presented in three ways and are known as vertical, horizontal and circular (or concentric) charts. Vertical organization charts look like family trees and are the most popular. An example is given in Figure 2.10. Horizontal charts are simply vertical charts turned on their side. Some firms prepare them to avoid conveying the impression of superiority, and to imply that everyone is pulling in the same direction. Figure 2.11 shows a horizontal organization chart. Circular, or concentric, charts place the most senior people in the middle of the organization with the others spreading outwards from them. It avoids the lines of authority which can be offputting. An example is laid out in Figure 2.12.

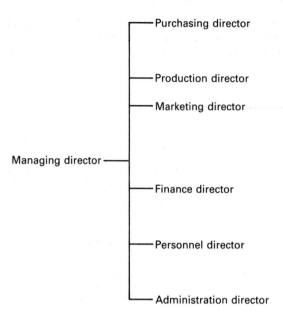

Figure 2.10 A vertical organization chart

2.6 Rapid revision

Answers	Questions
–	1 What are the three main types of business structure?
1 (a) Functional structures; (b) divisional structures; (c) matrix structures.	2 What is a functional structure?
2 It is one in which a business is organized into departments by function – purchasing, production and so on.	3 What is a divisional structure?
3 It is one in which a business is run on the basis of product or geographical divisions, with each division operating as a separate concern.	4 What is a matrix structure?
4 It is a combination of a functional and a divisional structure.	5 Who's who in a board of directors?

Figure 2.11 A horizontal organization chart

Figure 2.12 A circular organization chart

5 A chairman is in charge and has a deputy who takes over when he or she is absent. Executive directors are senior people from within the company, usually heads of departments. Non-executive directors are normally former executive directors or experts in their field.

6 What departments typically exist in an average-sized company?

6 (a) Purchasing; (b) production; (c) marketing; (d) finance; (e) administration; (f) personnel.

7 Who works in a purchasing department?

7 Perhaps, (a) a purchasing director; (b) a chief buyer; (c) a stock controller; (d) buyers; (e) a stock supervisor; (f) a warehouse supervisor; (g) storekeepers; (h) clerks.

8 Who works in a production department?

8 Possibly, (a) a production director; (b) a designer; (c) a production planner; (d) a quality controller; (e) a maintenance engineer; (f) draughtsmen; (g) a production engineer; (h) a production supervisor; (i) operatives; (j) a production controller; (k) inspectors; (l) clerks; (m) technicians.

9 Who works in a marketing department?

9 Often, (a) a marketing director; (b) a market research manager; (c) researchers; (d) an advertising manager; (e) copywriters; (f) artists; (g) a sales manager; (h) sales representatives; (i) a customer services assistant; (j) a distribution manager; (k) drivers; (l) mechanics; (m) clerks.

10 Who works in a finance department?

10 Typically, (a) a finance director; (b) a cost accountant; (c) a wages supervisor; (d) a financial accountant; (e) a credit controller; (f) clerks.

11 Who works in an administration department?

11   Usually, (a) an administration director; (b) an office manager; (c) a security manager; (d) a data processing manager; (e) receptionists; (f) secretaries; (g) clerks; (h) guards; (i) computer programmers; (j) systems analysts.

12   Who works in a personnel department?

12   Normally, (a) a personnel director; (b) a training officer; (c) a health and safety officer; (d) a welfare officer; (e) an employment officer; (f) clerks; (g) inspectors; (h) canteen staff; (i) counsellors; (j) nurses.

13   What is authority?

13   It is the capacity to exercise power that is accepted by others.

14   What is responsibility?

14   It is an obligation to complete specific tasks or duties.

15   What is a span of control?

15   It refers to the number of employees that one person is able to control effectively.

16   What does delegation involve?

16   It involves transferring various decisions and/or tasks from a superior to a subordinate.

17   What is a centralized business?

17   It is one in which a tight knit group of people exercise authority.

18   What types of relationship exist in a business?

18   (a) Line relationships; (b) staff relationships; (c) lateral relationships; (d) functional relationships.

19   What is a line relationship?

19   It is a simple and straightforward one between a superior and a subordinate.

20   What is a staff relationship?

20   It is one which exists between a superior's personal assistant and his or her subordinates with whom the p.a. does not have a line relationship.

21   What is a lateral relationship?

21 It is a relationship between two employees working together at the same level.

22 It is a relationship that exists between a person in one department and someone else in another.

23 It is a diagram which illustrates the structure of an organization.

24 (a) Vertical charts; (b) horizontal charts; (c) circular charts.

22 What is a functional relationship?

23 What is an organization chart?

24 What types of organization chart can be drawn up?

25 Go over the questions again until you know all of the answers. Then move on to the next section.

3
Business activities

3.1 What does a business do?

Quite simply, the definition of a business as 'an organization which produces and/or distributes goods and/or services for profit' aptly sums up what each and every business does. It makes, it buys, it sells or whatever, all to make money! Typically, it initially establishes the objectives that it wants to achieve in the future and then sets about doing business successfully by promoting the right products at the right prices in the right places. Whatever its approach, it also has various responsibilities to certain organizations and individuals in the business environment, and it must fulfil these if it is to continue trading. At the same time, any firm can enter into decline at some stage and to avoid this a business must be able to spot danger signals and remedy the causes – otherwise it will fail.

3.2 The objectives of a business

Business objectives are simply those goals which a firm sets for itself with regard to sales, profits and so on, in the short-, medium- and long-term over the next year, three years and thereafter. A whole host of different goals may be established but tend to boil down to three over-riding ones in most instances – to survive, to make a profit, and to grow. Whatever other ones may be stated in public or in private can usually slot under one or more of these umbrella headings.

To survive

The initial aim of any start up business, large or small, has to be to survive. This is especially evident in smaller concerns run by sole traders and partnerships, particularly in difficult or recessionary times. A sole proprietor takes a workshop from which he manufactures handmade furniture. He wants to become known in the marketplace, be regarded as a reliable and friendly supplier and bring in enough money to pay the bills and live on. He, like every other small business person you might talk to, wishes to tick over and to be here next year, or whatever. In essence, he or she just wants to survive.

Larger businesses are not that dissimilar, although it is likely that the owners and managers will have thought more about prospects before setting up, will have greater financial resources at their disposal and will take a longer rather than a shorter-term perspective than their smaller counterparts do. They may be happy, or at least willing, to accept losses in the first one or two years if these will enable them to secure their position within the market and then allow them to move on to their next major objective, which is to make a profit.

To make a profit

At some stage, and generally speaking, the sooner the better, a business needs to make a profit. Quite simply, its income must exceed its expenditure, leaving enough money to plough back into the firm for new equipment, updated machinery, better stock and so on and to provide the owners with a decent return on their investment. Some firms wish to maximize their profits so far as possible, whereas others are satisfied with satisfactory profit levels.

1 Maximized profits

It is often assumed that each and every business is in relentless pursuit of as much profit as it can obtain, regardless of anything and anyone else, and occasionally this is true. A firm may seek to increase sales by volume or value, to reduce costs to the bare minimum, to make the most efficient use of resources available and so forth, all to achieve the main goal of deriving the greatest possible profit.

2 Satisfactory profits

The common perception of a profit obsessed business is not always accurate or indeed fair. It may have a number of other objectives which need to be fulfilled in order to make a profit, but which simultaneously act as constraints upon profit maximization. As examples, to keep employees happy, to improve working conditions and to promote a first class public image are all objectives which need to be achieved if a business is to be successful and profitable, but which can also limit its profits. Similarly, a shopkeeper may shut at five o'clock when profits are satisfactory rather than at nine o'clock when they are maximized, because he wants to go home and enjoy life!

To grow

Once a firm is stable and profitable, the owners and managers will want it to expand and grow on the rough and ready principle that a bigger business will sell more and make larger profits, thus enabling it to continue its growth. It may aim to grow via various routes.

1   Horizontal integration

This involves a firm expanding across the same level in which it currently operates within the production and distribution of goods. Thus, a producer of raw materials may produce a greater quantity, a manufacturer could move to a larger factory and a retailer might open another shop all with the aim of meeting increasing demand for their products and services within the marketplace. To all intents, the business does the same as before but on a grander scale. There are limits to horizontal growth though. It may be restrained not only by the availability of raw materials, satisfactory office space and so on but also by the size of the market. After all, there are only a certain number of customers wanting to purchase so many goods.

2   Vertical integration

A business may want to grow vertically, expanding into other levels within the production and distribution chain. As an example, a manufacturer may integrate backwards (or upstream) by producing its own raw materials or could integrate forwards (or downstream) by starting or buying retail outlets to sell its goods direct to end users. In some instances, a firm can become *fully integrated*, producing and distributing products from start to finish. A good illustration of this is with breweries, some of which produce the barleys and hops that are the raw materials for beer, malt and brew the beer and then sell it via their own public houses.

As often as not, vertical integration takes place not just because a firm wishes to grow but also as a result of problems with suppliers and/or customers. Typically, suppliers may produce goods of mixed quality, at variable prices and could deliver them late, time and again. Customers may want larger discounts, longer credit terms and might not display and promote the goods to the firm's satisfaction. They may even be slow and reluctant payers. Eventually, the business decides to act to eliminate these difficulties – and to expand at the same time. As with horizontal integration, vertical growth is limited by various factors, most notably by the total size of the market.

3 Conglomerate integration

This type of integration, or diversification as it is better known, entails a firm expanding into different product and service markets. Such diversification can be *concentric* whereby a business produces similar goods and services to its existing ones. For example, a firm that manufactures razor blades, household scissors and the like may diversify into garden shears, spades and rakes, all sold via the same hardware stores. *Pure diversification* occurs when unrelated products and services are produced and offered, such as when a firm diversifies from household furniture to paints. Often, conglomerate integration becomes a goal when horizontal and/or vertical integration have reached their limits.

It is interesting to hear sole proprietors and partners talking and to study the promotional material of larger concerns in order to discover what they have to say about their objectives. It is common to find that image conscious firms sell themselves as caring concerns, out to 'provide our customers with the first class service they deserve' and so forth. Perhaps so, but a realist may claim that they have an ulterior motive: to attract more customers and their money, or whatever. The bottom line objectives of any business are much the same; to survive, make a profit and grow, no more and no less!

3.3 Doing business successfully

Very many ingredients are required if a business is to be successful – experienced owners and managers, satisfactory finance, a good location, hardworking and skilled employees, sufficient customers, not too much competition, supportive local authorities and government and so forth. The list goes on and on, and is virtually never ending. However, many firms believe that the best way of working towards success is 'to promote the right product at the right price in the right place'. If they get that product-price-promotion-place mix absolutely correct, then they will be well on course to survive, profit and grow. It will certainly be of considerable help, and may enable them to overcome shortcomings and mistakes elsewhere.

The right product

A 'product' has been defined as 'a good or service which is offered to customers'. A description of the right product may be that it is 'a good or service which is offered to customers *and* which satisfies their wants or needs'. Thought needs to be given to various areas, including:

1   Product line

This refers to the number of versions of a product that are going to be provided by a firm in order to satisfy the wants or needs of its customers in a marketplace. As an example in the car market, Vauxhall Motors provides many different versions of its popular Cavalier model to please various groups. Some people want to drive a Cavalier with a powerful engine, others are more concerned with appearance. Some wish to pay more, others less, and so on.

2   Product group

This phrase relates to the combination of product lines that join together to make up a firm's offering to a particular market. Hence, Vauxhall Motors provides Cavaliers, Astras, Corsas and so forth for that motor car market while producing other product lines which make up alternative product groups for other markets such as trucks and lorries.

3   Product mix

This simply refers to all of the product groups and lines that combine to form its total offering across all markets. The concern's product mix may be interrelated or extremely diverse, depending upon its range of business operations and activities.

The right price

Price may be defined as 'the amount of money that customers pay for a product or service'. The right price could said to be 'the amount of money that customers are happy to pay for a product or service, *and* which provides a satisfactory profit for the supplier'. With this dual aim in mind, a business has to make decisions about the prices it will charge for its goods along with any discounts, delivery charges, payment terms and conditions and the like. Various pricing methods may be employed by a firm. These three are the most common:

1 *Cost based pricing*

This method simply ties the price of a product or service to the costs incurred in producing and distributing it, and makes an allowance for the profit required too. Quite obviously, no business is going to want to sell its goods at a loss – although one or two may be sold as *loss leaders* to attract customers to others in the range – so all prices must be tied to costs to a certain degree.

2 *Demand based pricing*

Here, a business relates its prices to the demand for its products and services. If the demand from existing and would-be customers is high, prices can be raised. Conversely, when demand is low, prices will need to be dropped accordingly. Many firms practise what is known as *price discrimination*, whereby they vary their prices between types of customers, locations and so forth, charging what they can where they can.

3 *Competition based pricing*

With this method, a concern links its prices to those charged by rival firms. Clearly, if there are many competitors in the market all offering comparable goods and services, then a firm will need to be aware of rival prices. If it sets a higher price than the others, customers will simply go elsewhere, and vice versa. Should a concern have few competitors in the marketplace, then logically it should be able to charge more.

The right promotion

Promotion has been described as 'the ways in which a product or service is brought to the attention of customers'. The right promotion may be defined as 'the ways in which a product or service is brought to the attention of customers and which persuades them to purchase that product or service.' The phrase 'at a fair and reasonable cost to the supplier' could be added to this definition as well. The promotional mix comprises various features:

1   *Advertising*

This involves promoting a product or service via a host of media such as television, the radio, newspapers, magazines, posters and the cinema. Advertisements need to be seen or heard by the right people, attracting their attention, seizing their interest, installing desire and persuading them to take action – no easy task!

2   *Sales promotion*

This covers such measures as free samples, money-off offers, 'two for the price of one' deals, trading stamps, in-store demonstrations and point of sale displays – anything which will grab the attention of customers, and stimulate demand for a product or service!

3   *Packaging*

This is a useful promotional tool, often overlooked or at best ill considered by businesses. The packaging of a product should not only protect it during distribution, but also be sufficiently well designed and attractive to draw customers to it, and persuade them to buy it. As an example, one washing powder is much the same as another but can be distinguished by its appealing packaging.

4   *Face-to-face selling*

Here, sales representatives or agents go out 'in the field' to sell the product to existing and prospective customers. Often, this approach can be very successful as the firm's representatives can show, demonstrate and explain the uses of the product, answer questions, deal with worries and doubts, and so on.

5   *Public relations*

With this, a firm tries to create a favourable image of itself and its goods in the marketplace. Typically, it does this by feeding media such as television, the radio and the press with news and information about its operations and activities, in order to show it in a good light. Stories ranging from its environmentally friendly disposal of waste matter to the sponsoring of a local junior football team will all help to build up goodwill.

The right place

Place really refers to 'the ways in which a product or service is delivered to customers'. The right place would extend this description to 'the ways in which a product or service is delivered to customers so that it is always readily available to them'. The phrase 'at a minimal cost to the supplier' might be tagged to the end of this description too. Several distribution channels can be identified:

1   *Manufacturer-wholesaler-retailer-buyer*

With this channel, a manufacturer makes the product and sells it in bulk to a wholesaler who breaks stocks down into retail packs for a retailer who sells it to the final buyer, or end user.

2   *Manufacturer-wholesaler/retailer-buyer*

Here, the manufacturer makes a bulk sale to a business which combines wholesale and retail functions, selling direct to the consumer of the product.

3   *Manufacturer/wholesaler-retailer-buyer*

With this, a manufacturer makes the product and then sells it in retail sized quantities to a retailer who resells it on to end users. Hence, manufacturing and wholesaling functions and activities are combined.

4   *Manufacturer/wholesaler/retailer-buyer*

Here, a manufacturer performs the successive functions of making, wholesaling and retailing goods, selling them direct to the consumers.

3.4   Business responsibilities

Whatever the objectives of a firm may be – and never forget that whatever might be stated in public, in private it almost invariably aims to survive, make a profit and grow – it is responsible for its actions to various other organizations and individuals. No business can do what it wants in pursuit of its goals, regardless of the environment in which it operates. It has numerous responsibilities to the following groups in particular, and may be made accountable to them by law if it fails to fulfil these responsibilities in a proper manner.

Shareholders

Not surprisingly, a company, and more specifically its board of directors, has a responsibility to its owners, and in various ways. Most notably, it has to be sufficiently profitable to continue trading successfully, and to provide shareholders with an agreeable return on their investment in the form of annual dividends. Also, it needs to win universal confidence in its activities within the marketplace so that share values are maintained or improved. If shareholders are dissatisfied with the performance of a company and its directors then they can act to overthrow the board or replace certain directors at the next annual general meeting.

Employees

Staff are entitled to be paid in full and on time and to expect their firm to honour the other employment terms and conditions which exist between them, relating to hours of work, overtime, paid holidays and time off, maternity and sickness leave and pay, and so on. Similarly, they have a right to be able to work in an environment which is healthy and safe, free from faulty machinery, run down equipment and other dangerous surroundings. A host of employment and health and safety laws – such as the Employment Acts of 1980, 1982, 1988 and 1989 and the Health and Safety at Work Act of 1974 – protect employees, with rogue firms subject to legal action, fines and adverse publicity in the media, which is often the greatest deterrent of all. In extreme cases, such as when health or lives are in danger, a firm can even be closed down.

Creditors

A business has a responsibility to repay those organizations and individuals to whom it owes money. Typically, these *creditors* as they are known will include banks or other financial institutions which have supplied funds to set up and/or continue to run the concern and suppliers which have handed over goods or provided services on credit, expecting to receive payment for them at a later date. Those firms which do not pay their bills on time or at all can be taken to court by creditors seeking to enforce payment. If they do not then pay, the court may authorize a debt collecting agency to seize their possessions to settle the debts. For sole traders and partnerships, this might mean homes being sold to meet the firm's commitments.

Customers

Those organizations and people who buy products and services from a business are entitled to receive first class goods which are also safe and reliable, and provided on any terms and conditions which may have been previously agreed. Thus, if a customer orders a leather settee from a furniture store and a delivery date of 30 June is agreed, then that settee must be made of leather (not plastic), should be safe (without catching fire if a cigarette is dropped onto it), reliable (without fading or splitting within months), and arrive by the end of June. A wide range of consumer laws – such as the Sale of Goods Act of 1979 and the Trade Descriptions Act of 1968 and 1972 – exist to protect customers from unscrupulous businesses, with legal activities, fines and adverse publicity likely to follow for those businesses which fail to comply with the laws of the land.

The State

Each and every business, or its owners in smaller firms, has an obligation to the State, most notably to Customs and Excise and to the Inland Revenue. It has to maintain honest and accurate books and records, submit accounts and/or returns for VAT and tax purposes and pay any VAT and tax due on time. Those firms which are slow to fulfil their obligations, typically by sending in late returns and payments, may have to pay surcharges and additional interest on monies due. Those who attempt to defraud Customs and Excise and the Inland Revenue by understating profits may be subject to substantial fines and even imprisonment in some circumstances.

Neighbours

Often overlooked, those individuals and/or firms which live or work close to a business have rights too. A business should act in a fair and reasonable manner towards them at all times. As examples, having noisy lorries loading and unloading early in the morning, carrying out loud activities which disturb the peace and quiet and opening until late at night might be considered to be unreasonable behaviour, especially by those in the immediate vicinity. The local authority's planning regulations and bye-laws will restrict business activities for the common good, with notices being served on those businesses which fail to act in accordance with the law and enforcement action being taken against those who choose to ignore such notices.

The community

Similarly, a business also has a wider responsibility to the community as a whole, as well as to its immediate neighbours. Thus, if a manufacturer receives raw materials and despatches finished goods by road, lorry drivers should be instructed to avoid driving through residential areas wherever possible. Also, waste matter left over from the production of finished products must be disposed of in a responsible manner, rather than being discharged without restraint into the nearest river or landfill site. In recent years, national government has passed increasingly tough laws regulating the disposal of waste that pollutes the environment.

3.5   The decline of a business

Any firm can enter into a decline, and for innumberable reasons. It is wise for the owners and managers of a concern to be aware of danger signals and, more importantly, the causes that lie behind them, as well as how to remedy them so that the business can continue to survive, profit and grow. If not, the firm will fail, and have to cease trading.

Danger signals

Anything out of the ordinary and which is unanticipated should be a cause of concern to a business – not necessarily a huge concern, but one that is worth at least a second thought or further investigation. Typical danger signals include fewer customers, falling sales, rising expenditure, lower profits, increasing stock levels, more debts, longer payment times and a shortage of cash. Often these will be temporary situations which are simply part of the ebb and flow of business life but they could be symptoms of a deeper, long-term malaise.

Causes

The reasons why a business is not doing as well as anticipated may be numerous, and are not always easy to identify, especially by owners and managers who are too closely involved with the concern to take an objective viewpoint and who could even be the cause of the problems. The most common reasons for business failure can be attributed to the following:

1 *Bad management*

Quite simply, managers may not be good enough to manage successfully, making one wrong decision after another. A whole host of mistakes may be made and could include going into partnership with inappropriate partners who have insufficient skills, knowledge and experience to do the job they are expected to do, employing people who are just not suited to the work, and structuring the organization in an inefficient manner. Perhaps they try to make the business grow too fast, manufacturing new products or entering different markets without first having conducted sufficient research to ascertain if they are likely to be profitable enough.

Also, managers may borrow money to fund rapid growth rather than consolidating for a period, and be unable to repay the capital and interest as quickly as required by the lender. They may site the business in an inappropriate location, too far from customers who prefer to go to a rival who is closer. They might employ too many people such as partners, friends and relatives who are difficult to dismiss and whose wages bite into profits too much. Managers may insist on continuing to sell goods and offer services which are no longer demanded by buyers, who wish to purchase updated items nowadays.

Few owners and managers will admit to their failings though. Business problems are the fault of 'that useless partner' or 'those lazy workers' rather than the owner who took them on in the first place. Possibly, difficulties are attributed to 'that heartless bank manager' or 'the funny customers in this town', never to the foolish manager who rushed into the loan agreement or moved the concern to that back street location. It is those businesses with owners and managers such as these which are most likely to fail because those in control can identify the symptoms but never the underlying cause – themselves!

2 *The changing environment*

Self-inflicted though many wounds are, there is little doubt that some difficulties are genuinely beyond the control of those in charge of a firm and may be attributed to outside influences. Interest rates and/ or business rates may rise substantially so that modest profits are turned into losses. The landlord of the premises occupied by the firm might wish to redevelop the property, forcing the business to seek other premises in less suitable or more costly surroundings. Employment laws may be passed or amended forcing businesses to perhaps pay more money to their staff or to make expensive alterations to their property to maintain health and safety standards.

The demand for certain products may shift possibly because new technology has been developed which produces better quality or different items – some firms may be unable to afford the equipment and machinery needed to manufacture these products, and will thus fall behind with sales and profits. More competitors might enter the marketplace taking away customers from a firm, suppliers may go out of business forcing a concern to purchase inferior items from elsewhere which are less popular with their customers. New consumer legislation could be passed which obliges firms to manufacture goods to more stringent standards. It all costs money, which can make the difference between profits and losses.

In practice, business problems can rarely be attributed to just one reason, or a particular group of reasons under the heading of 'bad management', 'the changing environment' or whatever. More often than not, they result from a mixture of reasons, building one on top of the other and which become increasingly difficult to separate and identify as time passes especially if owners and managers adopt a subjective rather than objective stance, as can happen.

Remedies

Not surprisingly, almost all businesses experience problems from time to time but, assuming that these can be spotted correctly and early enough, most of the firms are able to survive them, and go on to make a profit and grow, as planned. Obviously, a remedy for one problem may be irrelevant to (or could even worsen) another, but several common remedies can be identified:

1   *New management*

Those managers (and employees) who have made errors or who are unable to rise to the challenge of a changing environment may be replaced. Shareholders may vote to change the board of directors or individual directors at the company's annual general meeting. Managers can transfer or even dismiss incompetent staff, as appropriate. Unfortunately, sole proprietors and partners are less able and willing to accept this drastic remedy, and are thus more likely to continue their decline.

2 *More capital*

Often, an injection of fresh finance perhaps from shareholders or a bank can rectify a difficult situation, enabling the business to invest in the equipment needed to manufacture new products, to ride out early trading losses in a different marketplace, to move to a better location, or whatever. There is a risk that a firm is simply delaying the inevitable and even exacerbating the situation by adding loan repayments to its forthcoming expenditure, but this may be considered to be a risk worth taking in the circumstances.

3 *Reducing costs*

A sensible approach for all firms, not just those in temporary difficulties, is to minimize costs as far as possible. Tighter financial control may involve a range of (sometimes unpleasant) actions such as switching full-time jobs to part-time positions, making staff redundant and so on, but it could ensure the all important survival of the firm, without which there would be no jobs at all.

4 *Re-organization*

It may be that restructuring the business can rectify some or all of its problems, with departments merging to become more efficient and cut costs, and personnel being transferred out of jobs and into other ones for which they are better suited. Often, re-organization is little more than a euphemism for closure with loss-making plants and divisions being shut down so that those parts of the company which have been supporting them can continue on a profitable basis.

5 *Revised objectives*

Often overlooked but worth considering, it may be wise just to amend the firm's objectives, perhaps lowering them to more realistic levels. In some instances, the business may not be in real trouble, but is simply not achieving its targets which may have been too ambitious in the first place. That local shopkeeper may have to be content with conquering the town, rather than the world!

6 *New products and services*

Most goods have a similar life cycle being introduced amid a blaze of publicity followed by (rapid) growth and a period of steady sales ending with a decline and eventual disappearance. Each stage may differ in length but the ending is almost always inevitable as replacement products and services appear. A firm should forever be seeking ways of improving its range of goods, being prepared and able to update or replace them before competing goods do.

7 New markets

Similarly, a business should continually be aware of other markets that are or may become profitable in the near future. All markets and the internal and external influences upon them are forever changing, and it is sensible for a business to be prepared to move from one to another as appropriate, whenever the changing situation warrants such actions.

Failure

Of course, danger signals and the causes of problems are sometimes not spotted until it is too late to take corrective action, or occasionally are not recognized at all. Sadly, businesses in these circumstances may then cease trading, either through their own choice, or because individuals and firms to whom they owe money force them to via the courts. A business might be regarded as having failed when it is *insolvent* and its liabilities exceed its assets. Under the terms of the Insolvency Act of 1986, different rules apply to the termination of firms depending on their status, as follows:

1 Sole traders

Those individuals who are insolvent can either come to a voluntary arrangement with their creditors, or go bankrupt. A voluntary arrangement is simply an agreement between the individual and his or her creditors whereby they accept reduced or delayed payments. A proposal will be prepared with the aid of an accountant or solicitor who is experienced in these matters, and will be put to the court for permission to proceed. If granted, the plan is then presented to the creditors who may or may not agree to it. Should they refuse, the individual may be made bankrupt.

Bankruptcy proceedings may commence when the individual or creditors concerned approach the court. A creditor may do this if it is owed £750 or more by the individual, not an especially large sum nowadays. If a bankruptcy order is made by the court, a trustee is appointed to collect the individual's assets and sell them to meet his or her debts. Do not forget that these assets include business and personal belongings, such as the family home and car. Bankruptcy is a very traumatic experience and one which is hard to imagine unless experienced.

2 Partnerships

A partnership may terminate along the same lines as an individual's business or in accordance with the terms and conditions detailed in the partnership agreement. In addition, a partner (or partners) may apply to a court to have the partnership dissolved on various grounds. Valid grounds for dissolution might include a partner's mental instability, constant breaches of the partnership agreement and personal or professional misconduct which might harm the business, and any other 'just and equitable' reason. If a partnership ends, assets should be sold to pay off any liabilities and debts, individual loans to partners and capital contributions by partners in that order. The residue should then be divided up in the same proportions as profits once were.

3 Companies

Like a partnership, a company can be wound up on a voluntary basis or in a compulsory manner, by court order. A *liquidator* will be appointed to take charge of the company, collect its assets, pay off its debts and distribute any remaining funds to shareholders, as appropriate. Money is distributed in a strict order of sequence. Preferential creditors such as the Inland Revenue demanding taxes and employees requiring wages are paid first. Then, the other creditors such as banks and trade suppliers are paid. Next, preference shareholders receive their share followed by the ordinary shareholders who, in reality, may be given nothing at all.

It should never be forgotten that the closure of a business has many effects, and it is important to think about these. Take the sole trader as an example. He or she may lose his or her home, is now out of work and must answer to the court until he or she is discharged from bankruptcy in three years. After that, he or she may find it hard to begin again with another business loan, mortgage for a home and so on – few will lend money to or want to trade with a known failure. His or her family will suffer too – they may have to move out of a luxurious home into substandard and rented accommodation, live without a car, treats, days out, holidays and so on.

Others are affected too – employees are on the scrapheap (and their families suffer as well), customers may have to go further afield for goods and services, suppliers lose a valuable source of income, a landlord might be left with a vacant property which is difficult to re-let and neighbours could be unhappy being next to an empty unit which creates the impression of an area in decline. The list is almost endless.

3.6   Rapid revision

Answers	Questions
–	1 What does a business do?
1 It produces and/or distributes goods and/or services for profit.	2 What are the overriding objectives of each and every business?
2 (a) To survive; (b) to make a profit; (c) to grow.	3 In what ways might a business grow?
3 (a) Horizontally; (b) vertically; (c) by diversifying.	4 What is horizontal integration?
4 It is the growth of a business across the same level in which it currently operates within the production and distribution chain.	5 What is vertical integration?
5 It is the expansion of a business into other levels within the production and distribution chain.	6 What is conglomerate integration?
6 It is the growth of a business into other product and service markets.	7 What are the key ingredients of doing business successfully?
7 (a) The right product; (b) the right price; (c) the right promotion; (d) the right place.	8 What does a business need to think about if it is to provide the right product?
8 (a) Product line; (b) product group; (c) product mix.	9 What are the three most common pricing methods which may help to produce the right price?
9 (a) Cost based pricing; (b) demand based pricing; (c) competition based pricing.	10 What might the right promotion consist of?

10 (a) Advertising; (b) sales promotion; (c) packaging; (d) face-to-face selling; (e) public relations.

11 What distribution channels might get the products to the right place?

---

11 (a) Manufacturer-wholesaler-retailer-buyer; (b) manufacturer-wholesaler/retailer-buyer; (c) manufacturer/wholesaler-retailer-buyer; (d) manufacturer/wholesaler/retailer-buyer.

12 What organizations and individuals is a business answerable to?

---

12 (a) Shareholders; (b) employees; (c) creditors; (d) customers; (e) the State; (f) neighbours; (g) the community.

13 What are the danger signals that suggest a business is in trouble?

---

13 Typically, (a) fewer customers; (b) falling sales; (c) rising expenditure; (d) lower profits; (e) increasing stock levels; (f) more debts; (g) longer payment times; (h) cash shortages.

14 What are the most common reasons for business failure?

---

14 (a) Bad management; (b) the changing environment.

15 What are the remedies for business difficulties?

---

15 Possibly, (a) new management; (b) more capital; (c) reducing costs; (d) re-organization; (e) revised objectives; (f) new products and services; (g) new markets.

16 What is insolvency?

---

16 It is a state of affairs which exists when liabilities exceed assets, and debts cannot be paid.

17 What happens when a business is insolvent?

---

17 It will cease trading on a voluntary basis or in a compulsory manner, by court order.

18 Who are affected by the closure of a business?

---

18 Everyone, including (a) owners; (b) managers; (c) employees; (d) customers; (e) suppliers; (f) landlords; (g) neighbours.

19 Go over the questions again until you know all of the answers. Then move on to the next section.

Part Two
Business Resources

4
Financial resources

4.1 What are financial resources?

Financial resources is an expression which describes those funds that are used by a business to acquire the assets which it needs to trade successfully, and to settle the liabilities which accrue during its trading activities. These funds may consist of *investment* or *share capital* put in by the owners or subscribed by shareholders, along with *loan capital* provided by lenders, such as a bank or other financial institutions.

With regard to financial resources, a firm will initially calculate its financial needs before looking at types and sources of finance, and matching them together. As a simple example, a business does not want to borrow a large sum of money from one of the owner's relatives if that person is going to want to have the money repaid in a month. It would be far better to approach a bank or whoever else is willing to forward sufficient funds and spread repayments over a 10- or 20-year period, or whatever. Then, the concern has to set about raising finance, using it wisely and accounting for it to the Inland Revenue and other interested bodies such as Customs and Excise and the Registrar of Companies.

4.2 Calculating financial needs

Each and every firm has to work out how much money it needs to start trading and to continue on a successful basis. By and large, businesses do this by anticipating and budgeting for income and expenditure over a forthcoming period of time. Budgeting serves several purposes in addition to helping a concern to calculate its financial requirements. In particular, it encourages planning and provides the firm and all of its employees with a financial framework to work within and towards. Hopefully, the various departments and their personnel will pull together to ensure that budgets are adhered to, and the business stays on course for financial success. Several types of budget can be recognized:

1   *The sales budget*

This budget anticipates likely sales over a future period, and may be broken down in various ways – perhaps by product and/or service, by types of customer or by geographical location.

2   *The distribution budget*

Here, the expected costs of warehousing, transporting and distributing goods are set out. Often, the distribution budget will be tied up within the sales budget.

3   *The selling costs budget*

This budget will lay down the estimated costs incurred by advertising and promoting products and services, and through employing a salesforce to go out 'on the road' to meet customers face to face. As with the distribution budget, it may be linked to the sales budget.

4   *The production budget*

Working back from the initial sales budget, this particular budget can detail the types and numbers of items which may need to be manufactured or processed, and the costs of overheads, labour and materials which go into making them.

5   *The purchases budget*

Closely related to the production budget, this specific budget will set out the expected purchases of raw materials and finished goods which go into the production process.

6   *The administration budget*

This budget details the cost of the administration department, its personnel and its varied and numerous functions.

7 *The capital expenditure budget*

Here, the anticipated expenditure on new and/or replacement fixed assets of ongoing use to the firm such as equipment, machinery and vehicles is itemized for the period concerned.

8 *The cash budget*

Of considerable significance, this budget highlights the firm's cash position by setting down the expected inflows of cash from sales and the outflows for purchases. Any cash surpluses or, more importantly, deficits can thus be seen in advance.

9 *The master budget*

As the name implies, the master budget draws together all of the information from the other budgets that have been prepared to show the firm's financial position at the end of the period if, and it is some-times a big if, everything goes according to plan.

As a consequence of this budgeting activity, a firm will be better placed to decide exactly how much finance it needs to set up and operate, and when it is required. It can then go on to look at different types of finance that are available to it, and where these may be obtained.

4.3 Types of finance

Whatever the size of a business and regardless of its various financial needs in the short, medium and long term, there are numerous types of finance which are, by and large, available to one and all of them. Most firms will take advantage of the following types, at one time or another.

Loans

A loan is an advance of a specified sum of money usually for a set period of time, and at a fixed or variable rate of interest. With a fixed interest rate, a business will have to pay interest of perhaps 10 per cent per annum whatever happens whereas with a variable rate it may go up or down from possibly five to 15 per cent according to prevailing economic conditions. The advanced money, or capital, and the interest are normally repaid by monthly instalments. Depending on the risks involved, a loan may be *secured* or *unsecured*. With a secured loan, the borrower must deposit some collateral with the lender – anything from a gold watch to the deeds of a property – so that if repayments are not made, it can be sold to cover the debt. An unsecured loan requires no such security, although the lender will press the borrower very hard to sell any assets if repayments are not made.

Most businesses will take out a loan when starting to trade in order to buy premises, equipment, machinery or whatever, and will want to spread out payments for as long as possible in order to keep plenty of cash circulating to finance day-to-day needs. A five- to 10-year term is commonplace. The choice, if one exists, between picking a fixed or variable interest rate is a difficult one and a decision largely depends upon the owners' views of what will happen to interest rates in the future. A fixed rate does allow the firm to know what must be paid and when, although there is a chance that it will end up paying more than it needed to if rates subsequently fall. In practice, the difference between a secured and unsecured loan is small, perhaps being limited to a slightly lower interest rate for a secured one. A failure to meet repayments will usually result in legal action being taken against the borrower to force him or her to sell secured *and* unsecured assets to settle the debt – so in that respect they are much the same.

Overdrafts

An overdraft is an arrangement whereby an individual or firm can borrow as much as they want from a lender up to a mutually agreed, total amount – easier said than done! A fixed or variable rate of interest is applied to the existing balance on a daily basis and any interest and administration charges due are settled by the borrower every month or quarter. They tend to be cheaper than loans. Normally, an overdraft facility is granted for a specific period of time and any outstanding sum due is repayable in full on demand. Like loans, overdrafts may be secured or unsecured. The vast majority of firms have overdrafts operating on an almost indefinite basis, using them to finance working capital.

Grants, subsidies and schemes

Often overlooked or poorly investigated, there are many grants made available by local and national government to persuade businesses to set up, or to trade in a given area. For example, *regional enterprise grants* have been given to small firms locating in neglected areas in order to help them pay for plant, machinery and the like. Local and national government have also subsidised new and growing concerns in a variety of ways such as by paying part of their production costs, employees' wages and export activities. There is an enormous amount and range of free finance available for those firms willing and able to seek it out.

Various schemes also exist to help firms raise finance in one form or another, again available for those businesses which go out and find them. The best known example is the government's Loan Guarantee Scheme which aims to encourage banks to lend money to small firms which cannot provide sufficient security to obtain a loan on the usual terms. Under this scheme, the government acts as a guarantor for the bulk of the loan with the bank forwarding the rest on an unsecured basis. If the money is not repaid, the government will settle most of the debt.

Trade credit

This is a well established business practice whereby suppliers agree (sometimes after a little arm twisting) to defer payment for goods and services for a period of time, typically 30 days or the end of the month following delivery. Buyers can then make use of their purchases, perhaps even repackaging and selling them, before payment falls due. Many businesses survive only by taking advantage of these credit facilities – they do not have the money to pay for goods 'up front' and cannot settle the bills unless and until those items are resold. Often, firms abuse these credit facilities by extending them without permission and even buying elsewhere if suppliers consequently complain or hold up deliveries of new stocks.

Not surprisingly, suppliers try to speed up payments and reduce the credit made available to businesses purchasing from them by offering *prompt payment* or *early settlement* discounts – perhaps five per cent off the bill for paying within seven days or two and a half per cent for settling within 30 days. Whenever products and services are purchased, buyers have to decide whether it is better to pay perhaps 95 per cent of the bill now and possibly incur additional overdraft interest and administration charges or to pay 100 per cent in 30, 60 or even 90 days and not use the overdraft facility as much, or at all.

Hire purchase

With this type of finance, which is also called *instalment credit* on occasions, an individual or firm buys an item by paying an initial deposit followed by a series of fixed monthly payments to cover the balance, plus interest and administration charges. Usually, 'hp' agreements are spread over three to five years, and are subject to exorbitant interest rates, typically of between 25 and 30 per cent. Smaller firms tend to buy items such as photocopiers and fax machines on hire purchase although the excessive interest charges do not make this a sensible option. Paying cash from an overdraft facility may be wiser, especially if a five to 10 per cent 'cash in hand' discount can be negotiated with the seller.

Leasing

In many respects, this is comparable to hire purchase. Here, one business rents, or *leases*, machinery, equipment or whatever to another firm for a monthly fee. Ownership of the item is retained by the lender or lessor while being used by the borrower, or lessee. At the end of the agreement or beforehand if a replacement is required, the lessor will take back the item. Clearly, leasing costly equipment can be a sensible policy for a firm to pursue as it may then use the items without having to tie up money, and is an especially wise move if the goods lose their value quickly, and are soon outdated and superseded by new models.

Factoring

This increasingly popular business practice involves a business handing over its account handling to another organization, commonly known as a *factor*. On receipt of invoices due to be paid by a firm's customers, the factor provides that firm with a cash payment of about 85 per cent of the total value of the invoices. The balance less a handling fee of between three and 10 per cent is forwarded by the factor when the invoices have been paid. For a business, the prompt payment of the bulk of the monies combined with less time and effort spent on chasing debts normally outweigh the costs involved with factoring. It can be very beneficial, releasing cash quickly for those firms operating on a tight budget.

Invoice discounting

A variation on factoring, this takes place when a business simply sells its unpaid invoices to a specialist organization at a discount rate of perhaps 20 per cent or more of their face value. The organization buying the invoices is then responsible for chasing and collecting payments and makes a profit for itself once a success rate of 80 per cent or whatever has been surpassed. As with factoring, the business which sells its unpaid invoices benefits from early cash settlements, albeit at a rather substantial price.

Shares

A company is financed initially by shares purchased by its shareholders and can then raise additional funds by selling more shares to current shareholders or to new ones approved of by the existing shareholders in a private limited company or to the general public in a public limited company. With a private limited company, it is likely that close and trusted business colleagues of the present shareholders will be approached personally, and asked to buy into the company. For a plc, advertisements and prospectuses will be issued and other large firms will probably invest, seeking a safe and steady return on their investment rather than hands-on involvement. Clearly, a new share issue which is taken up is a good sign, and may persuade other lenders to forward finance too, if it is still required.

Two main types of share may be offered – *preference* and *ordinary* shares. Preference shares give their holders a guaranteed dividend, whereby they receive a set return of perhaps 10 per cent of their investment each year. Thus, these shares represent a very safe investment. However, preference shareholders are not usually permitted to vote and will not share in any surplus left over if the company ceases to trade. Ordinary shareholders may receive a dividend if any profits remain after preference shareholders have obtained their returns but are just as likely not to receive anything in a poor trading year. Obviously, these shares represent a riskier investment, but do at least enable their holders to vote and to share in any surpluses on the cessation of business.

Various common terms are used with regard to the issuing and take-up of shares, and it is sensible to be aware of them. *Authorized capital* is the total value of the shares which a company is permitted to issue, as detailed in its Memorandum of Association. *Issued capital* is the value of the capital issued to shareholders in the form of shares, whether preference or ordinary ones. The amount of capital which has been paid for becomes known as *paid up capital* and the proportion which does not have to be or has not yet been paid is called *unpaid capital. Reserve capital* is the unpaid capital which cannot be called up unless the company is about to stop trading and has debts which need to be settled.

Debentures

A debenture is a fixed interest loan to a company, secured against one or more of that company's assets. With a fixed charge, a particular asset such as a computer or a printing machine is pledged as security and might be seized and sold to meet the company's obligations if necessary. With a floating charge, the lender, who might be a major shareholder, has a claim on any company assets if the capital and/or interest payments are not made as agreed. Some debentures are repayable, or 'redeemable', at a specified date in the future, typically 10 years from the day of issue. Others are irredeemable, and never need to be repaid – the lender receives interest payments forever!

4.4 Sources of finance

Whatever types of finance are sought by a business, they will inevitably come from one or more of a variety of sources, most often these:

Self

Most businesses, from the sole trader up to the public limited company, can finance some or even all of their operations and activities from their own existing resources, one way or another. Savings, redundancy monies, inheritances, gifts from family and friends and so on may all be used, especially when starting a concern. Once trading, finance can be self-generated in a host of ways such as selling outdated and/or under-used assets, lowering staffing and stock levels, reducing trade credit to customers and ploughing back profits rather than taking them out of the firm. It could even be generated by investing existing money elsewhere – perhaps buying and selling shares in another growing company, all at a substantial profit!

Banks

These are the main source of finance for the vast majority of businesses as they offer a wide range of short-, medium- and long-term finance, as well as other services such as investment advice. Commercial, or 'clearing', banks such as Barclays, Lloyds, Midland and National Westminster with their network of high street branches are usually the first (and last) port of call for most entrepreneurs. Larger concerns may approach merchant banks which in many respects provide the same (or very similar) facilities and services as clearing banks, but for corporate rather than personal or small business customers.

Venture capital organizations

Sometimes, a firm will require finance for what are considered to be high risk activities such as expansion into new products or markets. As likely to fail as they are to succeed, these plans are notoriously difficult to finance from conventional sources such as high street banks, especially in recessionary times. Thus, a business will need to obtain what is termed as venture capital from specialist organizations, some of which are independently owned and run, while others are subsidiaries of commercial banks.

By specializing in venture capital investments, these organizations acquire expertise in evaluating high-risk projects and are able to make wiser and ultimately more profitable choices because of the knowledge they have accumulated over many years. Often, they focus on a specific trade or industry to reduce further the risks by building up extensive experience in just one particular field. Usually, venture capitalists are funded by other financial institutions such as pension funds, which do not have any or sufficient expertise in a given marketplace.

Venture capital is most often provided as a mix of loan and share capital. In some instances, the venture capital organization may even require a controlling interest in the firm by acquiring more than 50 per cent of its shares. Whatever its stake, it will inevitably demand to be an active participant in the overall running of the business rather than being a passive adviser as most lenders tend to be. The British Venture Capital Association is the trade body that represents and acts on behalf of those financial organizations operating in this field.

Government

Whether at a local or national level, the government is a key source of finance for businesses, especially new and growing ones. This assistance may be available on either a direct or indirect basis. An obvious example of direct financial aid would be a grant to encourage a firm to base itself in a given area, in the hope that this will help to stimulate the local environment by bringing money, jobs and trade into the area. On an indirect basis, the government may guarantee a loan forwarded to the business by a third party, as happens when a high street bank provides finance to a firm under the terms of the popular Loan Guarantee Scheme.

Suppliers

Without doubt, nearly all suppliers to a business act as an (unofficial) source of finance for it, unless they demand 'cash on delivery' when goods and services are supplied (in which case the firm may simply look elsewhere for stock). At the same time, that business probably acts as a source of finance for the next firm in the production and distribution chain, and in much the same way. In effect, each one is propping up the next!

Finance houses

These are financial institutions which specialize in providing hire purchase and leasing facilities. They usually act in liaison with suppliers in order to provide the facilities. Typically, a small business owner might approach a supplier to buy some office equipment or whatever on hire purchase. The supplier provides the goods in exchange for a deposit but subsequent monthly payments are made by the small business direct to the finance house. In the event of the firm defaulting on payments, it is the finance house and not the supplier which will take the necessary legal action to recover the debt.

Factors

These tend to be specialist financial organizations with considerable experience in account management and debt collection. Clearly, they face a difficult task in making money with most firms only wanting to hand over their accounts because they have substantial numbers of customers delaying or refusing to pay bills. Factors need to be selective in the accounts which they take on, and charge a high, across the board fee on all accounts – difficult *and* easy ones to collect!

Insurance companies

General insurance companies offer insurance cover against the risk of loss or damage to personal and business assets. They issue insurance policies to provide for various contingencies, in exchange for premiums, some of which are subsequently used to settle claims under the terms of those policies. To maximize income and profits, these companies invest their accumulated funds either in quickly disposable assets in case of a sudden influx of claims as occurred after a hurricane swept through Britain in October 1987 or in long-term assets such as company shares which are potentially more profitable if selected carefully. In either event, much of their funds are used (indirectly) to finance businesses.

Long-term insurance companies were originally concerned with providing cover against loss or damage to life and limb, and were thus better known as life and accident insurance companies. Nowadays, this constitutes only a small proportion of their work, as most policies sold are designed to generate long-term savings for policyholders, typically over a 10-year period or more. Like general insurance companies, these organizations seek to secure as high a return as possible from the monies invested through them so that their commission is maximized and they therefore invest in long-term securities such as shares in growing and successful companies.

Pension funds

These institutions specialize in managing personal and corporate pension schemes, collecting contributions from individuals, employees and employers, investing them wisely and making payments to retired beneficiaries in due course. Their investment approach is similar to insurance companies, although as payouts are likely to be in 20 to 40 instead of in 10 years, company shares are an even more appropriate investment for them. Indeed, they are the largest share owning group in the UK. Pension funds are represented by the National Association of Pension Funds which acts on their behalf when dealing with fellow financial institutions and the government.

Unit trusts

These organizations operate a number of investment funds, buying and selling securities such as UK and overseas companies' shares. Parts, or *units*, of these funds are sold to investors, and are subject to an initial management and ongoing annual fees. Buyers, or *unit holders* as they become known, tend to be small investors drawn from the general public. The values of the funds and therefore the units vary according to the fluctuating values of the securities. Units can be resold by their holders, hopefully at a profit. The Unit Trust Association is the representative body of these organizations in the UK.

Investment trusts

Contrary to their name, these are not trusts but companies. Their main activity is investing in fellow companies, often overseas. As with unit trusts, they are attractive to smaller investors. Sometimes, they also provide specialist forms of finance direct to businesses, most notably venture capital. Investment trust companies in the UK are represented by an organization known as the Association of Investment Trust Companies.

4.5 Raising finance

For most firms, raising funds will involve approaching a bank or another lender who will expect to receive a *business plan* which will help them to reach a decision. This plan, or business proposal, is a document which sets out the (prospective) commercial and financial activities of a concern, and verifies them so far as possible with detailed supporting material in appendices. Often, the business owner or manager fills out a pre-printed form such as the one reproduced as Figure 4.1. Alternatively, he or she draws up one beneath the following sections and headings.

The commercial section

Obviously, all business plans are different but in most instances this information will be given in the commercial section of a proposal:

1 The background to the business: when, where and why it began trading, how it has progressed, its major achievements and the obstacles it has overcome. If it is a new concern, an explanation should be given about why it will be successful and how, where and when it will commence trading. If a firm is being purchased, details ought to be provided about the reasons for its sale and the asking price.
2 The business premises: why the site was selected, whether the property is rented or bought outright, its price, any terms and conditions associated with renting or buying it, size, shape and any equipment, machinery and vehicles which are owned, or need to be purchased.
3 The products and services offered: what they are, how they contributed to stock levels and sales turnover, how and where they are made or bought, buying and selling prices and sales and promotional methods. They should also be compared and contrasted with competing goods and services in terms of respective

Figure 4.1 A pre-printed business plan form

BARCLAYS BUSSINESS PLAN FORM

Use this form to help you structure your own business plan.

INTRODUCTION

THIS BUSINESS PLAN FORM AND THE ACCOMPANYING APPENDICES HAVE BEEN SUBMITTED TO SUPPORT OUR APPLICATION FOR AN £8000 OVERDRAFT FACILITY FOR OUR FIRST TRADING YEAR. THEY CONTAIN FULL COMMERCIAL AND FINANCIAL DETAILS ABOUT OUR PROPOSED BUSINESS ACTIVITIES AND OBJECTIVES.

DETAILS OF THE BUSINESS

Name of business   COCO CARRI-BAGS

Business address   12 ESBURY INDUSTRIAL ESTATE, PORTMAN WAY, ESBURY, YORKSHIRE   LE26 3BH

Format (limited company, sole trader etc.)   PARTNERSHIP

Type of business   MANUFACTURER

Telephone   TO BE CONNECTED

Date business began (if you have already started trading) TO COMMENCE 1 SEPTEMBER 1991

Business activities WE SHALL PERSONALLY MANUFACTURE AND MARKET OUR OWN UNIQUE RANGE OF LADIES FASHION BAGS, KNOWN AS CARRI-BAGS WITHIN THE TRADE AND TO THE PUBLIC.

PERSONAL DETAILS

Name   CORINNE CORRIGAN

Address   13 SHOTLEY DRIVE, TRIMLEY YORKSHIRE LE12 8NG

Telephone (home) 0394 59241   Telephone (work) ══════

Qualifications HIGHER NATIONAL DIPLOMA IN FASHION AND DESIGN, 2 'A' LEVELS IN ART ('B' GRADE) AND BUSINESS STUDIES ('C' GRADE) PLUS 6 MISCELLANEOUS GCSE'S ('C' GRADES)   Date of Birth 14 SEPTEMBER 1970

Relevant work experience SALES ASSISTANT (SATURDAYS) FOR SMARTIES FASHIONS, THE SQUARE, ESBURY SINCE FEBRUARY 1987 MARKET RESEARCH INTERVIEWER (HOLIDAYS) FOR REGIONAL OPINION POLLS, 60 HIGH STREET, TRIMLEY SINCE JUNE 1989.

Business experience A SECOND YEAR, HND ASSIGNMENT INVOLVED SETTING UP OUR OWN BUSINESS. I DESIGNED, MANUFACTURED AND SOLD CARRI-BAGS TO 12 FASHION SHOPS IN YORKSHIRE

Courses attended 'RUN YOUR OWN BUSINESS' AND 'BETTER BOOK-KEEPING' - 20 WEEK COURSES HELD AT THE ESBURY INSTITUTE ON TUESDAY AND THURSDAY NIGHTS

Details of key management personnel (if any)

Name RAJESH MUNGLANI	Name ══════
Position PARTNER	Position ══════
Address 13 SHOTLEY DRIVE	Address ══════
TRIMLEY, YORKSHIRE	
LE12 8NG	
Date of birth 18 OCTOBER 1970	Date of birth ══════
Qualifications HND - FASHION AND DESIGN	Qualifications ══════
'A' LEVEL - ART ('C' GRADE)	
'A' LEVEL - ECONOMICS ('C' GRADE)	
4 GCSE's - ('C' GRADES OR ABOVE)	

Figure 4.1   (continued)

Relevant work experience HE HAS RUN HIS OWN MARKET STALL (LADIES FASHIONS) IN BRADSHAW PARK ON EVERY SATURDAY AND SUNDAY SINCE JANUARY 1989

Relevant work experience ════

Present income NIL - MARKET JUST EVICTED

Present income ═══

What skills will you need to buy in during the first two years? ACCOUNTANCY SKILLS - DRAWING UP ANNUAL ACCOUNTS, TAX ADVICE ETC - FROM AN ACCOUNTANT. LEGAL SKILLS - PREPARING A PARTNERSHIP AGREEMENT, PERUSING OUR LEASE ETC - FROM A SOLICITOR.

PERSONNEL

Estimate the cost of employing any people or buying any services you may need in the first two years

Number of people	Job function	Monthly cost	Annual cost
PARTNERS (2)	ALL DUTIES	£ 433 (APX)	£5200
YTS TRAINEES (2)	MISCELLANEOUS TASKS	£ 87 (APX)	£1040
ACCOUNTANT\SOLICITOR	ADVICE \ ASSISTANCE	£ 100	£1200

(Remember to include your own salary and those of any partners you may have in this calculation)

PRODUCT/SERVICE

Description THE CARRI-BAG IS A MULTI-PURPOSE BAG FOR WOMEN AVAILABLE IN BLACK, PINK, GREY AND PEACH, IT MAY BE USED AS A HANDBAG, SPORTS HOLDALL, BABY CHANGER OR SHOPPING BAG. WHEN NOT IN USE, IT CAN BE FOLDED UP AND TUCKED INTO A POCKET.

Contribution of individual products or services to total turnover

Product	% Contribution
BLACK CARRI-BAG	30
PINK CARRI-BAG	20
GREY CARRI-BAG	20
PEACH CARRI-BAG	30

(the figures in this column should add up to 100)

Break down the cost of materials (if any)

Product A

Materials (including packaging, labelling etc.)	Cost
OUTER AND INNER MATERIAL	£6·00 (3 METRES × £2 PER METRE)
ZIPS, TRIMS AND PACKAGING	£1·00

*Selling price for Product A: £14·00   (£7·00 COST PRICE)

Product B ════

*Selling price for Product B: ════

Product C ════

*Selling price for Product C: ════

(*These are assumptions)

Where did you get your estimates from?

Material	Source
OUTER AND INNER MATERIAL	GAYTHER AND HICKS (WHOLESALERS) LTD,
ZIPS, TRIMS AND PACKAGING	96 ESBURY INDUSTRIAL ESTATE, ESBURY

Figure 4.1 (continued)

MARKET

Describe your market　WE SHALL SELL TO INDEPENDENT FASHION STORES WHICH APPEAL TO 16-35 YEAR OLD FEMALES. THE MAIN USERS OF OUR PRODUCT WILL BE STUDENTS, CAREER WOMEN AND YOUNG MOTHERS LOOKING FOR AN ATTRACTIVE, ALL PURPOSE BAG AT A COST CONSCIOUS PRICE.

Where is your market?　THE CARRI-BAG SHALL BE SOLD WITHIN A 25 MILE RADIUS OF ESBURY, BETWEEN THE TOWNS OF WHITTON, BURLEIGH AND WALTON

Who are your customers?　INDEPENDENT RETAILERS SEEKING GOODS WHICH ARE NOT IN THE MULTIPLES, CAN BE BOUGHT IN LIMITED NUMBERS AND ARE DELIVERED ON TIME

How big is your market?　THERE ARE 64 SUITABLE RETAIL OUTLETS IN THE REGION - 24 WILL CONSTANTLY STOCK OUR PRODUCT, 28 ARE INTERESTED IN IT, 12 ARE NOT.

Is your market growing, static or in decline?　GROWING — THERE WERE 50 OF THESE SHOPS IN AUGUST 1989 RISING TO 57 IN 1990 AND NOW 64 IN 1991.

Itemise the competitive products or services

Competitor's name　＿＿＿＿＿＿＿＿＿＿

Competitive product/service A

Name　HANDBAG　　　　　Price £15 - £25 (LEATHER)

Strengths IT IS AN ESTABLISHED PRODUCT　Weaknesses TOO SMALL FOR PRACTICAL USE
IT APPEALS TO ALL FEMALES IN OUR MARKET　IT DOES NOT HAVE ENOUGH COMPARTMENTS
IT IS AVAILABLE IN VARIOUS COLOURS/STYLES　IT CANNOT (USUALLY) BE ADJUSTED OR
Competitor's name ＿＿＿＿＿　FOLDED AWAY FOR EASY STORAGE

Competitive product/service B

Name　SPORTS HOLDALL　　　Price £15 - £25 (ACCORDING TO BRAND)

Strengths IT IS AN ESTABLISHED PRODUCT　Weaknesses HEAVY AND BULKY TO USE
LEADING BRANDS PURCHASED FOR IMAGE/STATUS　IT DOES NOT HAVE (M)ANY COMPARTMENTS
IT IS AVAILABLE IN VARIOUS COLOURS/STYLES　IT IS DIFFICULT TO ADJUST AND STORE
Competitor's name ＿＿＿＿＿　ONLY APPEALS TO SPORTING TYPES

Competitive product/service C

Name　BABY CHANGER　　　　Price £15 - £25

Strengths USUALLY LIGHTWEIGHT AND STRONG　Weaknesses IT IS NOT WIDELY STOCKED
IT NORMALLY HAS A NUMBER OF SECTIONS　IT CANNOT (NORMALLY) ADJUST OR FOLD
IT IS AVAILABLE IN VARIOUS COLOURS/STYLES　ONLY APPEALS TO YOUNG MOTHERS.

What is special about your own product or service?　IT IS A NEW, INNOVATIVE PRODUCT WHICH DOES NOT HAVE ANY DIRECTLY COMPARABLE RIVALS AT THE TIME OF WRITING WE HAVE APPLIED FOR A PATENT TO TRY TO MAINTAIN THIS UNIQUE POSITION FOR AS LONG AS POSSIBLE. NOTE THE 'PRODUCT PROTECTION CORRESPONDENCE' IN THE APPENDICES.

Advantages of your product or service over

Competitor A　IT IS MORE VERSATILE, APPROPRIATE IN ANY CIRCUMSTANCES.
IT IS LARGER AND MORE SPACIOUS THAN EACH OF THEM.

Competitor B　IT IS LIGHTER THAN ALL OF THEM
IT HAS MORE COMPARTMENTS THAN ANY OF THEM

Competitor C　IT CAN FIT INSIDE A JACKET OR TROUSER POCKET
SEE 'PRODUCT SPECIFICATION CHARTS' IN THE APPENDICES.

Figure 4.1　(continued)

What is your sales forecast for the

*1st three months?

Units 864 (288 PER MONTH)   Invoiced value £12096 (EXCLUDING VAT)

*2nd three months?

Units 1008 (336 PER MONTH)   Invoiced value £14112 (EXCLUDING VAT.)

*3rd three months?

Units 1152 (384 PER MONTH)   Invoiced value £16128 (EXCLUDING VAT)

*4th three months?

Units 1296 (432 PER MONTH)   Invoiced value £18144 (EXCLUDING VAT)

(*These are assumptions)

(See the section on sales forecasting on pages 14-15 of FINANCIAL PLANNING FOR YOUR BUSINESS)

Explain how you have arrived at these estimates THEY ARE BASED ON ORDERS RECEIVED FROM 24 FASHION SHOPS AND DISCUSSIONS WITH 28 OTHER STORES WHICH HAVE EXPRESSED A FIRM INTEREST IN STOCKING CARRI-BAGS (SEE 'CUSTOMER ORDERS' AND 'CUSTOMER RESEARCH FINDINGS' IN THE ATTACHED APPENDICES)

Give details of any firm orders you already have WE HAVE ORDERS FROM 24 INDEPENDENT RETAILERS, EACH REQUESTING 1 BOX OF 12 CARRI-BAGS PER MONTH AT £168 PLUS VAT PER BOX (REFER TO 'CUSTOMER ORDERS' IN THE APPENDICES)

MARKETING

What sort of marketing do your competitors do?

Competitor A ⸺.
_____

Competitor B ⸺
_____

Competitor C ⸺
_____

What sort of marketing or advertising do you intend to do?

Method	Cost
PERSONAL VISITS AND DEMONSTRATIONS	OUR TIME PLUS £168 PER ANNUM (PETROL)
PRESS RELEASES - PAPERS, TRADE MAGAZINES	OUR TIME PLUS MODEST POSTAGE/STATIONERY
ENTRY IN THE LOCAL 'YELLOW PAGES'	FREE OF CHARGE

Why do you think that these methods are appropriate for your particular market? NO RETAILER WILL BUY AN INNOVATORY PRODUCT FROM A NEW FIRM WITHOUT A DEMONSTRATION PRESS ARTICLES MAY BE SEEN BY POTENTIAL CUSTOMERS. RETAILERS LOOK IN 'YELLOW PAGES' FOR SUPPLIERS

Where did you get your estimates from?

Method	Source
PERSONAL VISITS, DEMONSTRATIONS, RELEASES	SELF ASSESSMENT
ENTRY IN THE LOCAL 'YELLOW PAGES'	BRITISH TELECOM (PUBLISHERS)

PREMISES/MACHINERY/VEHICLES

Premises:

Where do you intend to locate the business and why? 12 ESBURY INDUSTRIAL ESTATE — OUR WORKSHOP IS INEXPENSIVE AND CLOSE TO OUR SUPPLIER AND CUSTOMERS (VIA M1)

What sort and size of premises will you need? LEASEHOLD PREMISES - WE SHALL NOT CONSIDER A FREEHOLD PROPERTY UNTIL WE CAN FULLY ASSESS OUR LONG TERM NEEDS. 900 SQUARE FEET - THIS PROVIDES US WITH SUFFICIENT SPACE FOR SHORT TERM GROWTH.

Figure 4.1 (continued)

What are the details of any lease, licence, rent, rates and when is the next rent review due? 3 YEAR RENEWABLE COUNCIL LEASE, £2,700 PER ANNUM FOR RENT AND RATES, NO RENT REVIEWS (SEE OUR 'LEASEHOLD AGREEMENT' IN THE APPENDICES)

Machinery/Vehicles:

What machinery/vehicles do you require? INDUSTRIAL SEWING MACHINES AND RELATED ITEMS TO ACTUALLY PRODUCE THE CARRI-BAGS. A VAN TO DELIVER THEM EACH MONTH AND VISIT PROSPECTIVE STOCKISTS IN OUR AREA

Are these to be bought or leased and on what terms? THE SEWING EQUIPMENT/MACHINERY IS TO BE BOUGHT OUTRIGHT FOR £5000 (PLUS VAT) ESBURY POLYTECHNIC'S FASHION DEPARTMENT IS SELLING THEM TO US AT APPROXIMATELY 20 PER CENT BELOW EQUIVALENT COST PRICES PRIOR TO ITS CLOSURE. THE VAN IS ALREADY OWNED

How long is their lifespan? THE SEWING MACHINES AND RELATED ITEMS ARE ESTIMATED TO HAVE A LIFESPAN OF 5 YEARS (REFER TO OUR 'SUPPLIERS PRICE LISTS' IN THE APPENDICES) SIMILARLY, THE VAN OUGHT TO LAST US FOR THIS PERIOD OF TIME AS WELL.

RECORD SYSTEM

Describe records to be kept and how they are to be kept up to date? WE SHALL USE THE 'COMPLETE TRADERS ACCOUNT BOOK' (THOMPSONS) TO MAINTAIN INCOME, EXPENDITURE AND VAT RECORDS (SUPPORTED BY INVOICE, RECEIPT AND BANK STATEMENT FILES) THIS WILL BE FILLED IN ON A DAILY AND WEEKLY BASIS, AS APPROPRIATE. WE SHALL CHECK IT EACH MONTH TO SEE THAT WE ARE MEETING PROFIT AND CASH FLOW TARGETS (AND WILL TAKE ANY NECESSARY ACTIONS IF NOT)

OBJECTIVES

What are your personal objectives in running the business?

Short-term TO MAKE OUR OWN DECISIONS, CONTROLLING OUR PROFESSIONAL AND FINANCIAL FUTURE; TO BE ABLE TO EARN A REASONABLE LIVING FROM OUR SKILLS AND HARD WORK; TO DO WORK WHICH WE ARE SUITED TO AND ENJOY DOING.

Medium-term TO CONTINUE TO CREATE AND DEVELOP FASHIONABLE, PRACTICAL PRODUCTS; TO BE WIDELY RECOGNIZED AS TALENTED DESIGNERS WHO ARE ABLE ENOUGH TO TRANSLATE THEIR NOVEL IDEAS INTO FINANCIAL PROFITS

How do you intend to achieve them? BY ATTENDING FURTHER DESIGN COURSES IN THE EVENINGS TO BROADEN OUR KNOWLEDGE AND TALENTS; BY WORKING 24 HOURS EACH DAY, 7 DAYS PER WEEK IF NECESSARY TO ESTABLISH OURSELVES

What objectives do you have for the business itself?

Short-term TO INCREASE OUR CUSTOMER BASE FROM AN INITIAL 24 TO 36 ACCOUNTS BY THE END OF THE YEAR; TO MAINTAIN A HEALTHY CASH FLOW (AS SET OUT IN OUR 'CASH FLOW FORECAST' IN THE APPENDICES); TO ACHIEVE PROFIT TARGETS (AS PER THE 'PROFIT BUDGET' IN THE APPENDICES)

Medium-term TO CONTINUE TO EXPAND OUR CUSTOMER BASE AT A STEADY RATE OF 12-24 NEW ACCOUNTS PER YEAR, IN LINE WITH OUR PRODUCTION CAPABILITIES; TO CONSTANTLY IMPROVE CASH FLOW AND PROFIT LEVELS TO PREPARE FOR (POTENTIAL) LONG TERM EXPANSION AND DIVERSIFICATION.

Figure 4.1   (continued)

How do you intend to achieve them? BY COMBINING WELL PRICED, QUALITY PRODUCTS WITH A PERSONAL, FRIENDLY SERVICE; BY CAREFULLY MONITORING AND CONTROLLING THE LEVELS AND TIMING OF OUR INCOME AND EXPENDITURE.

What are your long-term objectives (if any)?

1. TO INCREASE SALES AT A MANAGEABLE RATE, EVENTUALLY SEEING THE CARRI-BAG STOCKED BY ALL INDEPENDENT FASHION STORES IN THE UNITED KINGDOM

2. TO BE ABLE TO CONCENTRATE ON DESIGNING NEW PRODUCTS, PROMOTING TRUSTED STAFF TO MANUFACTURE, SELL AND DISTRIBUTE CARRI-BAGS FOR US.

3. TO DIVERSIFY INTO COMPLEMENTARY PRODUCT LINES, SOLD THROUGH AN ESTABLISHED NETWORK OF INDEPENDENT RETAIL OUTLETS

4. TO EXPAND THE BUSINESS ONTO AN INTERNATIONAL BASIS, WITH OUR RANGE OF PRODUCTS AVAILABLE ACROSS EUROPE

5. TO NOT RUN BEFORE WE CAN WALK, ONLY DIVERSIFYING AND EXPANDING WHEN WE HAVE SUFFICIENT KNOWLEDGE, SKILLS AND EXPERIENCE TO SUCCEED

How do you intend to achieve them? AT THIS STAGE, WE ARE TAKING 1 (INEXPERIENCED) STEP AT A TIME AND CONCENTRATING ON ACHIEVING OUR SHORT (AND MEDIUM) TERM GOALS. ONLY IF THESE ARE REACHED WILL WE BE ABLE TO SET AND WORK TOWARDS SPECIFIC LONG TERM OBJECTIVES

FINANCE

Give details of your known orders (if any)

Date	Order	Details	Delivery date
1 =	FULL DETAILS OF ALL KNOWN	ORDERS ARE GIVEN	IN 'CUSTOMER
2 =	ORDERS' IN THE APPENDICES.		
3 =			
4 =			

Give details of your current business assets (if any)

Item	Value	Life Expectancy
BEDFORD RASCAL VAN	£1000	UP TO 5 YEARS

What will you need to buy to start up and then throughout your first year?

Start up

Item	Value
INDUSTRIAL SEWING EQUIPMENT, MACHINERY AND MISCELLANEOUS ITEMS	£5000 (EXCLUDING VAT)

Year 1

Item	Value
===	===
===	===

How will you pay for these?

		Value	Date
Grants	ENTERPRISE ALLOWANCE (C. CORRIGAN)	£2080	1 SEPTEMBER 1991 THROUGH
	ENTERPRISE ALLOWANCE (R. MUNGLANI)	£2080	TO 31 AUGUST 1992
Own resources	===	===	===
Loans	OVERDRAFT FACILITY	£8000	1 SEPTEMBER 1991 ONWARDS

Figure 4.1   (continued)

Creditors

What credit is available from your suppliers?

Supplier	Estimated value of monthly order	Number of days credit
GANTHER AND HICKS LTD	£2520 (MONTHLY AVERAGE)	30 *

*ALTHOUGH WE WILL PAY ON DELIVERY TO OBTAIN A 7.5% DISCOUNT(BUILT INTO FIGURES)

By reference to your Profit and Loss Budgets and Cashflow Forecasts, determine what your financial requirements are (ie. what overdraft or loan facilities are you looking for from Barclays?)

IN THE SHORT TERM, WE ARE SEEKING AN OVERDRAFT FACILITY OF £8000. IN THE MEDIUM AND LONG TERM WE ANTICIPATE ASKING FOR ADDITIONAL OVERDRAFT AND LOAN FACILITIES WHICH WILL HELP TO FUND EXPANSION AND DIVERSIFICATION. WE HOPE TO ESTABLISH A LONG TERM RELATIONSHIP WITH BARCLAYS BANK

What are you putting in yourself? A JOINT 'ENTERPRISE ALLOWANCE' FROM THE GOVERNMENT OF £40 PER WEEK EACH FOR 12 MONTHS (PROVIDING A TOTAL OF £4160)

What security will you be able to put up? NONE - ALTHOUGH WE WILL OWN ASSETS VALUED AT £6000. IN THE (UNLIKELY) EVENT OF BUSINESS FAILURE - AND WE ARE AWARE OF THE FAILURE RATE OF NEW VENTURES - THESE COULD BE SOLD TO REPAY YOU

OTHER

Accountant	ROBERT WILLIAMS (OF MITCHELL AND MOSSMAN LTD)
Address	YORK HOUSE, 6-8 YORK ROAD, ESBURY, YORKSHIRE LE26 4LZ
Telephone	0903 22407
Solicitor	MARIE PLATEK (OF TANNER, JONES AND MULLERY)
Address	48 SOUTH TERRACE, ESBURY, YORKSHIRE LE26 9TJ
Telephone	0903 22122

Legal status (ie. sole trader, partnership etc.) PARTNERSHIP

VAT registration WE ARE AWAITING CONFIRMATION OF OUR VAT REGISTRATION NUMBER

Insurance arrangements SIMON CHATFIELD (OF CHATFIELD AND SONS IN AMBERFIELD ROAD) IS ARRANGING A SMALL BUSINESS INSURANCE PACKAGE FOR US AT AN ESTIMATED COST OF £240 PER ANNUM.

+++ YOU'RE BETTER OFF TALKING TO ❀ BARCLAYS

NB. All figures exclude VAT. Published by Barclays Bank PLC (member of IMRO), Business Sector Marketing Department. Reg. No. 1026167. Reg. Office: 54 Lombard Street, London EC3P 3AH. BB470. Item Ref. 9971615A. AE. May 1990.

Figure 4.1   (continued)

advantages and disadvantages, with explanations of how any weaknesses will be eliminated in the future.

4 The owners and managers of the business: their respective educations, qualifications and work experiences plus descriptions of their various personalities, skills, knowledge and areas of expertise, and how these all gel together. Key employees should be referred to and detailed in the same manner.

5 The marketplaces: its size, the numbers and types of customers, the firm's existing and anticipated shares, internal and external influences and their possible and probable effects. It is also necessary to review the concern's rivals, and their backgrounds, activities, locations, premises, goods, services, customers and market shares. Positive and negative features should be viewed in comparison to the firm's own strengths and weaknesses, with suggestions made about how these drawbacks can be overcome.

6 The business objectives: in the short, medium and long term. The short term may be regarded as the forthcoming year with the medium term seen as up to five years, and long term thereafter. To survive is probably the immediate aim of almost all new businesses, with making a profit following on from that once the firm has become established.

The financial section

Again, each business proposal is unique but the following details will almost inevitably feature prominently in the financial section of every one of them, one way or another:

1 A profit budget. This is simply a form which outlines anticipated sales, costs and profits (or losses) over a given period of time, usually one year. Typically, a lender would expect to receive a month-by-month budget for the next year with quarter-by-quarter summaries for the subsequent two years so that they can see where repayments are coming from. Figure 4.2 is an illustration of a profit budget form.

2 A cash flow forecast. This shows how cash comes into and goes out of the business over a period of time, normally one year. Many small firms fail not because they are unprofitable but as a result of cash flow problems. A business may sell its goods but then has to wait three months or more for payments. Meantime, bills have to be settled. With expenditure constantly exceeding income, the cash eventually dries up and the firm has to stop trading. An example of a cash flow form is reproduced as Figure 4.3.

3 The financial requirements: total money needed and when, type

PROFIT BUDGET FOR:				MONTH

	MONTH		MONTH		MONTH
	BUDGET	ACTUAL	BUDGET	ACTUAL	BUDGET
SALES (a)					
Less: Direct Costs					
Cost of Materials					
Wages					
GROSS PROFIT (b)					
Gross Profit Margin ($^b/_a$ x 100%)					
Overheads					
Salaries					
Rent/Rates/Water					
Insurance					
Repairs/Renewals					
Heat/Light/Power					
Postages					
Printing/Stationery					
Transport					
Telephone					
Professional Fees					
Interest Charges					
Other					
TOTAL OVERHEADS (c)					
TRADING PROFIT (b) – (c)					
Less: Depreciation					
NET PROFIT BEFORE TAX					

NB. All figures exclude VAT. Published by Barclays Bank PLC (member of IMRO), Business Sector Marketing

Figure 4.2   A profit budget form

| TO | | | | | | | |  BARCLAYS |

	MONTH		MONTH		MONTH		TOTALS	
ACTUAL	BUDGET	ACTUAL	BUDGET	ACTUAL	BUDGET	ACTUAL	BUDGET	ACTUAL

Department. Reg. No. 1026167. Reg. Office: 54 Lombard Street, London EC3P 3AH. BB470. Item Ref. 9971615B. AE. May 1990.

Figure 4.2 (continued)

CASHFLOW FORECAST FOR:				MONTH

	MONTH		MONTH		MONTH
RECEIPTS	BUDGET	ACTUAL	BUDGET	ACTUAL	BUDGET
Cash Sales					
Cash from Debtors					
Capital Introduced					
TOTAL RECEIPTS (a)					
PAYMENTS					
Payments to Creditors					
Salaries/Wages					
Rent/Rates/Water					
Insurance					
Repairs/Renewals					
Heat/Light/Power					
Postages					
Printing/Stationery					
Transport					
Telephone					
Professional Fees					
Capital Payments					
Interest Charges					
Other					
V.A.T. payable (refund)					
TOTAL PAYMENTS (b)					
NET CASHFLOW (a-b)					
OPENING BANK BALANCE					
CLOSING BANK BALANCE					

NB. All figures include VAT. Published by Barclays Bank PLC (member of IMRO), Business Sector Marketing

Figure 4.3   A cash flow form

| | TO | | | | BARCLAYS | | | |

	MONTH		MONTH		MONTH		TOTALS	
ACTUAL	BUDGET	ACTUAL	BUDGET	ACTUAL	BUDGET	ACTUAL	BUDGET	ACTUAL

Department. Reg. No. 1026167. Reg. Office: 54 Lombard Street, London EC3P 3AH. BB470. Item Ref. 9971615C. AE. May 1990.

Figure 4.3 (continued)

and amount of finance required, the firm's financial input, what the money will be used for, how and when it will be repaid and the security that is available to set against borrowings. As a rule of thumb, a lender will want to see half of the finance needed being provided by the firm itself, and as much security as possible to cover loans and overdraft facilities.

The appendices

All of the commercial and financial statements incorporated within the business plan must be verified, and perhaps developed further, within the appendices. These are what might be included:

1   The business: three years' annual accounts, up-to-date books and records showing stock, assets, monies owed and owing, the business transfer agent's details, an accountant's assessment.
2   The premises: a map showing location and surroundings, the estate agents' property details, the freehold deeds or leasehold agreement, a solicitor's assessment, a surveyor's report, photographs of the premises, equipment, machinery and vehicle details.
3   Products and services: samples or illustrations of the goods, suppliers' price lists, quotes of various costs, retail price guides, advertising and promotional literature. Similar material could be provided for rival products as well.
4   Owners and managers: curricula vitae, copies of certificates and diplomas, testimonials from previous employers and associates, a partnership agreement, a solicitor's assessment of this arrangement.
5   The marketplace: customers' orders, customers' sales records, a map highlighting the location of customers and competitors, photographs of rivals' premises, competitors' sales guides and other literature.
6   The finance: profit budgets, cash flow forecasts, trade association correspondence about likely sales, costs, profits and so on, quotes and estimates of anticipated expenditure, proof of capital and security available.

4.6   Using finance

Having calculated its financial requirements and set out the planned uses of its finances when drawing up a business plan, it is sensible for a firm to monitor carefully its financial resources on an ongoing basis. *Variance analysis* is the rather offputting name given to the straightforward task of comparing the differences between the budgeted and actual results. There are four key areas of concern.

1 *Sales-revenue variance*

As suggested by its name, this represents the difference between the budgeted and actual value of sales achieved over a given period of time. This variance can be attributed to *sales-price variance* where the selling price was different from the anticipated price and/or *sales-volume variance* where sales were not as expected.

2 *Materials-cost variance*

Here, there is a difference between the estimated and actual cost of materials. This may be because of *materials-quantity variance* where a smaller or larger quantity than expected was used and/or *materials-price variance* where the quantity was as anticipated, but the actual prices were more or less than had been budgeted for.

3 *Overhead-cost variance*

As the name implies, this is the difference between the anticipated overhead costs of a product or service and the actual overhead costs. This could be because actual expenditure is more or less than the budgeted amount, which is termed *expenditure variance* or because output is higher or lower than expected, which is known as *volume variance*.

4 *Labour-cost variance*

With this, there is a difference between the estimated and actual labour costs of a product. The difference can be associated with *labour-rate variance* where the wages paid are higher or lower than expected and/or with *labour-efficiency variance* where more or less time is spent than was anticipated.

Whether differences are attributable to sales, materials, overheads or labour variance (or more likely a mix of them), a firm will need to remedy matters as soon as possible, spotting the causes and seeking to rectify them as quickly as it can – otherwise profits may soon turn into losses, and the concern will enter into a permanent and terminal decline concluding in business failure.

4.7   Accounting for finance

All businesses need to keep accurate and up-to-date books and records
of their financial activities, subsequently drawing up accounts and
analysing them. This can help a firm to spot potential problems in
advance such as high stock levels which tie up working capital and
increasing sums of money owed by customers which restrict cash
flow. Also, the Inland Revenue and Customs and Excise will want to
see accounts for income, corporation and value added tax purposes.

The books

Numerous facts and figures must be noted down regularly. A small
business may keep the following books, which are much the same as
those kept by larger concerns, albeit in a much simplified manner:

1   *The cash book*

Here, the owner or manager would detail takings, money banked,
cash paid for stock and cash paid for expenses, all on a day-to-day
basis. This would be followed by weekly cash summaries, for week-
by-week comparisons.

2   *The bank book*

Then, he or she might record monies into and out of the firm's bank
account, on a daily and weekly basis. Expenditure could be divided
up between rent, stock, electricity, gas and so on, to see what has
been spent under the various headings.

3   *The VAT book*

Day-to-day sales might be noted here, with the VAT element separated for easy reference when VAT returns have to be submitted to
Customs and Excise. Stock purchases, overheads and expenses would
be detailed too, with their relevant VAT sums.

4   *The wages book*

Gross wages, deductions, net wages and so forth should be recorded
for each employee, whether employed on a temporary, part-time or
full-time basis.

5 *Creditors and debtors lists*

Details of those organizations and individuals to whom money is owed and who owe money to the business ought to be noted down so that payments can be made and debts chased, as and when appropriate.

6 *Orders, invoices and receipts files*

Separate files should be maintained for orders, invoices and receipts, placed in alphabetical order, and then by dates. These will help to verify accounts should the Inland Revenue or Customs and Excise query them.

7 *Assets lists*

Equipment, machinery, vehicles, fixtures and fittings purchased should be noted, with their dates of purchase, prices paid, and so on. A proportion of these sums can be set against the firm's profits, thus reducing its tax bill.

The accounts

By maintaining clear and accurate books, it should be relatively easy to use the accumulated data as the basis for quarterly and annual accounts:

1 *The trading account*

This is a financial statement which simply lists the sales, cost of sales and gross profit (or loss) of a business over a trading period. Sales are easy to calculate by referring to the books. Cost of sales is worked out by taking the stock held at the beginning of the period, adding purchases and deducting the stock left at the end of the period. Sales less cost of sales leaves the gross profit, or gross loss, as seen in Figure 4.4.

2 *The profit and loss account*

Usually compiled with and following on from the trading account, this second statement shows the gross profit, overheads and net profit

Sales		£58 000
Opening stock	£20 000	
Purchases	£25 000	
Closing stock	£15 000	
Cost of sales		£30 000
Gross profit		£28 000

Figure 4.4   A trading account

(or loss) over a given period. Gross profit is taken from the trading account. Overheads such as rent, rates, repairs, maintenance and so on are then set out and after being totalled are deducted from the gross profit to leave the net profit or net loss. Obviously, the firm's various expenses are easy to add together if full and complete records have been maintained. An example of a profit and loss account is given in Figure 4.5.

3   The balance sheet

This statement lists a firm's assets and liabilities at a specific date, and indicates how its activities during the preceding period of time have been funded. Fixed assets are those items such as equipment and machinery which are of ongoing use. Current assets are items such as stock and cash that increase and decrease regularly. Current liabilities are debts which have to be settled in the near future, typically to banks and suppliers. Subtracting current liabilities from current assets leaves net current assets or net current liabilities. These are then added to or deducted from fixed assets to give net assets or net liabilities.

The lower part of the balance sheet highlights where the money has come from to run the concern over that period of time. A financed by section might comprise sums made up of the owners' capital, profit from the profit and loss account, and loans from banks or other sources. The owners' personal drawings for day-to-day living expenses are subtracted from these sums to reach a final figure that should be the same as the net assets or net liabilities. An example of a balance sheet is shown in Figure 4.6.

The ratios

A multitude of simple ratios can be applied to a firm's accounts to see how well it is doing. The business should do this itself to spot

Gross profit		£28 000
Overheads:		
Rent, rates	£8000	
Wages	£3000	
Transport	£1300	
Electricity, gas	£1200	
Printing, stationery	£1000	
Telephone	£800	
Depreciation	£600	
Accountancy fees	£600	
Postage	£500	
Insurance	£400	
Repairs, maintenance	£300	£17 700
Net profit		£10 300

Figure 4.5 A profit and loss account

Fixed assets		£1 800
Current assets:		
Stock	£15 000	
Debtors	£4 000	
Cash in hand	£ 500	
	£19 500	
Current liabilities:		
Creditors	£4 500	
Bank overdraft	£3 000	
	£7 500	
Net current assets		£12 000
Net assets		£13 800
Financed by:		
Capital	£12 000	
Profit	£10 300	
Drawings	(£8 500)	
		£13 800

Figure 4.6 A balance sheet

areas for improvement, and possible problems. The Inland Revenue may do it too, in order to see if the figures are in line with comparable concerns. If not, the firm may be suspected of 'cooking the books' and an investigation could follow. Key ratios include:

1   *Gross profit*

This is often expressed as a percentage of sales, allowing for easy comparison alongside the average for that trade or industry:

$$\frac{\text{Gross profit}}{\text{Sales}} \times 100 = a \text{ per cent}$$

2   *Expenditure*

It is useful to take each area of expenditure and view it as a percentage of sales:

$$\frac{\text{Expenditure}}{\text{Sales}} \times 100 = b \text{ per cent}$$

3   *Working capital*

A business needs to know if it is solvent and can pay its way:

Current assets − Current liabilities = Working capital

Of course, if all current liabilities had to be settled tomorrow, a firm would find it difficult to convert stock into cash very quickly, so it is sensible to exclude this sum from the calculation:

Current assets − Stock − Current liabilities = Working capital

4   *Stock turnover*

In any business, stocks should be kept as low as possible, freeing cash and making the most efficient use of funds:

$$\frac{\text{Opening stock} + \text{Closing stock}}{2} = \text{Average stock}$$

$$\frac{\text{Cost of sales}}{\text{Average stock}} = c \text{ times per year}$$

5 *Creditors and debtors*

It is wise to be aware of the speed with which bills are paid, by and to the firm:

$$\frac{\text{Creditors}}{\text{Purchases}} \times 365 = d \text{ days}$$

$$\frac{\text{Debtors}}{\text{Sales}} \times 365 = e \text{ days}$$

4.8 Rapid revision

Answers	Questions
–	1 What are financial resources?
1 They are the funds that are used by a business to acquire the assets which it needs to trade successfully, and to settle the liabilities which accrue during its trading activities.	2 What types of budget are drawn up to help a firm calculate its financial needs?
2 (a) A sales budget; (b) a distribution budget; (c) a selling costs budget; (d) a production budget; (e) a purchases budget; (f) an administration budget; (g) a capital expenditure budget; (h) a cash budget; (i) a master budget.	3 What are the main types of finance available to a business?
3 (a) Loans; (b) overdrafts; (c) grants, subsidies and schemes; (d) trade credit; (e) hire purchase; (f) leasing; (g) factoring; (h) invoice discounting; (i) shares; (j) debentures.	4 Which are the major sources of finance for a firm?
4 (a) The firm; (b) banks; (c) venture capital organizations; (d) government; (e) suppliers; (f) finance houses; (g) factors; (h) insurance companies; (i) pension funds; (j) unit trusts; (k) investment trusts.	5 What is a business plan?

5   It is a document which sets out the commercial and financial activities of a concern, and verifies them so far as possible with detailed supporting material in appendices.

6   What should a business plan consist of?

---

6   (a) A commercial section; (b) a financial section; (c) appendices.

7   What should be included in the commercial section?

---

7   Information about (a) the firm's background; (b) the business premises; (c) products and services; (d) owners and managers; (e) the marketplace; (f) the firm's objectives.

8   What should be put in the financial section?

---

8   (a) A profit budget; (b) a cash flow forecast; (c) details of the firm's financial requirements.

9   What should be incorporated in the appendices?

---

9   Anything that can verify details provided about (a) the business; (b) the premises; (c) the products and services; (d) the owners and managers; (e) the marketplace; (f) the finance.

10   What is variance analysis?

---

10   It is the comparison of the differences between budgeted and actual results.

11   What are the main areas of concern with regard to variance analysis?

---

11   (a) Sales-revenue variance; (b) materials-cost variance; (c) overhead-cost variance; (d) labour-cost variance.

12   What books should be kept by a business?

---

12   (a) A cash book; (b) a bank book; (c) a VAT book; (d) a wages book; (e) creditors and debtors lists; (f) orders, invoices and receipts files; (g) asset lists.

13   What accounts need to be drawn up by a firm?

---

13   (a) A trading account; (b) a profit and loss account; (c) a balance sheet.

14   What is a trading account?

---

14   It is a statement which lists the sales, cost of sales and gross profit or loss of a business over a trading period.

15   What is a profit and loss account?

15 It is a statement which shows the gross profit, overheads and net profit or loss of a business over a trading period.

16 What is a balance sheet?

16 It is a statement which lists a firm's assets and liabilities at a specific date, and indicates how its activities during the preceding period of time have been funded.

17 What ratios should be applied to a firm's accounts to see how well it is doing?

17 In brief, (a) gross profit; (b) expenditure; (c) working capital; (d) stock turnover; (e) creditors; (f) debtors.

18 Go over the questions again until you know all of the answers. Then move on to the next section.

5
Physical resources

5.1 What are physical resources?

Generally speaking, the term *physical resources* is an all purpose one which really encompasses any physical item that is used by a business during its operations and activities – a ballpoint pen is as much a physical resource as a huge warehouse is! More specifically, physical resources can be broken down into various groupings, most notably land, premises and equipment. Land refers to the geographical land, the sea bed and the natural resources such as oil and minerals found within them. Premises covers the buildings that are on the land, whether shops, offices, warehouses or factories. Equipment relates to the equipment and machinery of long-term use to a firm as well as to the raw materials, component parts and finished products that come and go as a business buys, manufactures and sells goods and services for profit.

So far as the owners and managers of a firm are concerned, their interest in physical resources extends primarily to thinking about and then deciding where to locate the business, how to choose the right property for them and how to select equipment of use to the concern. They also want to know something about their rights, duties and restrictions with regard to owning or renting physical resources. Last, but most definitely not least, they wish to contemplate the disposal of physical resources, whether land, buildings or outdated and inefficient pieces of equipment and machinery.

5.2 Locating a business

Whether the owners or managers of a new or growing business want to locate (or relocate) it in the North or South, a city or a village, a high street or a back street, there are numerous influential factors which should be taken into account before a decision is made. The most common influences on this important decision are easy to identify, as seen in Figure 5.1 and as follows.

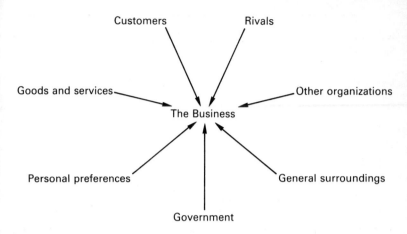

Figure 5.1 Influences on the choice of business location

Goods and services

The presence or absence of various goods and services in a particular locality may persuade or dissuade the owners or managers of a business into or from basing it there. Some firms have to locate near to the goods that are bought and used in their activities, especially those that are difficult to transport, for whatever reasons. For example, cement works are most often sited near to chalk and limestone deposits which are the key raw materials for manufacturing cement, and are heavy and therefore time consuming and costly to move from one place to another.

Similarly, businesses may find that it is worthwhile to be located near to essential services – perhaps a labour force from which suitably qualified and experienced employees can be recruited, a financial network for banking, foreign exchange and insurance assistance, and a transport system so that finished products can be distributed quickly and efficiently, by road, sea or air. In certain instances, a firm might even be based as far away as possible from various services. As an example, it might be unwise to be located in an area where the workforce has a reputation for strikes and associated problems that delay or halt production.

Customers

For most businesses, the proximity of (would-be) customers is an overriding concern, since an absence or an insufficient number of customers will mean they cannot be established or run on a viable, long-term basis. For example, a newsagent is more likely to succeed on a crowded housing estate than in a quiet country lane, miles from local residents and passers-by. Of course, some firms offering highly specialized products and services can locate where they want to be, as they know that customers will travel from far and wide for what they are selling. As examples, a portrait painter or a craftsman making furniture by hand will draw in customers attracted by their unique skills, wherever they are working.

Rivals

Owners or managers may choose to have their firm trading close to or far from (prospective) competitors. There could be sound reasons to locate as near as possible to rivals. Typically, the owners can see that their business is better than the competition in some way which should ensure that customers will buy from it rather than from the rivals. As an example, a small shop run by a husband and wife team may open close to a large, national store because they can be more flexible with their opening times, stock and prices and may offer a more personalized service, thus allowing them to survive and make a reasonable living from their endeavours.

Sometimes, a particular area becomes known for a trade or specific products and services, and customers flock to it because of this. For example, if a town has six estate agencies and five are close together in one street with the other based some distance away, then most housebuyers will find it convenient to call into the five that are near to each other, but not the one on the far side of the town. Any new estate agent who is planning to open an agency in the area may be advised to base it close to the five agencies, rather than the one on its own.

Alternatively, it could be more sensible to locate away from any rival businesses. Perhaps the owners or managers of a new firm can recognize that their concern is not sufficiently different or better than existing businesses, and by starting up will simply divide the trade into smaller proportions so that none of the firms achieve an acceptable sales turnover, leaving all of them fighting for survival. Each and every concern that is successful has something to distinguish it from its immediate competitors, and unless owners and managers can identify that extra ingredient, they will not, or certainly should not, open for business in that vicinity.

Other organizations

Usually, businesses are more successful when they are based near to other organizations which will attract potential customers into the area, or at least not deter them from visiting it. Complementary

• Churches	• Furniture stores
• Playgroups	• Pet shops
• Schools	• Bakers
• Colleges	• Greengrocers
• Hospitals	• Fishmongers
• Health centres	• Butchers
• Universities	• Grocers
• Dentists' surgeries	• Delicatessens
• Street markets	• Health food stores
• Farms	• Public houses
• Banks	• Off licences
• Building societies	• Restaurants
• Post offices	• Fast food restaurants
• Stationers	• Cafes
• Men's fashion shops	• Booksellers
• Ladies' fashion shops	• Antique dealers
• Children's clothes shops	• Jewellers
• Nursery goods stores	• Pawnbrokers
• Toy shops	• Photographers
• Newsagents	• Hardware stores
• Confectioners	• Car repairers
• Travel agencies	• Tyre and exhaust centres
• Camping goods stores	• Car accessories stores
• Sports goods stores	• Other organizations

Figure 5.2 Organizations which can help or hinder a business

concerns may be looked for – after all, babywear, children's and ladies' fashion shops mix together well, and will pull in customers for each other. A babywear shop, a fishmonger and an undertaker will not. Looking at the list or organizations in Figure 5.2, imagine that you are going to open a shop selling clothes, posters, compact discs or whatever interests you, and decide which of these organizations would be a help or hindrance to that business, and mull over the reasons why.

General surroundings

Likewise, surroundings can help or hinder a business and influence its success or failure, and most owners and managers will thus contemplate what else is in an area before settling there. Often, a plus for one business is a minus for another. For example, a new pelican crossing on a busy road between a supermarket and that babywear shop would encourage people to cross over to the smaller shop, to its benefit. However, an adjacent off licence which obtained much of its

• Traffic lights	• Taxi ranks
• Pelican crossings	• Railway stations
• Yellow lines	• Telephone boxes
• Parking meters	• Post boxes
• One-way systems	• Bottle banks
• Roundabouts	• Benches
• Roadworks	• Newspaper sellers
• Car parks	• Public lavatories
• Pedestrianized areas	• Parks
• Bus stops	• Other surroundings

Figure 5.3   Surroundings which can help or hinder a firm

income from car drivers who pulled over, popped in and drove away quickly would lose trade because of the accompanying parking restrictions. Checking out Figure 5.3, think about how these various factors that comprise the general surroundings would affect your chosen business, or perhaps not have any effect at all. Sometimes, even petty influences can make a difference – people like to walk on the sunny side of the street and those firms on that side will do better than those on the dull side. Strange, but true.

Government

Local authorities and central government can play a big part in the decision-making process of owners and managers choosing where to locate their firms, by offering financial discounts and incentives to businesses that locate 'here' rather than 'there'. As examples, a local council might give rent-free periods and/or reduced rents to firms moving into a newly-built industrial estate. The government also provides various grants and other concessions to firms moving to certain areas, in an effort to boost local economies, by drawing in money, job opportunities and trade to these communities.

Personal preferences

Clearly, the owners of a business should contemplate many factors before picking the right location, from the proximity of raw materials through to the benefits of obtaining grants and other concessions from local or national government. As often as not though, the final decision has as much to do with personal preferences as anything else, especially with regard to small concerns run by a sole proprietor or a partnership. Typically, the sole trader starts trading in an area because he or she has always lived there and does not want to move away from family and friends. Perhaps partners pick a locality which offers them a good lifestyle, where house prices are low, the pace of life seems slower and the environment appears to be cleaner. Logic and clear reasoning do not necessarily prevail when the final decision is made, which may be why so many smaller firms fail to succeed.

5.3   Choosing a property

Once the owners or managers of a business have decided where it should be located, they will then usually need to look for a suitable property in that area, which they can afford to buy or rent on a permanent basis. Premises – whether a shop, a warehouse or a factory – can be divided into two categories, namely freehold and leasehold properties. Thought has to be given to which type of property is most appropriate for that particular business, before considering any other factors and making a choice.

Freehold premises

These are premises that are legally owned outright by a party. Being a freeholder, as the owner is often called, offers various, key benefits. They can do what they want with their property, redesigning or extending it to suit their individual requirements, subject only to the laws of the land. Also, they do not have to pay rent or carry out the many duties or comply with the numerous restrictions that tenants in rented premises have to do. If or when the property is eventually sold, a substantial profit may be made, assuming that prices have risen during the period of the freeholder's ownership.

There are drawbacks involved with owning freehold premises though. The purchase price may be prohibitive and could stretch financial resources to breaking point, with money used to buy the property instead of being kept in reserve for lean trading times. If the premises are purchased with financial assistance, perhaps a bank loan or building society mortgage, and repayments are not maintained, the property could be repossessed with the owner losing not only the premises but a business and even a home as well. If the business is unsuccessful, the property may be hard to sell, becoming a liability rather than an asset. In a sluggish market, it could have to be sold at a considerable loss – not an unusual occurrence in the 1990s.

Leasehold properties

These premises are rented, or 'leased', to a party by the legal owner for an agreed period of time. The party renting the property is known as the leaseholder. Freeholders and leaseholders involved in a landlord–tenant relationship are also sometimes referred to as lessors and lessees. Often, a new lease (or leases) is granted when a freeholder builds or converts premises and seeks an occupier (or occupiers) for a certain timespan, perhaps five, 10 or 20 years. For the tenant, the advantages of a new lease are that initial capital expenditure is relatively low and newly built units tend to be standardized, easy to customize and require limited maintenance and repairs for the immediate future. However, if property prices rise, the tenant makes no profit from this, while rents are likely to increase over the years, often at a disproportionate rate.

A tenant who wishes to vacate premises during the term of a lease can sell (or assign) that lease to a would-be tenant for an appropriate financial sum (or premium), subject only to the landlord's permission which should not be unreasonably withheld. The premium charged will simply reflect the supply of and demand for that particular type of property at that precise moment. In favour of an assigned lease, the incoming tenant acquires readymade premises in an established area. Against it, the premium may be high if the property is in demand, and they will still be subject to the same terms and conditions as the outgoing tenant.

If an existing tenant is unable to find a buyer for a lease, they may try to sub-let it, thus creating a freeholder–head leaseholder–sub-leaseholder relationship. There are some pros for the sub-leaseholder, especially if premises are shared. Costs and excess space are minimized and complementary concerns such as a photographic studio and a picture framing business can help to draw in customers for each other. However, there are cons as well. The head leaseholder's inability to sell the lease may be a bad sign, perhaps indicating that the property is poorly located or has other drawbacks. Also, the rent charged may be excessive so that the head leaseholder can skim off a profit. Worst of all, the sub-leaseholder may find it difficult to renew the sub-lease on its expiry as the head leaseholder may want to re-occupy the premises in more favourable times.

Size

Quite obviously, the size of the premises is a key concern. They need to be large enough for the firm to operate and carry out all of its activities successfully. For example, a partnership which is to open a shop will want to make sure that the property has enough room to accommodate counters, shelves, showroom stock, aisles, storeroom stock, delivery bays, staffrooms and so on. At the same time, the property should not be too big – it may convey added status but the extra (and unnecessary) rent, heating and lighting costs and so forth all need to be paid for and could mean the difference between a profitable and an unprofitable concern.

Shape

Perhaps surprisingly, the shape of the premises may need to be assessed in a careful and thorough manner before a decision is made. Take that shop as an example again. The partners might seek a unit which is a basic square or rectangle so that they can set out the store as they want to. Properties with nooks, crannies, pillars and posts may be rejected as these would prohibit the most effective layout – and possibly encourage shoplifters who would use them to hide or at least obscure their activities.

Miscellaneous factors

Of course, a whole host of miscellaneous other factors will influence the final choice. Those budding shopkeepers may want a property with a large window to display goods, high ceilings to stack items up the walls, storage space to the rear, upstairs or downstairs, a back door and yard for stock deliveries and even living accommodation above or below the business area. Cost is the bottom line in many instances – a freehold property is too expensive, leasehold premises are not, one is the right size and shape but very costly, another is a little smaller and rather cramped but is more affordable, and so on.

5.4 Selecting equipment

Whatever they do, all firms need to invest to some degree in equipment, machinery and stocks. *Fixed capital investment* on assets of long-term use to a business such as equipment and machinery must occur to replace old and inefficient items, and to help to produce more or better quality products. *Working capital investment* on assets of short-term use such as raw materials, component parts and finished goods for resale has to take place if the business is to trade successfully, and make sufficient profit to survive, and then prosper.

When selecting equipment, machinery, stocks and so forth, the owners and managers of a firm will consider many factors – among them whether suppliers have a good name and a sound reputation

	Year one (£)	Year two (£)	Year three (£)	Yearly average (£)
Sales income	10 000	7 500	5 000	7 500
Production costs	5 000	4 000	3 000	4 000
Gross profit	5 000	3 500	2 000	3 500
Depreciation	2 000	2 000	2 000	2 000
Net profit	3 000	1 500	0	1 500

Machine: Cost £7000; estimated lifespan 3 years; residual value £1000; depreciation £7000 − £1000 = £6000 ÷ 3 years = £2000 per year

Accounting return: £1500 (average profit) ÷ £7000 (cost) × 100 = 21.4 per cent per annum

Figure 5.4   An accounting return

for quality and behaviour, if the items will do the job properly and be first class and reliable, whether the terms and conditions of the deal are favourable. Of overriding concern especially for items of long-term, continuing use, is whether they will be a worthwhile investment, or not. Most firms will carry out an *investment appraisal* before choosing equipment, machinery or whatever. Several methods can be used.

Accounting return

This involves working out the likely annual profits resulting from the investment in relation to its cost. Figure 5.4 shows such a calculation which suggests an accounting return of 21.4 per cent per annum. This can then be compared with other possible returns from alternative investments, and a selection decision made. Obviously, there are many ifs and buts involved with calculating an accounting return – the sales, costs, lifespan of the item and so on are all uncertain. Thus, firms will make optimistic, realistic and pessimistic estimates per investment to illustrate a range of potential outcomes, prior to making a choice.

Payback period

With this method of appraisal, a business calculates how long it will take for an investment to generate sufficient money to recoup its original outlay (if at all). As a basic example, if a machine or whatever costs £10 000 and generates cash from the sale of goods made by it at a rate of £5000 by the end of the first year and £5000 again

	Outflow (£)	Inflow (£)
Year one	6000	1800
Year two	–	1800
Year three	–	1800
Year four	–	1800
Year five	–	1800
Total	6000	9000

Figure 5.5   A projected cash flow

by the end of the second year then its payback period is two years. Again, various estimates are made before different investment possibilities are compared and contrasted, and a final decision is made about them.

Discounted cash flow

The phrase *cash flow* simply refers to the monies which come into and go out of a business, as sales are made and bills are paid. A firm which has a good (or positive) cash flow receives money from sales before its bills have to be settled, and is never short of cash. A concern that has a negative cash flow, is 'strapped for cash' or whatever, does not obtain money from its sales until after its bills have to be paid, and is always struggling to make ends meet – and will consequently find it hard to survive for very long, let alone prosper.

A discounted cash flow is just an anticipated cash flow which has been adjusted (or discounted) to reflect present day values. It works on the principle that £100 today would be worth £110 next year if that sum was invested now at an interest rate of 10 per cent, £121 in two years and so on. Clearly, most investments involve a large outlay of money now with returns spread out over several years and the size of these returns may sound impressive until discounted to the present time. Not surprisingly, discounting cash flows can make investment appraisal much easier and more accurate. Figures used need to be realistic though. Too high, and net present values will be less than their true worth, and some quality investments will be rejected. Too low, and net present values will be ridiculously high, and various unwise investments will be made.

An example of how discounted cash flow works with investment appraisal is as follows. Imagine a firm is looking at a new machine. It will cost £6000 and has an expected lifespan of five years. It should generate an inflow of cash of £1800 per annum as seen in Figure 5.5.

	Outflow (£)	Inflow (£)	Discount rate (10%)	Discounted inflow (£)
Year one	6000	1800	0.9091	1636.38
Year two	–	1800	0.8264	1487.52
Year three	–	1800	0.7513	1352.34
Year four	–	1800	0.6831	1229.58
Year five	–	1800	0.6208	1117.44
	6000	9000		6823.26

Figure 5.6 A discounted cash flow

It appears to be a sensible investment as total inflows exceed out-flows by £3000 (£9000–£6000). However, this cash flow does not allow for the effects of time upon money in that £1800 in five years is worth much less than the same sum today. A more accurate assessment involves discounting the sums at an appropriate rate, as in Figure 5.6. It can be seen that the net present value is at £6823.26 – not quite such an appealing prospect as it once was.

5.5 Rights, duties and restrictions

The old and rather sexist cliché 'An Englishman's home is his castle' is not wholly accurate these days, if indeed it ever was. Those businesses (and individuals) which own and/or occupy land and premises and use equipment and machinery on them have numerous rights, duties and restrictions that they must be aware of and adhere to if they are not to fall foul of the law. Wide ranging and detailed though these are, the key areas of interest are as follows.

Rights

Under the terms of the Landlord and Tenant Act 1954, both parties acquire certain rights (and therefore duties to each other) when agreeing to and signing a lease. Some of these rights (and duties) are expressed in writing. Typically, the landlord is entitled to receive rent and any other payments due such as a service charge for cleaning communal areas on the agreed dates. He or she has the right to expect the property to be used only for its agreed purpose. The premises should also be maintained in good order, repaired and re-decorated to workman-like standards as and when necessary.

The tenant is entitled to exclusive possession of the property and ought to be allowed to assign the lease or sub-let the premises to another party subject to the landlord's written permission which should not be unreasonably withheld. Rent reviews will take place at regular intervals when the rent will be duly amended to reflect existing market conditions. The two sides will go to a mutually acceptable third party (or parties) to arbitrate in the event of unresolved disputes.

Numerous implied rights (and duties) are assumed to exist when a leasehold agreement is signed. For example, the landlord has the right to expect the tenant to pay any rates, taxes and insurances relating to the property that are not the landlord's responsibility. Also, he or she is entitled to assume that the tenant will treat the premises in a fair and reasonable manner, as any other decent tenant would do. In return, the tenant has the right not to be harassed in any way nor to have the property devalued by the landlord's actions. Both sides are entitled to take legal action to obtain compensation if their rights are infringed, or even to terminate the lease in extreme circumstances.

Duties

In addition to the express and implied duties in the lease, occupiers also have other responsibilities, most notably to lawful visitors, trespassers and employees. Under the terms of the Occupier's Liability Act 1957, they have a common duty of care to all lawful visitors, whereby they must ensure that those visitors with express or implied permission to come onto the property are either reasonably safe and free from dangers or are given sufficient warning of and dangers to make certain that they remain reasonably safe. For example, this might be achieved by erecting a large sign, although thought needs to be given to whether children or ethnic groups would notice or understand it.

This Act does not extend to cover those visitors who are on a property unlawfully and are better known as trespassers. Duties to these people can be found in what is referred to as common law or case law, where the results of earlier court cases act as precedents for subsequent ones. A similar duty of care must be provided for unlawful visitors if, and only if, the occupier is or ought to be conscious of the dangers to trespassers and is aware of the presence of a trespasser, or that one may enter the property. In such situations, the occupier is expected to offer reasonable protection to them.

The Health and Safety at Work Act 1974 sets down the duties that employers, and therefore many occupiers, must fulfil with regard to their employees. So far as is reasonably practicable, they must ensure the health, safety and welfare of staff by supplying safe work systems, plant, machinery and equipment plus a secure environment and working conditions for them. Employers with five or more employees have to compose a written health and safety statement outlining their rules and procedures. Also, sufficient additional information, guidance and supervision has to be offered to staff on an ongoing basis so that standards are upheld.

Restrictions

There are many restrictions which limit an owner's or occupier's use of their land, premises and equipment. When a property is sold it is common for one party to impose certain restrictions (or restrictive covenants) on the other, or sometimes upon each other. The seller (or vendor) may restrict the buyer to manufacturing or selling just one particular type of product, or range. The purchaser could force the vendor to agree not to open a competing business within a set time and distance from his or her firm. If a reasonable restrictive covenant is breached, the injured party can sue for damages via the courts and/or seek an injunction to rectify the matter. Agreeing not to start a rival newsagent's 'within the next two years' is reasonable, 'never' is not. 'Within a one mile radius' is reasonable, 'in the same county' is not.

Easements are rights that exist over land either expressly as a consequence of an agreement or transaction or by implication if they have existed for 20 years or more. As examples, one party may sell part of his or her land to another party subject to the proviso that he or she can continue to enjoy vehicular access over that portion of the land. Alternatively, a farmer might have allowed ramblers to cut across his unused bottom field for over 20 years and is obliged to let them continue, even if he now wishes to grow crops there.

A business can fall foul of the crime of statutory nuisance. Various nuisances fit into this category, such as emitting waste, noise and vibrations into the air, onto land or into waterways, having insufficiently ventilated, unclean and overcrowded premises and keeping goods and/or animals on land in such a manner that they are harmful to good health. Empowered by the Public Health Act 1936, Noise Abatement Act 1960, Clean Air Act 1964, Control of Pollution Act 1974 and their updates and successors, the Environmental Health Departments of local authorities are responsible for checking, dealing with complaints and inspecting premises in their area. On identifying an offence, they can serve an abatement notice requiring it to cease. If no action is taken, a court order may be obtained or they can employ a sub-contractor to carry out any necessary work, with costs charged to the offender.

A public nuisance may be defined as 'an act or omission that materially affects the comfort and convenience of members of the public'. This encompasses many crimes and includes serving or selling food in unhygienic surroundings, causing an obstruction and carrying out dangerous activities in proximity to the public. For example, a business that built a golf course next to a road might discover that this is classified as a public nuisance if pedestrians and car drivers find themselves under fire from mis-hit golf balls. In many instances, public nuisances are termed and thus tackled as statutory nuisances.

A private nuisance is 'an unlawful interference with another party's use of, enjoyment of or rights over or in relation to land'. For example, if a property is allowed to fall into disrepair then neighbours may claim that this interferes with their enjoyment of their own land and they could sue the creator of the nuisance for damages and seek an abatement of the nuisance and an injunction to prevent its repetition. To succeed, the injured party must show that there has been an indirect interference with the enjoyment of land perhaps by proving the existence of excessive noise, that it has caused some form of physical or psychological damage, is unlawful (and allowances would be made by a court for undue sensitivity, its reasons and locality) and of an ongoing nature.

The existence of the Town and Country Planning Act 1977 means that an owner or occupier who wishes to carry out any material alteration of buildings on land or their use must apply for planning permission from the local authority in order to do so. Prior to granting permission, the authority will want to be sure that the area and its inhabitants will not be adversely affected, local services such as gas are readily available and that the land is not needed now or in the future for socially beneficial schemes such as roads or schools. Changes or developments that take place without permission can result in enforcement notices being served via the courts to restore the land or buildings to their original state.

Local authorities also possess considerable powers with regard to the compulsory purchase of land. Owners can be forced to sell their property to the local authority in order that a socially advantageous development can be carried out. On objection, a public enquiry will take place and an inspector will consider all views before making a recommendation to the appropriate government minister, whose decision is final.

5.6 Disposing of physical resources

At some stage, a business will inevitably want to dispose of the physical resources that it has acquired and used as it trades. It may wish to sell its freehold premises, terminate the lease on a rented property or scrap its equipment and machinery.

Selling freehold premises

Selling a freehold property is relatively straightforward, assuming that someone wants to buy it! The firm will simply have the premises valued by commercial estate agents, who specialize in dealing with commercial properties such as shops, offices, factories and warehouses. Often, the business will approach residential estate agencies which sell houses, bungalows, flats and the like, and who may employ someone with expertise in the commercial property market.

Selecting a valuation which sounds realistic – typically one that is in proportion with other comparable properties that have been sold in the same area – the concern will employ an agency to sell the premises on its behalf in return for a (negotiable) flat fee or more likely a percentage of the sale price, perhaps two per cent or thereabouts. The commercial estate agent will then promote the property – sending particulars to interested parties on his or her mailing list, putting photographs in his or her windows, placing advertisements in newspapers and magazines and so forth. Prospective buyers will come forward and one of them may make an acceptable offer which is taken up by the firm. It is straightforward – if a deal can be agreed by the buyer and the seller!

Terminating a lease

A leaseholder who wants to vacate premises – perhaps in order to move to a larger and more prestigious property – can assign or sublet the lease to another individual or firm, doing this in much the same way that a freeholder does when he or she sells his or her premises outright. An estate agent who deals with commercial property will value it, and advertise the premises in his or her window, the local press and specialist publications, anywhere it might be seen by a prospective purchaser. A would-be buyer and the seller must then meet and negotiate a mutually acceptable deal. Simple though it appears, it can be a long, drawn out process, taking months or even years.

Whoever the lessee is towards the end of the lease will soon learn that it does not simply cease to exist on the expiry of its 10, 15 or 20 year term. It continues automatically on the same, basic terms and conditions unless and until it is terminated in accordance with the Landlord and Tenant Act 1954. The landlord can do this by serving a written notice on the tenant between six and 12 months before the termination date specified in it. Such a notice must contain a statement that the landlord is unwilling to grant a new tenancy, a date of termination which has to be at least six months hence and not earlier than the expiry date of the original term and a request for the tenant to confirm by counter-notice within two months that he or she is willing to vacate the premises on the stipulated date.

Alternatively, the tenant can serve a written notice on the landlord. This should include a termination date for the existing tenancy which must be at least six months ahead, a request for a new tenancy (if appropriate), details of its proposed terms and conditions and a statement asking the landlord to confirm acceptance or to outline his or her grounds for objection by counter-notice within two months. Whether the landlord or the tenant has initiated action, it is hoped that the two parties will be able to settle the matter amicably and between themselves. Most of them do.

If agreement cannot be reached either to vacate the property or to issue another lease on acceptable terms and conditions then the dispute may be referred to arbitration if a third party has been specified within the lease or (more likely) to a court. If a new tenancy is to be rejected and the tenant is therefore to vacate the premises, the landlord must persuade the court that there are sufficient grounds for this. This grounds may be many and varied – some are almost certain to guarantee judgement in the landlord's favour, others depend on the discretion of the court.

The landlord is likely to succeed if he or she is willing to provide the tenant with suitable, alternative accommodation or intends to carry out construction work on or demolish and reconstruct (a substantial part of) the premises or wishes to occupy them himself or herself as a personal or business residence. Other grounds that may be considered valid but are more dependent on the discretion of the court would be if the tenant had persistently delayed paying rent or had failed to maintain and repair the property or had committed another substantial breach of contract or if the tenancy related to part of a property which the landlord now wished to reclaim to relet as a whole unit.

If the landlord's grounds for turning down a new tenancy are accepted by the court as being valid, then the tenant will be expected to leave the business premises on the set date. In such a situation, the tenant may be able to claim compensation from the landlord – a sum equal to the rateable value of the property (or twice the value for tenancies of 14 years or more) for the disturbance involved in moving out plus an additional amount if authorized improvements have been made to the premises during the tenancy which consequently improve their prospective letting value for the future.

Should a new tenancy be ordered by the court, then the landlord and tenant will be given the opportunity to reach an agreement between themselves. Failing this, the court has wide, discretionary powers in the matter and can determine the length of the new tenancy to a maximum of 14 years, the rent to be paid at the open market value and the other remaining terms and conditions. Any

	Opening value	Depreciation (£5000 ÷ 4 years)	Closing value
Year one	£5000	£1250	£3750
Year two	£3750	£1250	£2500
Year three	£2500	£1250	£1250
Year four	£1250	£1250	0

Figure 5.7   The straight line method

variations from the expired lease whether proposed by the landlord or the tenant will need to be justifiable if they are to be granted by the court. The overall aim of the court is to ensure a fair and mutually acceptable agreement is signed.

Scrapping equipment

Some fixed and working capital assets such as buildings in popular locations can increase (or appreciate) in value over time, although as a general rule most equipment, machinery and stock tends to depreciate (or fall in value) the longer it is kept and used. Eventually, their worsening condition resulting from wear and tear will mean they are unable to do what they are meant to do, and will need to be scrapped and replaced. Similarly, some equipment and machinery will become obsolete because technological changes and developments render them out of date and less efficient than newer models, and again will need to be replaced. In either event, a firm must look ahead and set aside money for these eventualities.

When equipment, machinery or whatever is purchased for business use, a firm can set the cost against the profits that it makes so that less tax is paid to the Inland Revenue, and these savings can be put to one side to replace the items at a later date. Depreciation is most often calculated in one of two ways: the straight line or the reducing balance methods. The straight line method divides the original or historic cost of the item by the number of years of its expected life and puts this depreciation charge against the profits made in each of those years (Figure 5.7). The reducing (or diminishing) balance method writes off a fixed percentage of the item's value for each accounting period (Figure 5.8).

Of course, both formulae base their depreciation charge on the original cost of the equipment or machinery and the cost of replacement is almost inevitably going to be far higher. Hence, a business

	Opening value	Depreciation (50%)	Closing value
Year one	£5000	£2500	£2500
Year two	£2500	£1250	£1250
Year three	£1250	£625	£625
Year four	£625	£312.50	£312.50

Figure 5.8 The reducing balance method

will need to make what is known as a revaluation provision to allow for the increased future outlay. A sensible concern will hold onto extra profits rather than distributing them to partners, shareholders or whoever, in anticipation of the additional costs to come. Clearly, the best way of making provision is to compare regularly what has been set aside for a replacement item in relation to what it then costs to replace, and to top up the reserves accordingly.

5.7 Rapid revision

Answers	Questions
–	1 What are physical resources?
1 They are the physical items that are used by a business during its operations and activities.	2 What is land?
2 It is the geographical land, the sea bed and the natural resources found within them.	3 What are premises?
3 They are the buildings that are on the land, including shops, offices, warehouses and factories.	4 What is equipment?
4 It is the equipment and machinery of long-term use to a business and the raw materials, component parts and finished products that come and go as that business trades.	5 What are the main influences on business location?

5 (a) Goods and services;
(b) customers; (c) rivals; (d) other
organizations; (e) general
surroundings; (f) government;
(g) personal preferences.

6 What are freehold premises?

---

6 They are premises that are
legally owned outright by an
organization or an individual.

7 What are leasehold premises?

---

7 They are premises that are
rented to a party by the legal
owner for an agreed period of
time.

8 What other factors will a firm
consider when it is choosing a
property?

---

8 (a) Its size; (b) its shape; (c)
miscellaneous factors; (d) its cost.

9 What is fixed capital
investment?

---

9 It is the financial investment in
assets of long-term use to a
business, such as machinery.

10 What is working capital
investment?

---

10 It is the financial investment in
assets of short-term use to a firm,
such as raw materials and
component parts.

11 What is an accounting return?

---

11 It is the likely annual profit
resulting from an investment in
relation to its cost.

12 What is the payback period?

---

12 It is the length of time that it
takes for an investment to generate
sufficient money to recoup its
original outlay.

13 What is a discounted cash
flow?

---

13 It is an anticipated cash flow
which has been adjusted to reflect
present day values.

14 What rights and duties do
landlords and tenants have?

---

14 (a) Express rights and duties
as set out in writing in the lease;
(b) implied rights and duties which
are assumed to exist when a lease
is agreed and signed.

15 What other organizations or
individuals does a tenant have
duties to?

---

15 (a) Lawful visitors;
(b) trespassers; (c) employees.

16 What other restrictions exist
with regard to a firm's use of its
physical resources?

16   It may be restricted by
(a) restrictive covenants;
(b) easements. It must also avoid
causing: (c) a statutory nuisance;
(d) a public nuisance; (e) a private
nuisance.

17   What happens on the expiry of
a lease?

---

17   It continues on the same terms
and conditions unless and until it
is terminated by the landlord or
tenant in accordance with the
Landlord and Tenant Act of 1954.

18   What happens if a landlord
and a tenant cannot agree on the
continuation or termination of a
lease?

---

18   The matter will be settled by a
court which will ensure a fair and
mutually acceptable agreement is
reached.

19   What is depreciation?

---

19   It is the fall in value of an
asset which occurs over a period of
time.

20   What are the two ways of
calculating depreciation?

---

20   (a) The straight line method;
(b) the reducing balance method.

21   What is the straight line
method?

---

21   It divides the original cost of
the asset by the number of years
of its expected life. This gives the
annual depreciation.

22   What is the reducing balance
method?

---

22   This sets off a fixed percentage
of the item's value for each
accounting period.

23   Go over the questions again
until you know all of the answers.
Then move on to the next section.

6
Human resources

6.1 What are human resources?

The term *human resources* simply refers to managers and employees within a business, and implies that they are viewed as resources in much the same way as finance, land, premises and equipment are, to be moved into, about and out of a concern as and when necessary, rather than as people with feelings, hopes and fears. Unfortunately, this is often true, especially in larger businesses when those at the top make decisions about workers at the bottom, without actually knowing them. They are just names or even reference numbers on a sheet of paper. Smaller firms encourage closer personal relationships between employers and employees but the bottom line in business is that staff are really just assets or liabilities, no more and no less than that.

Regarding people in this manner, most firms will compose and work to what is known as a manpower (or human resources) plan, to ensure that it has the right people in the right places at the right times. This involves a business calculating its immediate staff requirements in terms of numbers, ages, skills, qualities and so forth, comparing these needs with its current workforce. Next, it tries to assess its future workforce after promotions, transfers, retirements and so on, and contrasts this with its anticipated staff requirements. It can then set about recruiting staff, managing employees and ending employment as and when necessary, all against a backdrop of employment laws which act as guidelines for and (more likely) restraints on their activities.

6.2 Recruiting staff

Although a firm will normally take a rather theoretical, long-term overview of its staffing levels and types, responsibility for recruiting suitable employees will usually fall either to the personnel manager or more likely to the relevant department head in a larger concern, or to the sole trader or an experienced partner in a smaller one. Inevitably, they will adopt a practical, down to earth approach to the recruitment process, which will probably consist of the following steps.

Analysing the job

The personnel manager, head of department or whoever, will begin by assessing the job that needs to be filled. A host of questions will have to be answered such as these: What is the job title? Where is it located? What is its purpose? Whom is the employee responsible to, and for? What are the main tasks involved with the job? How should these be completed? Questions will also arise about the ideal employee. What skills must he or she possess? What type of background experience should he or she have? What other qualities are required? The manager (or whoever) will personally be able to answer some of these questions and can fill in the gaps by watching the job being performed, talking to fellow employees and the person who is leaving, as appropriate.

He or she should then be able to compose a job description which is a statement listing the job title, the job title of the employee's superior, the job title of the employee's subordinates and the purpose and main tasks of the job. This job description serves many purposes, enabling the manager to decide the type of person required to do the job and to prepare advertisements and application forms. Also, it will allow him or her to judge applications, assess interviewees and evaluate the successful recruit at work. Examples of job descriptions are given in Figures 6.1 and 6.2.

Referring closely to the tasks detailed in the job description and calculating the skills, knowledge and experiences needed to do each of them, the manager will then draw up an employee specification. This statement, also known as a job, person or personnel specification, simply details the type of person required, and the key attributes that he or she should have. These attributes may be split into essentials and desirables. Figures 6.3 and 6.4 show examples of employee specifications for the jobs described in Figures 6.1 and 6.2.

As with job descriptions, employee specifications have various uses. They may be used to design advertisements and to decide where to advertise. Applicants' details in application forms and candidates' comments during interviews can be compared alongside them. Interviews may be based around them, with comments about each interviewee being noted down next to the essential and desirable requirements. Later on, the new employee's performance can be assessed more effectively by perusing the specification, to see how he or she measures up to the ideal person.

Job title	: Office assistant
Responsible to	: Office supervisor
Responsible for	: N/A
Purpose	: To help the Office supervisor as required
Tasks	: To distribute incoming mail to the relevant departments and persons
	: To photocopy and file copies of incoming mail
	: To type letters as instructed
	: To maintain stationery supplies
	: To keep the office tidy
	: To run errands as directed
	: To photocopy and file copies of outgoing mail
	: To despatch outgoing mail
	: To carry out any other tasks as instructed by the Office supervisor
Prepared by	:
Date	:

Figure 6.1 A job description for an office assistant

Job title	: Sales representative
Responsible to	: Sales manager
Responsible for	: N/A
Purpose	: To maximize sales of nursery goods
Tasks	: To call on existing customers each month to obtain sales orders
	: To visit prospective customers every month to generate sales orders
	: To submit sales orders as instructed
	: To maintain sales records as directed
	: To attend sales meetings as and when required
	: To complete any other tasks as instructed by the Sales manager
Prepared by	:
Date	:

Figure 6.2 A job description for a sales representative

Job title	: Office assistant
Job holder	: Must have a clean and tidy appearance
	: Must have a friendly and outgoing nature
	: Must have four GCSEs ('C' grades or above), preferably including English Language and Mathematics
	: Must be able to type at 50 words per minute
	: Should have previous office experience
	: Should be able to work Saturday mornings, as and when required
Prepared by	:
Date	:

Figure 6.3   An employee specification for an office assistant

Job title	: Sales representative
Job holder	: Must have a smart appearance
	: Must speak clearly without speech impediments
	: Must have a clean driving licence
	: Must have a telephone
	: Must live in Yorkshire, or a neighbouring county
	: Should have previous sales experience
	: Should have some knowledge of the nursery goods trade
Prepared by	:
Date	:

Figure 6.4   An employee specification for a sales representative

Attracting applicants

Once the manager knows who is wanted, he or she will move on to decide where to advertise to reach the right types and numbers of potentially suitable applicants, hopefully at a fair price. Popular sources of recruitment are schools, colleges, careers centres and universities, newspapers, magazines and the radio, job centres and employment agencies – even word of mouth and notices in a shop window or on a factory gate! Clearly, the one(s) chosen will depend upon who and how many people the manager wishes to contact, and the money that has been allocated to be spent on advertising the job.

Making a choice is no easy task – what is right for one firm may be wrong for another. For example, a business wants to fill a highly skilled position, and looks at each source of recruitment in turn, including job centres and employment agencies. Job centre advertisements are seen by many types and numbers of people, and are free. This sounds ideal but it may mean that a large proportion of applicants will be unsuitable, as some people will simply apply because 'it's worth a letter' and 'anything's better than being unemployed'. Perhaps so, but these applications are a waste of the manager's (and the applicants') time and a drain on the firm's resources as they will all have to be received, dealt with and responded to.

Those advertisements in an employment agency, which might specialize in particular types of job such as temporary, computer and secretarial ones, may be costly but will be seen by a smaller and more specific audience than a job centre. This could be a wiser option for that firm seeking to fill a highly specialized post – each and every applicant might be a potential winner! Of course, the business advertising a general, unskilled post may prefer job centres to employment agencies. A chart comparing and contrasting various recruitment sources is shown in Figure 6.5.

The manager can do much to attract the right people and dissuade the wrong ones from applying by composing appropriate advertisements for the job. Whether they are for a school noticeboard or a national newspaper, the contents of advertisements should develop from the job description and the employee specification. Concise details ought to be given about the business, the job title and location, its purpose and tasks, the salary and fringe benefits, the type of person required and where, how and to whom to apply for the post. Such full information will enable readers to decide whether the company and job are suitable for them, and vice versa.

The style and design of advertisements may vary too. In general, they should be eye-catching to attract attention. A bold headline, a strong border, different styles and shades of print, a company logo, colour or an illustration may achieve this. Also, they should be interesting, making the reader wish to go on by telling him or her what they want to know. They must be truthful, mentioning not only the good points of the job but the bad ones as well. As important, they need to be brief, encouraging people to read to the end, and specific so that everyone knows exactly what is involved. An 'attractive salary' is too vague, '£10 000 per annum' is better. An example of a recruitment advertisement is given in Figure 6.6.

Shortlisting applicants

The manager will not want to spend his or her valuable time interviewing every applicant, and will therefore seek to reduce the number

	Types of people reached	Number of people reached	Advertising costs involved
Schools	Youngsters, keen but inexperienced. First time employees	Plentiful – a regular supply, year after year	None – details welcomed
Colleges	Mainly young people, 16 to 19 years old. Limited experience	Many – seeking temporary, part and full time work	None – keen to obtain adverts
Careers centres	Youngsters, school leavers at 16	Those school leavers who approach the careers centre – not as many as you think! Perhaps 1 in 10?	None – gratefully received
Universities	Usually younger people, 18 to 21 years. Some are older	Numerous, all looking for work to supplement grants, and after graduation	None – always welcomed
Newspapers	Depends on type of paper and position. Local paper means local people. Jobs section means active job hunters	Varied, depending on circulation of newspaper. Hundreds, thousands or millions!	Variable – a few lines may be £10, a full page £1000, or more
Magazines	Depends on type of magazine and position. Specialist magazine equals specialist readership etc.	Varied, depending on circulation of magazine. Probably hundreds or thousands	Variable – that £10 'classified' advert or the £1000 'display' advert
Radio	A broad mix of types, not just youngsters as is often assumed	Many, scattered far and wide – but how many people really listen to radio adverts?	Variable, according to number of adverts booked and their broadcasting times. Perhaps £15–£60 per single, 30 second advert
Job centres	Many – right and wrong types	Numerous, whoever goes in or looks at the notices in the windows	None – a free service
Employment agencies	Specific groups looking for temporary, secretarial jobs or whatever	Compact, usually only interested and potentially suitable people – and they should be screened by the agency.	Substantial – may be 10–20 per cent of the successful applicant's annual salary
Word of mouth	Various, depending on who is told. Often friends and relatives – not necessarily the best employees!	Limited, perhaps only a handful – unless they tell their friends and relatives and so on	None
Notices	All types – suitable and unsuitable people!	Potentially unlimited numbers – depending on location	None, apart from the notice!

Figure 6.5 Sources of recruitment: a quick comparison

BABYTIME

requires

OFFICE ASSISTANT

A vacancy now exists at our headquarters for an assistant to undertake a variety of duties in a small but busy office.

The successful applicant will be smart and friendly, able to type at 50 words per minute and have a minimum of 4 GCSEs ('C' grade or above) preferably including English Language and Maths. Previous office experience is desirable.

We offer the winning applicant a salary of £7000 per annum, 21 days annual holiday, a 5 day week with occasional overtime and a friendly work environment.

For an application form, write to Maureen Reynolds at Babytime Ltd, 26–30 Windmill Road, Woodleigh, Suffolk IP6 9EZ

Figure 6.6   A recruitment advertisement

of applicants to perhaps six who seem most suitable, and are worth interviewing. He or she may screen applicants in a variety of ways in order to produce a shortlist of candidates to be interviewed. Asking them to complete an application form is the most popular screening method. With questions and answers laid out in a set format, the manager can check swiftly if essential and desirable requirements are met, easily comparing applicants. The form may also be used as a guide in any subsequent interview.

There are disadvantages though. If the number, type and order of questions are wrong, some applicants will not reply and those who do will be harder to assess. The form needs to be based around the employee specification with simple, straightforward questions being asked so that answers are given which enable the manager to decide if the essentials and desirables are fulfilled. The form has to be short, asking enough questions to screen out unsuitable applicants but not so many that potentially suitable ones lose interest. Sufficient room should be provided for answers. The details of two referees must be requested who can comment on the applicant's strengths (and weaknesses). Figure 6.7 shows an example of an application form.

Alternatively, the manager may screen by letter, curriculum vitae or telephone. Letters of application allow him or her to assess applicants' writing styles and may take up less time than drafting an application form. However, some applicants might be poor writers but good at the job itself. For example, a salesperson is rarely employed for his or her literary skills! Curricula vitae (CVs) are simply outlines of applicants' lives which may provide information in a logical

Application for Employment

Position

Name

Address

Telephone number

Date of birth

Education

School/College	From	To	Qualifications

Employment

Employer	From	To	Job title/ duties	Salary	Reasons for leaving

Hobbies

Additional comments

Referees

Name	Name
Position	Position
Address	Address

Signature   Date

Figure 6.7 An application form

Dear Mrs Munglani

Thank you for your application for the post of office assistant. This is currently receiving our careful attention and we will be contacting you again in the near future.

Yours sincerely

Maureen Reynolds
Office supervisor

Figure 6.8   A letter acknowledging a job application

sequence making it easy to check requirements but do allow applicants to decide what to include, and exclude. The telephone is a speedy assessment method, useful for judging speech and conversational skills. Nevertheless, it encourages lots of casual calls from half interested applicants, and at all hours.

On receipt of applications, the manager will normally acknowledge them with a polite letter such as the one in Figure 6.8. This is not only courteous but good public relations – applicants may be customers too. He or she will then compare the applications with the job description, the employee specification and each other. Those who seem most ideal are invited in for an interview, with a letter like the one shown in Figure 6.9. Others are rejected in a pleasant and concise manner with a letter such as the one in Figure 6.10.

Interviewing candidates

Job interviews have three key aims: to enable the manager to decide which (if any) candidate is the right person for the job; to allow that candidate to calculate if this is the right job and company for him or her; and to promote an image of a good, caring business so that the best candidate will accept the job offer and rejected candidates will still think highly of the firm. Not surprisingly, this is easier said than done.

One-to-one or panel interviews may be used. A one-to-one (or individual) interview comprises one interviewer and one interviewee, as the name suggests. It is simple to arrange a mutually convenient time and place to meet, the interviewer will find it easy to control and lead the conversation and the interviewee should feel relaxed in an informal atmosphere. However, one interviewer may find it hard to reach a decision on his or her own, and could make the wrong

Dear Miss Thompson

I write to invite you to attend an interview for the post of office assistant at 11.30 a.m. on 9 February at the above address.

This interview should last for about 30 minutes and will be conducted by me.

Please telephone if the time or day are inconvenient for you and we can make alternative arrangements.

I look forward to meeting you next week.

Yours sincerely

Maureen Reynolds
Office supervisor

Figure 6.9 An invitation to a job interview

Dear Mr Baker

Thank you for your application for the post of office assistant.

We have considered your application carefully but regret to inform you that you have not been successful on this occasion.

However, we would like to thank you for your interest and wish you well for the future.

Yours sincerely

Maureen Reynolds
Office supervisor

Figure 6.10 A letter rejecting a job applicant

choice. Panel (or board) interviews consist of several interviewers and one interviewee. Interviewers – perhaps the personnel manager, department head and a specialist in the job – can share responsibilities and reach the right decision between themselves but interviewees may find it rather tense and nerve-wracking to face several people.

Interviews should be conducted in a quiet room where the two sides can concentrate on finding out about each other without being

---

Education, qualifications and training
- What did you like/dislike about your school?
- What else did you do at school, apart from studying?
- Why did you choose to study those subjects?
- Why did you attend that training course?
- How have you benefited from that training?

Past, present and future employment
- What did you enjoy/not enjoy about your last job?
- Why did you leave your last job?
- What part of this job most/least appeals to you?
- What makes you think you can do this job well?
- Where do you see yourself in five years?

Leisure activities
- What do you do in your free time?
- Do you belong to any clubs or societies?
- Do you like sports?
- What newspapers and books do you read?
- Have you any money-making schemes on the go?

Miscellaneous matters
- What are your likes and dislikes as a person?
- What are your strengths and weaknesses?
- What would you say to an angry customer returning faulty goods?
- How would you handle a disagreement with your boss?
- What would you do if you fell out with a colleague?

Figure 6.11   Interview topics and questions

disturbed by the telephone, outside noise or other interruptions. The interviewer should read through the job description, the employee specification and the appropriate application form, curriculum vitae or whatever before each interview, preparing a list of topics and questions to be asked which will help him or her to complete the picture of the interviewee. Typically, the topics covered might include education, qualifications and training, past, present and future employment, leisure activities and miscellaneous matters. Examples of the types of questions raised are given in Figure 6.11.

The interviewer will usually greet each interviewee with a smile, putting him or her at ease by chatting informally, perhaps about the business, its goods and services and the job itself. As the interviewer talks, he or she will guide the interviewee to the interview room, showing him or her to a seat. When the interviewee starts to converse freely, the interviewer will press ahead to discuss the various topics in turn, asking questions as and when appropriate. Ideally, the interviewer will try not to talk too much, concentrating instead on encouraging the interviewee to speak by smiling and nodding and listening to what is being said so that the interviewee can be compared with the employee specification.

When the interviewer has heard what he or she wants to know, the conversation will be moved on with another question, perhaps to the next topic. At the end, the interviewee will have the opportunity to ask questions which the interviewer should answer fully and honestly. Then he or she will signal the interview is over by standing up, thanking the interviewee for coming in and saying that he or she will soon be in touch. The interviewee will be shown to the door, and bid farewell in a warm and friendly manner.

After all of the interviews have been completed, the interviewer will have to make a decision, perhaps after consulting with colleagues who may have to work with the new recruit in some capacity. He or she will again study the job description, employee specification and all of the applications, while contemplating how each of them fared during the interviews. One will be selected, with two or even three others kept in reserve, just in case the favoured candidate turns down the job offer.

Making a job offer

A job offer can be made verbally or put in writing. It is sensible to make a written offer (or at least to follow a verbal offer with written confirmation) to avoid possible misunderstandings and confusion. An offer should contain information about the job title, the job location and the job title of the employee's immediate superior. Also, it should set out details about the salary, hours of work, holidays, any trial period, the date when work will commence and any conditions attached to the offer, such as satisfactory references or passing a medical examination. An example of a written offer is shown in Figure 6.12.

Most businesses will wish to take up references about the new recruit from former employers and other people of status before he or she starts work. Not surprisingly, the manager wants to check facts and verify his or her opinions about the chosen candidate. Letters should be sent or telephone calls made – for 'off the record' comments – which seek to discover information about the candidate's previous job, length of employment, conduct, timekeeping, abilities, honesty, health and reasons for leaving, as appropriate. The crunch question is, 'Would you re-employ him or her?' If the answer is 'no', the manager may have second thoughts.

Once the offer has been accepted and quality references have been given, the manager will then reject the remaining candidates in a friendly manner. He or she should be aware that these people may also be customers and might be ideal for other jobs in the coming

---

Dear Miss Thompson

Further to our recent meeting, I am pleased to offer you employment as an office assistant at Babytime's headquarters. You will be responsible to me, the office supervisor.

Your starting salary will be £7000 per annum, paid monthly in arrears into your bank account. Overtime will be paid at twice the hourly rate.

Your normal hours of work will be from 9 a.m. to 5 p.m., totalling 35 hours per week. You will be entitled to a one hour lunch break which must be taken between 1 p.m. and 2 p.m.

You will also be entitled to 21 days paid holiday per year, plus statutory holidays. Our holiday year runs from 6 April to 5 April.

Other, miscellaneous terms of employment will be provided on your first day of work.

I would be grateful if you would confirm in writing if you wish to accept this offer and when you will be able to commence work. Finally, can you also confirm that I may approach your present employers for reference purposes.

I look forward to hearing from you.

Yours sincerely

Maureen Reynolds
Office supervisor

Figure 6.12   A written offer of employment

months or years. They will not apply if they were offended on this occasion. A letter similar to the one in Figure 6.10 might be sent. Sensible managers never specify a reason for rejection as this can lead to ill feeling and arguments as some unsuccessful candidates try to convince them that they have made the wrong decision.

6.3   Managing employees

Once a business has recruited the right staff (in the right places and at the right times), it then has to manage them properly so that they are ready and willing to be transferred and promoted as and when required. A whole host of diverse issues comprise the all embracing term *staff management*, including the following.

Induction

The word *induction* simply refers to the process of installing a recruit into his or her new post and should be done as quickly and as efficiently as possible. Many firms arrange induction days when recruits are invited in and shown around so that they can meet new colleagues, see work being done and generally soak up the atmosphere. Special attention is given to a recruit on his or her first day and during the initial weeks with managers and fellow employees watching out for him or her, ready with advice and guidance as and when appropriate. Hopefully, this will help the person to settle in without disruption and to maximize his or her contribution to the firm at the earliest opportunity.

Contracts of employment

Within 13 weeks of starting work, staff who are employed for 16 hours or so per week (or who have been employed for eight hours each week for five years) are legally entitled to receive a written statement of the main terms and conditions of their employment. This statement should contain information about the employer's and employee's names, the date when employment commenced, the job title, the hours of work, the rate and intervals of pay, holiday and sickness pay and arrangements, pension arrangements, disciplinary and grievance rules and procedures and notice arrangements. Alternatively, some details may be set out in other, easily accessible documents to which reference should be made in the statement. An example of a written statement is shown in Figure 6.13.

Training

All employees need to be assessed on a regular basis, perhaps quarterly to begin with, and annually once they have been settled into the firm. Staff appraisal as it is better known enables the business to deal with employees' worries and to eliminate difficulties as far as possible. Any gaps which appear to exist in their knowledge or experience may then be rectified by additional training, perhaps by the firm itself or on day release courses at a local college, or whatever. If a business plans to transfer and promote employees up through the organization then it will need to groom them for their new positions well in advance.

Pay and financial matters

A firm's wages bill is likely to represent a substantial proportion of its total overheads, and it will therefore try to keep this bill as low

---

Statement of Terms of Employment

This statement sets out the terms on which Babytime Limited (the employer) employs Jane Thompson (the employee) from 7 March 1994.

1 The employee is employed as an office assistant.
2 The rate of pay is £7000 per annum, paid monthly in arrears into the employee's bank account.
3 The hours of work are from 9 a.m. to 5 p.m. from Monday to Friday inclusive, with lunchbreaks between 1 p.m. and 2 p.m.
4 The employee is entitled to 21 days paid holiday each year, to be taken at mutually agreeable times. The holiday year runs from 6 April to 5 April.
5 Disciplinary and grievance rules and procedures are detailed in the attached notes.
6 Statutory Sick Pay (SSP) is paid in accordance with legal requirements. The booklet 'Sick or Disabled' is attached for reference purposes.
7 The employer has made no provision for a pension scheme, and personal arrangements should be made by the employee.
8 Notice must be given in line with statutory requirements. The booklet 'Rights to Notice and Reasons for Dismissal' is attached for reference purposes.

Signature   Date

Signature   Date

Figure 6.13 A statement of the main terms of employment

as possible by not paying high wages which will bite into profits. At the same time, offering low wages can be equally damaging, as the business will find it difficult to attract and retain good staff. When setting pay, the concern will need to calculate what it can afford to pay, comparing this with what will attract and keep the right people and contrasting it with what rival firms pay, and the general state of the jobs market at the moment. It is a tough choice.

Whatever the pay, most employees who work for 16 hours or more each week (or from eight to 16 hours per week for five years) are entitled to receive itemized pay statements from the firm. These statements should set out (or itemize) the employee's gross wage, the amount and purpose of any deductions and the net wage. Usually, deductions will comprise income tax and national insurance contributions which have to be deducted by employers under the terms of the Government's 'Pay as You Earn' (PAYE) scheme and forwarded to the Inland Revenue each month.

Employees who earn more than a certain weekly wage – £54.00 in 1992/3 – may be entitled to Statutory Sick Pay from their employers for up to 28 weeks of sickness. SSP as it is commonly known is paid at one of two rates, depending upon income. As a 1992/3 example, those who earn between £54.00 and £189.99 each week may be eligible for £45.30 SSP per week. Employees earning £190.00 or more could be entitled to £52.50. Businesses may reclaim SSP sums from the State by deducting the appropriate amounts from national insurance contributions paid through the PAYE system.

Most employees who have been employed by the same firm for six months, earn more than a certain weekly wage and who stop work because of pregnancy are entitled to up to 18 weeks' Statutory Maternity Pay (SMP). Those who have worked for 16 hours or more each week for two years (or for eight to 16 hours per week for five years) may receive 90 per cent of their average weekly earnings for six weeks followed by a flat, statutory weekly rate for up to another 12 weeks. The rate for 1992/3 is £46.30. Those employed for between six months and two years may be eligible to receive the flat rate for up to 18 weeks. As with SSP, SMP can be claimed back from the State via the PAYE system.

Pregnant workers have other statutory rights too. They may be entitled to reasonable paid time off to attend antenatal clinics, regardless of the hours worked or their length of service. They could be allowed to return to work after the birth of their baby (although firms with five employees or less do not need to keep jobs available). They might be able to claim unfair dismissal if they are sacked because of pregnancy.

Holidays and time off

All employees expect a reasonable, paid holiday entitlement according to their status. Junior staff might start on 18 days (plus public and bank holidays), subsequently increasing to 30 days or more (plus statutory holidays), depending upon their position within the firm and/or their length of service. As well as giving reasonable paid time off to pregnant employees for antenatal care, it must be offered to those employees under notice of redundancy who have worked for 16 hours or more each week for two years (or eight to 16 hours per week for five years) who wish to look for work or training opportunities. Staff who perform public duties such as jury service are entitled to reasonable unpaid time off. Employees who suffer a bereavement ought to be given paid, compassionate leave for a reasonable period.

Rules and procedures

Rules help to establish the performance and behaviour levels that are expected of employees. Procedures enable firms to deal with situations which develop when rules have been broken and will also ensure that they are not breached again. Businesses need to set down disciplinary and grievance rules and procedures in writing, handing this information out to employees with their written statements of the main terms and conditions of employment and displaying it in prominent areas. Thus, staff should be fully aware of and conversant with all of the rules and procedures within that particular organization.

Disciplinary rules will vary from one firm to another, according to the individual situation. Whatever they comprise, the rules will spell out what the business considers to be unacceptable conduct. Unexcused lateness or absence, inappropriate appearance or dress and overlong tea and lunch breaks may be seen as minor misconduct which could lead to disciplinary procedures being implemented if repeated. Continual unauthorized lateness or absences, the inability to meet work standards and doing other work during the hours of employment could be viewed as serious misconduct which will initiate disciplinary action. Theft, abuse, assault, breaches of confidence and other extreme activities might be regarded as gross misconduct, warranting instant dismissal.

Minor or serious cases of misconduct will trigger a firm's disciplinary procedures. These should be fair and reasonable at all times and ought to aim to correct and then improve an employee's performance and behaviour rather than simply punishing him or her. Minor breaches might be dealt with informally, by talking to the person to find out the cause of the problem, outlining the standards required and mutually seeking ways of remedying the lapse and avoiding a recurrence in the future. This 'quiet word in the ear' approach is often sufficient to remedy the position.

If this approach fails, the business will have to take disciplinary action against the offending employee. This might consist of a formal oral warning followed by a written warning for repeated minor offences or serious misconduct, a final written warning for continued unsatisfactory conduct and dismissal as a last resort. The employer must behave in a fair and reasonable manner throughout though – asking for and listening to explanations, checking facts and seeing both sides of the situation before making a decision, detailing the reasons, explaining what is expected in future, and how this can be achieved. Warnings should be deleted from the records once the situation has improved and been sustained.

Grievance procedures should be fair and reasonable too. Dissatisfied employees ought to be encouraged to raise problems on an informal basis with their immediate superior, to see if they can be settled quickly and satisfactorily, without further action needing to be taken. If this does not seem to be successful, a meeting may take place between the aggrieved employee and a manager further up the line who will tackle the problem in a similar way to a disciplinary matter – asking for and listening to explanations and so on. The grievance could even be referred to a respected outsider if necessary, whose decisions might be binding on the two parties.

Motivation

Businesses must keep staff happy if they want to retain them, and motivated if they wish to get the best out of them. There are many ways of achieving this dual aim:

1 Pay

Money is important to everyone, and employees will judge their value by what they are paid in comparison with colleagues in the same firm, and in other businesses. Hence, pay must be fair and competitive. Incentive schemes whereby additional sums are paid for achieving greater success can be a powerful motivating force, persuading staff to work harder, sell more goods, or whatever.

2 Holidays

The number of days off that each employee is entitled to may be a cause of dissatisfaction if they do not feel they are being treated fairly. Offering extra days off for staff who reach targets or who are promoted may motivate employees too.

3 Increased job involvement

Giving employees more control and responsibility over their day-to-day work can be beneficial. Perhaps they might be allowed to vary their approach to a task and to become more involved in setting their work targets. Sometimes, training is seen as a reward for hard work and progress, while the possibility of regular promotion acts as a motivator as well.

4 Work environment

It is sensible for a firm to ensure that its premises are employee friendly. They must be well laid out with quality equipment and machinery and comfortable furniture. They should not be too hot, cold or noisy. As important as anything else, they have to be safe. Offering staff an active social life with works outings, office parties, sports and so on may be worthwhile.

5   Company cars

Larger concerns often give high ranking employees the use of a company car, although smaller firms will inevitably find this to be prohibitively expensive. As an alternative, these businesses might offer their staff assistance with the cost of travelling to and from work, especially for those who live some distance away.

6   Subsidized items

Many companies provide subsidized canteens or restaurants for their employees. Small businesses might offer luncheon vouchers or provide vending machines with hot food and drinks instead. Most concerns allow their employees a discount on their goods and services too, ranging from a nominal 10 per cent upwards.

7   Financial assistance

Some firms give their staff low cost or interest free loans for various purposes. Also they might provide sick pay schemes and health insurance plans to protect their employees in the event of sickness and/ or accidents. Businesses which offer some form of pension scheme for their staff will make them feel happy and contented – and motivated to stay put!

6.4   Ending employment

It is relatively easy to recruit staff but unless they wish to leave it is more difficult to end their employment. The law with regard to giving notice, dismissals and redundancies is very strict and must be followed precisely if a business does not want to find itself the subject of a claim made against it by an aggrieved, former employee at an industrial tribunal.

Giving notice

Those employees who work for 16 hours or more each week (or who have been employed for between eight and 16 hours per week for five years) are entitled to minimum periods of notice according to their length of service. After one month's employment, one week's notice must be given and this remains the statutory minimum until two years' employment has been completed. Thereafter, they have to be provided with an extra week's notice for every year up to a maximum of 12 weeks' notice. In return, employees who have been employed for a month or longer must give one week's notice. This notice period remains the same, regardless of their length of employment.

Often, employers and employees agree to give each other longer periods of notice, above and beyond the bare minimum required by law. Businesses must think carefully about offering or agreeing to this though. If a firm promises to give a longer notice period than is necessary, it may have a discontented employee on the premises for that much longer, disrupting colleagues, being surly to customers and so on. If he or she is paid off in lieu of notice, it will cost the concern more than it needed to. Should the employee agree to a longer period of notice but subsequently decide to walk out without honouring it, there is little that the business can do about it. In practice, it is hardly worthwhile trying to enforce the agreement against his or her wishes.

Usually, notice can be given by either party at any time, and may be made orally or in writing. Once notice has been given, the period of notice commences from the next day. The normal rate of pay applies during this time. If the employee has worked for the firm for six months or longer, he or she is entitled to ask for and receive a written statement outlining the reasons for a dismissal. This request may be made verbally or in writing, and has to be attended to within 14 days of such a demand.

As with all legal duties and obligations, there are a few exceptions. With regard to giving notice, either party may terminate the mutually agreed contract of employment if the gross behaviour of the other side warrants it. Examples of gross behaviour might include theft, sexual harassment and assault. Also, either party may waive their entitlement to notice should they wish to do so. In some cases, a business may prefer to get an angry and disruptive employee off the premises as fast as possible. As often as not, both the firm and the employee will agree that it is mutually beneficial to part company immediately. There is little to gain from delaying the inevitable.

Dismissals

For a firm to dismiss an employee *and* stay within the law, the dismissal must be termed 'fair'. In order to be fair, the business must have 'sufficient reason' to dismiss the employee and have 'acted reasonably' at all times. Sufficient reason might incorporate the employee's inability to do the job properly, continual minor or sudden gross misconduct such as stealing or fighting, legal reasons which prevent him or her doing the job such as a driving ban, redundancy where the job ceases to exist or any other substantial reason such as passing trade secrets to competitors. To act reasonably, the firm must give the employee every chance and assistance to improve, consider the possibilities of alternative employment and not discriminate because of sex, marital status or race.

An 'unfair' dismissal takes place when the business does not have a sufficient reason and/or does not act reasonably – *both* criteria must be met for the dismissal to be deemed to be fair. An employee who resigns because the business broke one of the major terms of his or her contract could also claim he or she was subject to a *constructive* and therefore unfair dismissal as the firm's behaviour effectively forced him or her to leave. A major term might involve pay or hours of work. Anyone who has been employed for 16 hours or more each week for two years (or for between eight and 16 hours per week for five years) and who is below retirement age may bring a claim against their employer for unfair dismissal at an industrial tribunal. To be found guilty may lead to the reinstatement of the employee or a heavy fine – equally unappealing prospects for the concern, and an incentive to behave.

Redundancies

If a job (or jobs) cease to exist perhaps because of a sustained trade recession, a business has to fulfil its legal responsibilities, attend to its moral obligations and may have to make redundancy payments too. Legally, the firm has to select people to be made redundant on a fair basis. 'First in, last out' or 'Last in, first out' is often used. Selected employees who have been employed for a firm for at least 16 hours per week for two years (or for between eight and 16 hours each week for five years) must be given reasonable time off to look for new work or retraining opportunities. If 10 or more workers are to be made redundant, the business has to notify the Department of Employment, so help can be provided to redundant workers.

Redundancy is an extremely traumatic experience for anyone who has experienced it, and firms have a moral duty to lessen the blow so far as possible. This approach makes business sense too – the morale of surviving employees will be weakened if they see their concern acting in a heartless manner. Similarly, a firm must never forget that redundant employees may be customers as well, or will at least talk to other people who are. Bad word of mouth comments may affect trade. Businesses should do what they can to help employees find alternative work – everyone should be given time off to seek other jobs and facilities ought to be made available to them. Secretarial staff could help to type letters of application, and so forth.

Those departing employees who have been employed by the firm for 16 hours each week for two years (or for eight to 16 hours per week for five years) and who are below retirement age, may be entitled to redundancy payments. The sum which may be due to each person is related to their particular age, current pay and length of service and ranges from half a week's pay to one and a half weeks' pay per completed year – whatever it is, it will prove to be costly for the firm.

Industrial tribunals

These are independent judicial bodies which exist to settle employment disputes. Seventy-five per cent of cases relate to unfair dismissals although other matters such as equal pay, race relations and redundancy payments are handled too. With regard to unfair dismissals, a tribunal which finds in favour of the sacked employee may order the firm to reinstate him or her in the same job on identical terms and conditions, to re-engage him or her in a comparable job on the same terms and conditions or to pay financial compensation, which could run into a five figure sum. Clearly, businesses must avoid such a situation, which is both costly and damaging in terms of adverse publicity. The best way of doing this is to have sufficient reason to do what it did and to act reasonably at all times.

6.5 Employment laws

Not surprisingly, numerous employment laws exist which control and restrain firms in their recruitment, management and dismissal of employees. These are some of the most prominent and influential ones, that must be adhered to at all times.

Employment Protection (Consolidation) Act 1978

This Act – amended and updated in parts by various Employment Acts in 1980, 1982 and 1988 – is still the cornerstone of employment legislation today, covering almost all employment issues of any relevance. The Act (and its successors) entitles employees to a written statement of the main terms of employment, itemized pay statements, statutory sick pay, maternity benefits, holidays and time off, statutory periods of notice, a written statement of the reasons for dismissal, redundancy pay and not to be dismissed unfairly. Some of these entitlements may be subject to qualifying conditions, such as the number of hours worked per week and/or the length of service.

Sex Discrimination Act 1975

It is unlawful to discriminate on the grounds of sex or marital status with regard to advertising for staff, recruiting, terms and conditions of employment, benefits and facilities, training, transfer, promotion, dismissal or redundancy. Unlawful discrimination can be direct or indirect. Direct discrimination occurs when a person is treated less favourably than another of the opposite sex or marital status would be in the same or similar circumstances. For example, a woman is refused employment because the firm regards the job as 'man's work'. Indirect discrimination takes place when requirements or conditions are set which favour people of one sex or marital status more than another. As an example, minimum height and weight requirements benefit men rather than women, as they tend to be taller and heavier.

This Act is applicable to both women and men, full and part timers, regardless of their length of service – no minimum periods of employment are necessary for the Act to be effective. Sex discrimination is only lawful if it is a 'genuine occupational qualification'. A person of a particular sex may be required for authenticity, to respect privacy or to maintain decency. For example, a firm may stipulate that an attendant in the female changing rooms at its leisure centre must be a woman. Other limited exceptions to the Act relate to jobs within private households and the armed forces.

Race Relations Act 1976

It is illegal to discriminate because of colour, race, nationality or ethnic origin in employment matters ranging from recruitment through to dismissal. As with the highly similar Sex Discrimination Act, racial discrimination may be either direct or indirect. Likewise, discrimination on racial grounds is only permitted if it is a genuine occupational qualification. As an example, a model of a specific ethnic origin may be required for authenticity. Private households and the Civil Service are not covered by the terms and conditions of the Race Relations Act.

Disabled Persons (Employment) Act 1958

Businesses with 20 or more employees have a duty to employ a quota of disabled people, as registered at job centres. The quota currently stands at three per cent of their workforce. It is not a legal offence to be below quota but those firms which are have a responsibility to take on suitable disabled people if they are available when vacancies arise. If a concern wants to recruit an able-bodied person instead, it has to obtain a permit from the job centre. Businesses with over 20 employees should keep records showing the numbers and names of staff with starting and finishing dates, and clearly identifying registered disabled people in their employment.

Equal Pay Act 1970

Employees are entitled to equal pay and terms and conditions of employment if the work that they do is the same, broadly similar or of equal value to that carried out by fellow employees within the firm. The Act applies to all employees, regardless of their jobs or the number of hours for which they are employed. The only legitimate exception exists when a business pays its staff a higher rate after they have worked in the organization for a certain period of time.

Health and Safety at Work Act 1974

So far as is reasonably practicable, firms have to provide safe work systems, plant, machinery and equipment plus comfortable working conditions and a secure environment for their employees. Those businesses which employ five or more people have to draw up a written health and safety statement in which rules and procedures in this field are outlined. It has to be displayed in a prominent position where each and every member of staff will see it. Sufficient additional information, guidance and supervision must be offered to employees on an ongoing basis so that health and safety standards are upheld.

Those businesses which breach the Employment Protection (Consolidation), Sex Discrimination, Race Relations, Disabled Persons (Employment) and Equal Pay Acts may be taken to an industrial tribunal by an aggrieved employee. If the tribunal finds in the employee's favour, the firm will have to remedy the matter and/or pay substantial financial compensation – and the resulting media coverage may be harmful to the concern's image and trading activities too. With regard to the Health and Safety at Work Act, businesses that break the law may be taken to court by the local authority and fined, or even closed down in exceptional circumstances when lives are at risk.

6.6   Rapid revision

Answers	Questions
–	1 What are human resources?
1 They are the managers and employees within a business.	2 What is the purpose of manpower planning?
2 Its purpose is to ensure that the firm has the right people in the right places at the right times.	3 What does manpower planning involve?
3 It involves (a) calculating immediate staff requirements; (b) appraising the current workforce; (c) assessing the future workforce; (d) anticipating future staff requirements; (e) recruiting the right people in the right places at the right times.	4 What does staff recruitment involve?
4 (a) Analysing the job; (b) attracting applicants; (c) shortlisting applicants; (d) interviewing candidates; (e) making a job offer.	5 What is a job description?
5 It is a statement which lists (a) the job title; (b) the job title of the employee's superior; (c) the job titles of the employee's subordinates; (d) the purpose of the job; (e) the main tasks of the job.	6 What is an employee specification?
6 It is a statement that details the type of person required for a job, and the attributes that he or she should have.	7 Which are the most popular sources of recruitment?
7 (a) Schools; (b) colleges; (c) careers centres; (d) universities; (e) newspapers; (f) magazines; (g) the radio; (h) job centres; (i) employment agencies; (j) word of mouth; (k) notices.	8 What information should be included in a recruitment advertisement?

8 Brief details about (a) the business; (b) the job title; (c) the location; (d) purpose and tasks; (e) the salary and fringe benefits; (f) the type of person required; (g) where, how, whom to apply to.

9 What types of recruitment advertisement will attract applicants?

9 Ones that are (a) eye-catching; (b) interesting; (c) truthful; (d) brief.

10 What are the main methods of screening applicants?

10 (a) Application forms; (b) letters of application; (c) curricula vitae; (d) telephone.

11 What are the aims of a job interview?

11 (a) To allow the interviewer to select the right person; (b) to enable the interviewee to choose the right job; (c) to help the company promote a good image.

12 What topics should be covered during a job interview?

12 (a) Education, qualifications and training; (b) past, present and future employment; (c) leisure activities; (d) miscellaneous matters.

13 What information should a job offer contain?

13 Details about (a) the job title; (b) the job location; (c) the job title of the employee's superior; (d) the salary; (e) the hours of work; (f) holidays; (g) any trial period; (h) date of commencement; (i) any conditions.

14 What issues comprise the term staff management?

14 (a) Induction; (b) contracts of employment; (c) training; (d) pay and financial matters; (e) holidays and time off; (f) rules and procedures; (g) motivation.

15 What motivates staff?

15 Many things, including; (a) pay; (b) holidays; (c) increased job involvement; (d) the work environment; (e) company cars; (f) subsidized items; (g) other financial assistance.

16 What is a fair dismissal?

16   It is one for which the employer has sufficient reason. He or she must also act reasonably at all times.

17   What would constitute sufficient reason to dismiss an employee?

---

17   Typically, (a) inability; (b) misconduct; (c) legal reasons; (d) redundancy; (e) any other substantial reason.

18   What might happen to a firm which unfairly dismisses an employee?

---

18   It could be taken to an industrial tribunal and forced to (a) reinstate the person in the same job; (b) re-engage him or her in a similar job; (c) pay compensation.

19   What are the most prominent employment laws in the UK?

---

19   In particular, (a) Employment Protection (Consoldation) Act; (b) Sex Discrimination Act; (c) Race Relations Act; (d) Disabled Persons (Employment) Act; (e) Equal Pay Act; (f) Health and Safety at Work Act.

20   What might happen to a business that breaks the law in this field?

---

20   It may be taken to an industrial tribunal which may force it to remedy the matter and pay compensation in many instances.

21   Go over the questions again until you know all of the answers. Then move on to the next section.

Part Three
Business Markets

7
Market principles

When you hear the word 'market', you will probably think of a street market, selling fruit and vegetables, clothes, bric-à-brac or whatever. At the same time, you will have heard talk of 'the housing market', 'the overseas market' and so on – and quite obviously these are not held on a street corner! A market can thus be many things – varying from something that can be physically seen to a vague and rather abstract concept. The best definition of it may be that it is 'an arrangement whereby buyers of goods and services are brought into contact with sellers of those goods and services'. Hence, this applies both to the street market and to the varied elements of the housing market comprising estate agents, local newspapers and so forth – anything which brings buyers and sellers together!

Most markets operate according to various basic principles which are equally applicable to the student buying a bag of apples from a market trader as they are to the company purchasing office premises from another private or public limited company. These principles are as follows:

1 Buyers are usually free to spend their money on whatever goods and services they wish to purchase and they will normally (but not always) choose to buy those ones that give them the most satisfaction for the money they have spent. Thus, that student bought apples rather than lemons because she will derive greater satisfaction from munching an apple than from sucking a lemon. The company purchases premises in the centre of town rather than on the outskirts as these will convey the status that owners want to put across.

2 Similarly, sellers are normally free to manufacture those products and offer those services which they want to provide, and they will therefore usually produce and sell the ones that are the most in demand with existing and would-be buyers so that they can continue to survive, profit and grow. Accordingly, the market trader

may prefer to sell apples rather than lemons and the estate agent might like to take on easy to sell, centrally-based properties rather than those in second-rate locations.

3   If more products and services are wanted by buyers than are being supplied by sellers, then buyers will bid against each other for the limited number of goods available, and prices will rise. This situation is sometimes called *a sellers' market*, as it is obviously good news for sellers! However, rising prices will persuade existing and new sellers to supply more products and services in order to make more money but will have the reverse effect as buyers will no longer need to compete and prices will fall.

4   Conversely, if more goods are being provided by sellers than are actually required by buyers, then sellers will be left with excessive stocks which cannot be sold. This position is often referred to as *a buyers' market*, as it is clearly to the buyer's advantage. In these circumstances, sellers will then have to cut prices in order to persuade buyers to purchase goods, and will also need to supply fewer products and services in future so that there are enough available for buyers, but no more.

7.2   Demand

Demand can be defined as 'the desire to buy products and services at a particular price over a given period of time, combined with the ability to pay for them'. It is important to note that demand must be linked to a specific length of time. It is meaningless to state that at a price of £100, 50 000 products are demanded unless this is put into context, by adding, 'per week', 'month', 'quarter' or 'year'. Also, customers must be able to pay for goods and services. No matter how much they may want a product, no real demand can exist if they do not have the money available to buy it.

Demand is influenced by various factors, of which the following are the most significant.

Price

Obviously, the price of a product or service usually has a direct and strong influence upon demand. As a general rule – and rules exist to be broken – a higher price means less demand and a lower price leads to more demand. All things being equal, demand is inversely related to price. Thus, when prices are high, fewer customers want and are able to purchase the goods, and vice versa. Of course, there are exceptions. Taking a Rolls Royce automobile as an example, a price rise may not have an adverse effect on demand and could even

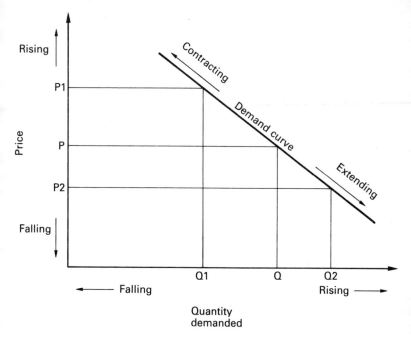

Figure 7.1 A demand curve

have a positive influence – a higher price is unlikely to put financial pressure on those customers already wealthy enough to purchase one, and it makes the car even more of a status symbol.

The normally close interrelationship between demand and price can be illustrated by a demand curve, as shown in Figure 7.1. This is a diagram which represents how demand increases or decreases as prices rise and fall, and is typically downward sloping from the top left to the bottom right of the graph. Looking at the example, when the price of a product is at P, the quantity demanded is at Q. If the price rises to P1, the quantity demanded will fall or 'contract' to Q1. Should the price be cut to P2, quantity demanded will increase or 'extend' to Q2. Note that the line is usually curved, rather than straight as drawn, since demand does not always respond in precisely the same proportion as a changing price. An eight per cent price rise does not necessarily mean an eight per cent fall in demand – it could be four or 12 per cent depending on circumstances.

Income

Not surprisingly, customers' incomes will be an influential factor upon demand too – no money, no demand! If incomes rise, customers will want and be able to purchase more products and services across the board so demand is boosted. Similarly, if incomes fall – perhaps when a business closes or people are made redundant – then they cut back, only wishing and being capable of buying the most essential goods and services. As always, there are exceptions. For example, a higher income can sometimes lead to a fall in demand for a particular product because a buyer wants to 'trade up' to a better item. He or she may buy silk shirts instead of cotton ones, a detached rather than a semi-detached house, and so on.

Taste

Often overlooked or ill considered, changing tastes and fashions can have a very profound impact upon demand for certain goods and services. This is most evident with clothes – no matter how cheaply they were priced, it is unlikely that string vests, corsets, longjohns and similar items of clothing are ever going to be in demand again! Clearly, when particular products and services come into fashion, demand will rise and will then fall away when they go out of fashion, months or perhaps even years later on.

Other goods and services

The prices of similar products and services can affect demand for particular goods because these other products and services are available as potential substitutes for customers. If the prices of a firm's goods and its rivals remain the same or in proportion with each other then demand for each of them will stay static, all things being equal. Should the price of one rise, demand may be transferred to another, which now offers better value for money and greater satisfaction for customers. Likewise, if the price of one falls, demand could be switched to it, as it appears more attractive than the rest.

As significant, if not more so in some instances, the prices of associated goods may influence demand for a concern's products and services as these goods are complementary to them. As a simplified example of this, if the price of petrol rocketed, the use and therefore the eventual purchase of cars would fall as drivers switched to public transport. Equally valid, if the price of gas rose dramatically, sales of gas cookers would slump, with buyers preferring to purchase electric ones. Of course, falling petrol and gas prices would have the opposite effect of increasing demand and sales of cars and gas cookers.

It is important not to forget that other, totally unrelated products and services are bought by customers and that their prices will have an effect on demand. After all, most customers, whether businesses or individuals, have limited incomes. Some spending will be essential, such as on rent, electricity, gas, water rates and so on. Other spending will be desirable, such as on clothes, home entertainment, eating out and so forth. If rents, clothes or whatever rise or fall in price, more or less money will be left over, thus increasing or decreasing demand for a firm's goods.

Population

The numbers and types of customers within the marketplace are inevitably going to play a part in the demand for particular products and services. This may be illustrated by looking at what might be loosely termed as 'the baby market'. If the birth rate falls, then logically the demand for baby clothes and nursery goods will fall as well, and vice versa when the birth rate rises. Similarly, if more boys are born, there will be a greater demand for blue baby clothes whereas more girls will mean more pink clothes are demanded. A rough and ready example – but an accurate one nevertheless.

Income, tastes, other goods, alternative services, population and any additional factors which might affect demand for a specific product or service are sometimes referred to as 'the underlying conditions of demand', and they can exert a significant influence, for better or for worse. This can be seen by the shifting demand curve in Figure 7.2. When the price of a product is at P, the quantity demanded is at Q, and if the price alters then the quantity demanded extends or contracts along demand curve D, as appropriate. However, if the price stays at P and an underlying condition changes so that demand falls, the quantity demanded moves to Q2, and the curve shifts to D2. Likewise, if demand rises, the quantity demanded moves to Q1 and the curve shifts to D1. Of course, demand does not necessarily change in proportion to shifting factors – hence a curved rather than a straight line.

7.3 Supply

Supply might be defined in a similar way to demand, namely 'the desire to make products and services available to customers at a specific price over a particular period of time, combined with an ability to provide them'. Again, it is sensible to put supply into context by associating it with a given length of time – 10 000 products per week, month, quarter, or whatever. In addition, businesses must not only be willing but also be able to provide the products and services required for supply to exist.

Like demand, supply is subject to numerous influences.

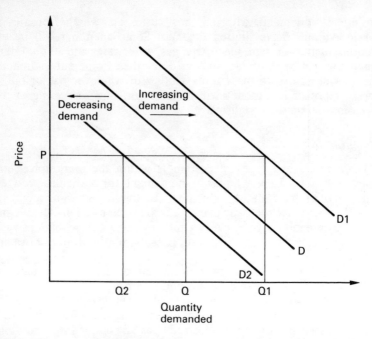

Figure 7.2   A shifting demand curve

Price

All things being equal, supply is directly related to the price of a product or service. Thus, if prices offered by customers are high, existing and new businesses will usually produce and supply more so that they increase their income and hopefully their profit during these good times. Conversely, if prices offered are low, existing firms will generally not wish to continue to provide as many goods if any at all as their income and probably their profit will slump during these bad times. They, and other businesses in the marketplace, will prefer to switch over to alternative products and services which currently attract higher prices and generate larger profits.

The relationship between supply and price may be seen in the supply curve set out in Figure 7.3. Indicating how quantity supplied increases or decreases as prices rise and fall, it usually slopes upwards from the bottom left to the top right of the graph. Studying this, when the price of a product is at P, the quantity supplied is at Q. If the price goes up to P1, the quantity supplied will rise (or extend) to Q1. If the price goes down to P2, the quantity supplied will fall (or contract) to Q2. Again, the supply curve is usually

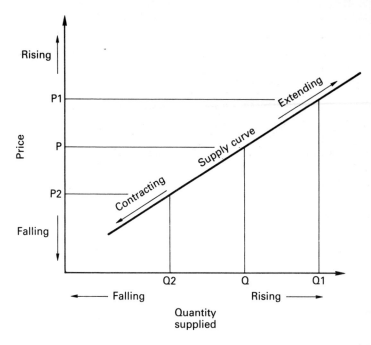

Figure 7.3 A supply curve

curved rather than straight as supply may not rise and fall in exactly the same proportions as price. A 10 per cent price rise could mean a five or a 15 per cent increase in supply, according to circumstances.

Costs

The costs of producing goods and services have a key influence upon supply. As a rough but ready rule, if the cost of obtaining finance, renting premises, employing staff, buying raw materials and so on rises, then a firm's ability to supply a given quantity of goods at a specific price is limited, and a smaller amount will be produced. Quite simply, if a shopkeeper's rent rises substantially, he or she will have less money left in the kitty to spend on stock for resale, and will have to carry a narrower range of goods. Similarly, if costs fall, a business can produce and supply more products and services. If that shopkeeper employs part timers to cover the busiest periods instead of full timers from nine until five, then he or she could spend more on resellable stock.

Objectives

A firm's goals – to survive, to make a satisfactory profit, to maximize profit and so forth – will naturally have an impact on its supply of goods and services. As a basic example, an aggressive and growing business may wish to maximize profits in the long term and will thus accept short-term losses if this will enable it to kill off its rivals so that it can seize a bigger share of the market in the future, and charge what it likes because no substitute products are still available. Hence, it may supply more goods at the same price – 'two for the price of one' deals perhaps – until competitors are forced out of business.

Other products and services

Some goods and services produced by a firm are so closely linked that an increasing supply of one may automatically increase or decrease the supply of another, as appropriate, and vice versa! For example, a farmer who breeds more chickens for the dinner table will simultaneously have more eggs to sell as well. A dairy herd farmer who supplies milk, butter and cheese to the market knows that if more butter is produced from a particular quantity of milk, then less cheese can be provided, and vice versa.

It is relatively easy to increase or decrease supplies of certain products and services, less so for others. A baker may be able to bake more bread and cakes simply by working longer hours whereas a farmer could be limited by the number of crops sown in previous seasons – it may take him or her years to boost supplies (and by that time they might not be in demand!). Of course, some firms are also able to supply alternative goods – ladies' clothes instead of men's clothes, toy prams rather than ordinary prams and so on. Thus, there is always a temptation to switch to different products and services if demand for them looks set to rise.

Once more, production costs, business objectives and other, miscellaneous factors are often called 'the underlying conditions of supply' and obviously have a considerable influence upon supply, as illustrated in Figure 7.4. When the price of a product is at P, the quantity supplied is at Q and if that price changes then the quantity supplied will move up and down the supply curve S, as relevant. Nevertheless, if the price remains at P and an underlying condition of supply alters so that supply falls, the quantity supplied moves to Q2, and the curve shifts to S2. Similarly, if supply rises, the quantity supplied moves to Q1 and the curve shifts to S1. As always, the effects of changes may be disproportionate thus resulting in curved rather than straight lines.

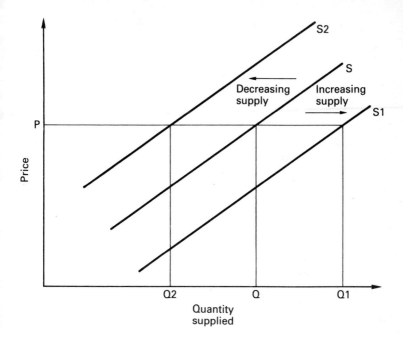

Figure 7.4   A shifting supply curve

7.4   Determining price

In a marketplace, the biggest single influence on demand and supply is price. Likewise, demand and supply interact to determine the price of a product or service. Demand, supply and price are all linked together and this can best be seen by looking at various charts. Figure 7.5 shows demand and supply curves for a particular product, with the demand curve representing the quantities that businesses are willing and able to supply at those prices. At price P, the two curves cross and it is at this price that demand and supply are said to be in equilibrium – the levels of demand and supply are perfectly matched, and everyone is happy!

Not surprisingly, this situation does not occur automatically. Typically, prices tend to fluctuate for some time before settling at or around the equilibrium price. Figure 7.6 illustrates what happens when the business sets a price which is too high – there is a demand for a smaller quantity of goods than is being supplied by the firm so a surplus of supply exists, and stocks remain unsold. In Figure 7.7 the business has again misjudged demand and set a price which is too low – customers are demanding more than the firm is willing

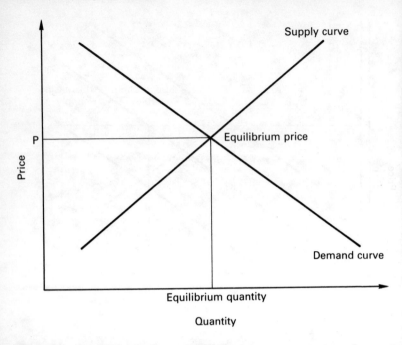

Figure 7.5   Equilibrium price and quantity

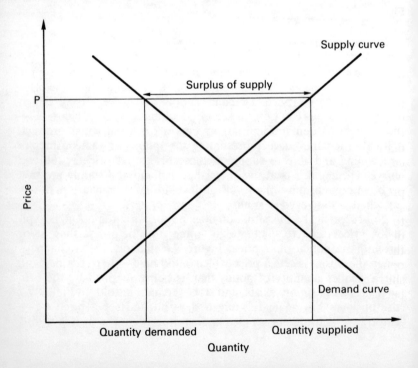

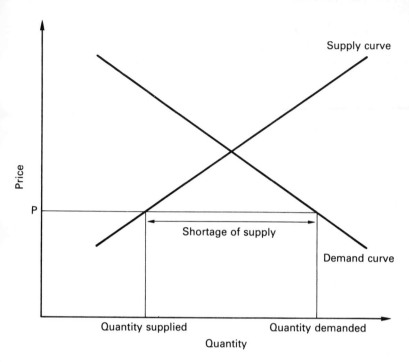

Figure 7.7 A shortage of supply

and able to supply at that price and a shortage exists, with queues forming!

In these circumstances, the business has various options available to remedy matters. If there is a surplus of supply, price can be reduced closer to the equilibrium price so that demand increases and the surplus quantities are purchased. Alternatively, the firm can reduce the level of supply to whatever is currently being demanded by customers. This alternative course of action is shown in Figure 7.8 where the supply curve shifts to the left and the price which was previously too high is now the equilibrium price.

Similarly, if there is a shortage of supply, price can be raised nearer to the equilibrium price so that demand decreases and those queues disperse! As an alternative, the business can boost supplies to match the existing demand from customers, if this is possible. Again, this option can be seen most clearly in Figure 7.9 where the supply curve shifts to the right and the price which was formerly too low now becomes the equilibrium price.

In theory, the market will reach its equilibrium position after some adjustment, and supply and demand will be synchronized perfectly at

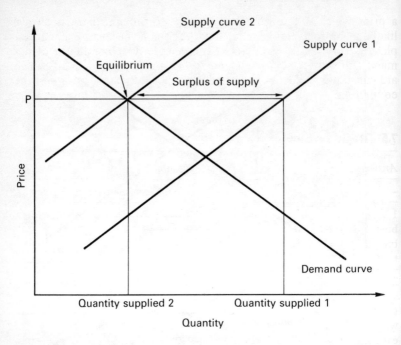

Figure 7.8 Reducing supply

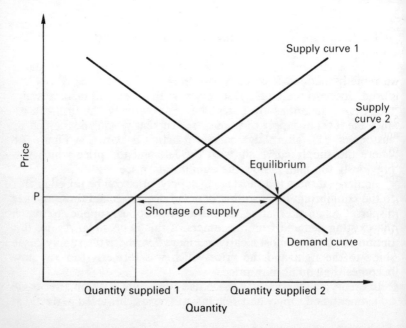

Figure 7.9 Raising supply

a price which suits both sides. In practice though, there is always likely to be some movement, however small, because the market-place is very fluid. Never forget those underlying conditions of demand and supply – tastes, income, other goods and the like – which are constantly changing and affecting supply, demand, price *and* the equilibrium.

7.5 Rapid revision

Answers	*Questions*
–	1 What is a market?
1 It is an arrangement whereby buyers of goods and services are brought into contact with sellers of those goods and services.	2 What are the principles of the marketplace?
2 In brief, (a) buyers are free to spend their money as they wish; (b) sellers are free to manufacture what they want; (c) if demand exceeds supply, prices will rise; (d) if supply exceeds demand, prices will fall.	3 What is a sellers' market?
3 It is a situation which exists when demand exceeds supply, and is to the seller's advantage.	4 What is a buyers' market?
4 It is a position which exists when supply exceeds demand, and is to the buyer's advantage.	5 What is demand?
5 It is the desire to buy products and services at a particular price over a given period of time, combined with the ability to pay for them.	6 What are the main influences on demand?
6 (a) Price; (b) income; (c) taste; (d) other goods and services; (e) population.	7 What is a demand curve?
7 It is a diagram which represents how demand increases or decreases as prices rise and fall.	8 What is supply?

8　It is the desire to make products and services available to customers at a specific price over a particular period of time, combined with an ability to provide them.

9　What are the key influences on supply?

9　(a) Price; (b) costs; (c) objectives; (d) other products and services.

10　What is a supply curve?

10　It is a diagram which represents how supply increases or decreases as prices rise and fall.

11　What are the biggest influences on price?

11　Demand and supply.

12　What is the equilibrium price?

12　It is the price at which demand and supply are perfectly matched and everyone is happy.

13　Go over the questions again until you know all of the answers. Then move on to the next section.

8
Forms of market

8.1 What forms of market exist?

Various types of market can be identified, the most prominent of which are called perfectly competitive, monopolistically competitive, oligopolies and monopolies. They each have their own individual mix of characteristics, derived from the following.

Barriers to entry

Numerous obstacles may exist in a market which need to be overcome by a firm wanting to enter that marketplace. These barriers to entry benefit existing businesses rather than newcomers. The most common barriers are the following:

1 Initial set-up costs may be prohibitively high. The investment in premises, equipment and machinery combined with the early trading losses that most start-up firms have to contend with may be just too costly, especially for smaller concerns operating with limited financial resources.
2 A lack of knowledge, information and experience plus the need to learn quickly in order to survive could dissuade many firms from trying to break into a market. The owners and managers of a business may be able to see that it is potentially lucrative but simply do not possess sufficient know-how to blend together the key ingredients necessary to be a success within it.
3 Various raw materials, component parts, finished products and even distribution channels may be controlled by key firms, unwilling to supply new entrants with these essential supplies or services. Forced to buy inferior raw materials, component parts or whatever, a newcomer's goods would not be competitive with other, existing products because of their lower quality.
4 If the costs of producing goods fall as the volume of production rises, the most economic level of operation may require entry on

a large scale if entrants are not to operate at a cost disadvantage. Put simply, a firm may have to produce lots of goods to sell them at low enough prices to be competitive – and might not be able to do this.

5   Customer loyalty to well-known products may be difficult to overcome – an entrant's goods are unknown and untested, and many current and would-be buyers will prefer to continue to purchase tried and tested products. Enormous sums of money are spent by entrants on advertising and promoting new goods in order to win over customers. These firms also cut prices substantially and operate at a loss for some time in an attempt to attract customers. Clearly, the costs involved with such policies are a significant barrier for most concerns.

Numbers and types of sellers

Some markets have many sellers, others only a few – or even just one in certain instances! These sellers may be large, and able to exert considerable influence upon the market, with regard to the goods and services provided, quantities supplied and price. Alternatively, they might be relatively small and insignificant in relation to the marketplace, and be unable to exert any noticeable pressure at all upon the principles of supply and demand. It may even be that customers will tell them what to do!

Product differentiation

A key characteristic of any market – and a distinguishing feature of each and every one of them – is the degree of product differentiation within them. As implied by the name, product differentiation simply refers to the ways in which firms distinguish the goods and services that they sell from others in the marketplace. This can be done by varying a product's appearance and qualities or by creating the impression that an item is different through advertising and promoting a certain aspect of it. For example, one soap powder may be much the same as another but it is perceived to be different because it is constantly promoted as 'the one with the clean, fresh smell'. Baloney – but effective baloney nonetheless!

Numbers and types of buyers

Not surprisingly, the quantity and type of buyers within a market will have a profound effect upon its individual character. As with sellers, some markets have a huge number of buyers, others relatively few. Again, they may be large and dominant, well able to influence the marketplace, or small and insignificant and unable to exert power on their own. If this is the case, sellers may be able to exercise greater influence than would be considered fair and reasonable.

Barriers to exit

There may be various obstacles within a market which stop firms from leaving it, or at least makes it hard for them to do so. The following are probably the most commonplace barriers to exit:

1 The investment in equipment and machinery needed to trade in a particular market may be so extensive that a business cannot really afford simply to stop using these resources. The items might be highly specialized and difficult to use for other purposes, and could be equally impossible to sell to other firms staying in that marketplace. It may be wiser to remain in the market, albeit making less profit than before.
2 Producing or offering only a single product or service may be a deterrent to leaving a market as it would mean that the concern would need to cease trading altogether. Those businesses which manufacture and sell a wide variety of goods may find it easier to exit from one market, as others remain available to it, and continue to be profitable.
3 Similarly, the degree of vertical integration that a firm has within a market is of some significance. Moving out of producing raw materials and component parts may be easy to plan but less easy actually to do if the business wishes to continue to sell the finished products which derive from them.
4 Sometimes, a concern which uses equipment and machinery to manufacture numerous products cannot afford to drop one of those items from its range even if it is becoming an unprofitable line. Having to spread production costs across the remaining products in the range may mean that they all become unprofitable, or at best fail to reach and sustain the required profits.

8.2 Perfectly competitive markets

A perfectly competitive (or perfect) market may be defined as 'a market with many small sellers and buyers, similar products and no barriers to entry or exit'. Strictly speaking, the phrase 'perfectly competitive' or 'perfect competition' refers to the absence of any restrictions upon competition rather than suggesting that this is an ideal market – although it is generally regarded to be at least preferable to the other types of market that can develop, such as a monopoly in which one firm dominates to the detriment of everyone else. In a perfect market, the following key characteristics can be readily identified:

1   Numerous buyers and sellers compete against each other so that no individual or group of buyers or sellers can exert undue influence. These buyers and sellers are small in comparison to the size of the marketplace, so that their activities are relatively insignificant.
2   Products and services are comparable in terms of price, quality and other features so no seller has a competitive advantage over rivals by supplying better goods. To all intents and purposes, buyers regard them as being identical and perfect substitutes for each other. They are as happy to buy one as to purchase another.
3   Buyers and sellers have roughly proportionate shares of the market so that no buyer or seller can dominate demand or supply, and therefore influence the price or market for their own benefit.
4   Buyers and sellers possess a full and complete knowledge of all aspects of the marketplace. Everyone knows who the buyers and sellers are, what products and services are available, and at what prices.
5   Sellers seek to maximize profits and are free to come into the market as and when they wish if this aim appears to be achievable. Likewise, they are equally free to leave the market if and when they want to. Whatever they wish to do is entirely up to them as no barriers or other restrictions exist.
6   Buyers are also free to enter the market whenever they want to, and may leave again just as easily. They are very price conscious and this is likely to be the overriding factor in their decision to join or depart from the marketplace at any given time.

The demand-supply-price principles of the marketplace are most evident in a perfectly competitive market. As an example, a seller cannot influence the price of its own goods. If too high a price is set, buyers will just switch to substitute products leaving the seller to amend price or supplies towards that equilibrium position. At the same time, there is little point in a seller cutting its prices when trading in a perfect market as it can sell all that it wants and is able to at the existing price. Needless to state, this type of market rarely exists, or at least not for long.

8.3   Monopolistically competitive markets

This market could be described as one where 'a large number of sellers offer different products and services to buyers'. In many respects, it might be said that it is a combination of a perfectly competitive and monopoly market. Each seller exercises a certain degree of power over its own products, while still being subject to various features of a perfect market. Monopolistic competition has these main characteristics:

1 There are numerous sellers competing for buyers and each one is large enough to exert some influence on the prices it charges for its goods and services. However, as there are so many sellers all with relatively modest shares of the market, the actions of one seller do not have any real or lasting impact upon the others, and the prices that they charge.
2 Products and services are different from those which are produced and supplied by other sellers in the marketplace. The difference may be real but is often slight, perhaps with one product being packaged in a more brightly coloured carton than another. As likely, the difference is imagined, with buyers believing an item to be different, and better, because of the clever or extensive way in which the seller advertises it.
3 Buyers are often many and varied in numbers and types, and may prefer some goods and services to others because of the differences that they have (or are perceived to have) in relation to the rest. Loyalty tends to build up in buyers towards their favourite products and price is not necessarily the major factor in their choice any more. However, they are still conscious of other goods and may be persuaded to change in some instances – such as when a seller abuses its customers' loyalties by hiking up prices too far.
4 There are few, if any, restrictions on entry to or exit from the market. Customer loyalty towards existing, known products and services could be one barrier to entry for would-be entrants to the marketplace. Usually though, sellers and buyers are free to come and go, as and when they wish to.

In this type of market, which is far more prevalent than a perfectly competitive one, the demand-supply-price principles still basically hold true. For example, if a seller raises price, some customers will remain loyal but a proportion will not. Similarly, if the seller drops its price, a number of customers will be attracted to its products away from its rivals, although others will stay true to the competitors' goods.

8.4 Oligopolies

An oligopoly could be best described as 'a market in which a small number of sellers supply goods and services to buyers'. It is the most common form of market in the UK and is especially evident in the car and tobacco markets where the five biggest businesses in each have a 92 and 99 per cent combined share of the respective market. These are the main features of an oligopoly:

1   Only a few sellers are in competition and each is large enough for its decisions and activities to have a considerable impact on fellow sellers and buyers, and the marketplace. There may be a wide range of buyers in terms of both numbers and types, but they are usually unable to exercise much influence in the market, if at all.

2   In a 'perfect oligopoly', products and services are the same or at least so similar that they are considered to be identical by buyers. Hence, they are perfect substitutes for each other. With an 'imperfect oligopoly', which is more prevalent, goods are either different or perceived to be different. As in a monopolistically competitive market, sellers promote and advertise these real or imagined differences to inspire loyalty from buyers, which may then be hard for other sellers to break.

3   There are inevitably numerous barriers to entry, almost invariably created by those few large sellers which are able to control the marketplace in a variety of ways. Those barriers relating to economies of scale, product differentiation and the withholding of essential and desirable supplies are most commonplace. Barriers to exit may exist too, particularly if it is necessary to go into the market in a big way, purchasing costly and highly specialized equipment and machinery to mass produce goods to achieve the required economies of scale to be competitive.

With the activities and actions of each seller being so influential on the others, price tends to be relatively rigid within an oligopoly. If one seller were to cut prices, the others would have to follow that lead to avoid losing buyers and a tit-for-tat price war could develop, with all sellers losing out in the end. At the same time a seller would not wish to raise prices, just in case the other sellers did not respond in the same manner, leaving that firm facing the prospect of its customers going elsewhere.

8.5   Monopolies

In theory, a monopoly exists when 'one seller controls the supply of a product or service for which no substitutes are available'. In practice, a seller is regarded as having a monopoly when it controls 25 per cent or more of the supply of a particular product or service. In such circumstances, it may liaise closely with the remaining sellers to manipulate supplies to the market to their own advantage. Hence, a rather more accurate definition of a monopoly might be that it is 'a situation which occurs when a small group of sellers act together to control the supply of a product or service for which no substitutes are available'.

In many ways, the differences between an oligopoly and a monopoly are very slight, if not almost non-existent in some cases. These are the main characteristics of a monopoly:

1 Although a monopoly may involve just one seller, it is more usual for two or three sellers to be trading, perhaps with one firm dominating and the other ones following its lead. There could be a large and diverse mix of buyers but these are unlikely to be powerful enough to influence the marketplace, to any significant degree.

2 Sellers supply products or services which are different from other goods in the marketplace, rather than simply being perceived to be different by customers because of product differentiation and clever advertising and promotional methods. For a monopoly to exist, buyers must really want – or more likely need – to purchase the monopolists' products or services.

3 Inevitably, monopolists will attempt to erect barriers to entry to the market in order to protect their dominant positions within that marketplace. One of the most common methods of doing this is to prevent new entrants from obtaining essential raw materials, component parts or whatever. Of course, other barriers to entry (and exit) may exist, varying from high set-up costs to prohibitive leaving costs.

Evidently, if a unique product or service is in demand, the seller is able to sell it at a higher price than would be possible if similar goods were available and/or its items were less popular. It is often said that a monopolist can restrict its output if necessary and charge whatever it likes in order to maximize profits. In essence this is true, although monopolists which provide essential goods are restricted from acting against the public interest in this way by the laws of the land. Of course, non-essential items tend to lose their appeal as prices rise again and again, until customers learn to live without them, or substitute products are eventually produced by rival sellers.

A quick comparison of the types of market is given in Figure 8.1.

8.6 Rapid revision

Answers	Questions
–	1 What are the main types of market?

	Perfectly competitive markets	Monopolistically competitive markets	Oligopolies	Monopolies
Barriers to entry	None	Few, if any	Many	Many
Sellers	Many, and small	Numerous, usually small	Few, typically large	May be one, or more likely a few
Product differentiation	None of note	Real, or imagined	Varies, products may be the same, or different	Real, often very distinct differences
Buyers	Numerous, and small	Many and varied	Numerous, often small	Many, and diverse
Barriers to exit	None	Limited, if at all	Many, in most instances	Many, in most cases

Figure 8.1   Types of market: a quick comparison

1   (a) Perfectly competitive markets; (b) monopolistically competitive markets; (c) oligopolies; (d) monopolies.

2   What are the distinguishing features of markets?

2   (a) Barriers to entry; (b) numbers and types of sellers; (c) product differentiation; (d) numbers and types of buyers; (e) barriers to exit.

3   What is a perfectly competitive market?

3   It is a market with many small sellers and buyers, similar products and no barriers to entry or exit.

4   What are the key characteristics of a perfectly competitive market?

4   In brief, (a) numerous buyers and sellers; (b) comparable products; (c) roughly proportionate market shares; (d) full knowledge of the market; (e) no barriers.

5   What is a monopolistically competitive market?

5   It is one in which a large number of sellers offer different products and services to buyers.

6   In short, (a) many sellers; (b) different products; (c) numerous buyers; (d) few restrictions.

7   It is a market in which a small number of sellers supply goods and services to buyers.

8   In essence, (a) a few, large sellers; (b) many small buyers; (c) identical or different products; (d) numerous barriers to entry; (e) various barriers to exit.

9   In a perfect oligopoly, goods are the same or very similar. In an imperfect one, goods are different or are perceived to be different.

10   It is a market where one seller controls the supply of a product or service for which no substitutes are available.

11   It is a market where a seller controls 25 per cent or more of the supply of a particular product or service and who works closely with other sellers to manipulate supplies to their own advantage.

12   In summary, (a) a few, powerful sellers; (b) numerous small buyers; (c) highly distinct products; (d) many barriers to entry; (e) various barriers to exit.

6   What are the main features of a monopolistically competitive market?

7   What is an oligopoly?

8   What are the major characteristics of an oligopoly?

9   What is the difference between a perfect and an imperfect oligopoly?

10   What is a theoretical definition of a monopoly?

11   What is a practical definition of a monopoly?

12   What are the predominant features of a monopoly?

13   Go over the questions again until you know all of the answers. Then move on to the next section.

9
Market practices

9.1 What are the practices of the marketplace?

Anyone in business will confirm that at times the marketplace might best be described as a jungle in which the strongest survive, and the weakest often do not. There is an element of truth in this exaggeration; after all, those businesses in a powerful position such as in an oligopoly or a monopoly situation will use their strength to the detriment of others, to prevent competitors from entering the market, and to force customers to pay higher prices than would be necessary in a more competitive environment. It may well be that the strongest business will effectively destroy its weakest competitors, as a large animal will eat smaller ones in a jungle.

Fortunately though, the marketplace exercises various constraints upon businesses within it so that they cannot abuse their power and do exactly what they want to customers and to competitors. Each and every business needs to know about the basis of business transactions with customers and the consumer protection laws which protect these organizations and individuals against exploitation. Similarly, they have to be aware of competition policies and laws in the UK, which aim to protect firms against anti-competitive behaviour. Last, but by no means least, they ought to be conscious of the regulatory bodies in this field, and their activities.

9.2 Business transactions

Some transactions between businesses and their customers are very informal, often developing from little more than a brief conversation. As an example, a customer walks into a sole trader's furniture shop, sees a sofa bed that he likes, is happy to pay the stated price and places an order for one. The sole proprietor asks for and is given a £50 deposit, orders the settee from the manufacturer and promises the customer that it will be delivered within a month. Three weeks later, the manufacturer delivers the sofa bed to the shop and the sole trader takes it to the customer's home and he pays the outstanding sum in cash. The transaction is straightforward, and both parties are satisfied.

Other transactions between sellers and buyers are much more formal, entered into after tough bargaining and with each side's rights and responsibilities set down in writing. For example, a small company wants its fleet of cars to be serviced regularly by a local garage. The purchasing director of the company meets with the garage owner and they thrash out a detailed written contract covering such topics as the frequency and amount of work carried out, prices charged and delivery and collection arrangements. Everything is spelt out clearly and concisely and heaven help anyone who does not do what they are supposed to do!

Whether informal or formal, verbal or in writing, transactions between businesses and customers are legally binding and enforceable agreements and if one party breaches the terms and conditions of such a contract, the other can cancel it and/or claim compensation through the courts. Thus, if that sofa bed had not arrived at the agreed time, the customer could have scrapped the contract, and demanded his money back. Similarly, if that local garage had carried out the agreed work but had not been paid, it could take the company to court to recover the money plus costs and might cancel the contract altogether (which would probably be a wise course of action).

For a business transaction to be a legal and valid contract, it must comprise the following elements.

Intention

Both parties must have intended to enter into a legally binding agreement with each other. In most instances, intention is obvious and can be seen to exist. The company with the fleet of cars and the garage owner have clearly intended to enter into a contractual relationship with each other, otherwise they would not have signed the contract! Sometimes, intention is less obvious or simply does not exist. In the sale of a freehold property, it is normal to agree to contract at some stage in the future by selling 'subject to contract'. Thus, the agreement is not (yet) legally binding and until contracts have been exchanged, either party can withdraw as and when they wish.

Offer

One side has to make an offer to the other one. The offer must be certain and distinguished from what is legally known as *an invitation to treat* which in plain English is an invitation for prospective buyers to make an offer which may, or may not, be accepted. As an example, the shopkeeper who sets out goods on display is not making an offer but inviting an offer – quite a different thing! An offer may terminate or be terminated on rejection by the other party, could lapse if it was subject to acceptance within a stated period of time or might be withdrawn at any stage prior to acceptance.

Acceptance

An offer must be accepted without conditions. If the party receiving the offer responds along the lines of 'Yes, I accept your offer subject to the condition that . . .' then this is not an acceptance of that offer. It is in effect a counter offer which terminates the original one. That initial offer will have to be made again if it is to be accepted – this time without any conditions being made by the recipient.

Consideration

Both sides need to provide what is legally termed as 'consideration'. Quite simply, each party must give or do something for the other one. As a basic example, when goods are sold, consideration takes the form of payment for those items, and vice versa the items for that payment! Both seller and buyer have provided consideration for the other. Of course, consideration need not necessarily involve the exchange of money and products, although it often does. Sometimes, the two parties may carry out services for each other, to their mutual benefit.

Capacity

Just as important as intention, offer, acceptance and consideration is that those entering into a contract have the legal authority (or capacity) to do so. Otherwise, it will be invalidated. Thus, a minor under the age of 18 may not have the capacity to enter into an agreement. More significantly, a company which engages in activities which exceed those that are set out in its Memorandum of Association may be regarded as trading *ultra vires* and without the capacity to enter into associated agreements.

Genuineness

It is equally important that both parties go into a contractual relationship on a voluntary basis rather than under duress, undue influence or as a result of one party making misrepresentations about the deal to the other. If a publishing company persuaded an author to let it publish his or her book on the understanding that 'thousands of copies' would definitely be sold and subsequent statements showed single figure sales, then a court might agree that misrepresentation had been made, and declare the contract null and void, thus enabling the author to take the book to a more reputable publisher.

9.3 Consumer protection laws

The harsh realities of the marketplace are such that some businesses will try to exploit their customers, perhaps by selling sub-standard or dangerous products, providing misleading information about services, or whatever. The ways in which a proportion of firms attempt to cheat are innumerable and diverse but fortunately are becoming better known and more widely publicized nowadays, especially in the media. A host of statutes have been passed which provide the framework for consumer protection in the UK. Some of the key Acts are described in the following.

Sale of Goods Act 1979

To comply with the terms of this Act, goods sold must be 'as described', 'of merchantable quality' and 'fit for a specified purpose'. 'As described' means that they have to match their description. A customer who orders a floral settee from a business must not be sent a striped one. 'Of merchantable quality' indicates that they have to be fit for their normal use. A lawnmower must cut grass. 'Fit for a specified purpose' means that they have to be suitable for any purpose specified by a customer before the sale and agreed with by the seller. As a simple example, if a customer asks whether a tube of glue can be used for sticking a broken heel back onto a shoe and a shopkeeper says that it can, then the glue has to be able to do it satisfactorily.

Weights and Measures Act 1985

It is an offence to use any weighing or measuring equipment or machinery which provides inaccurate readings. Similarly, it is an offence to give short weights or measures. A half pound bag of jelly beans must contain no less than the weight paid for! The Act also sets out how certain goods should be packaged and marked. For example, pre-packed products must have a written statement on the package which gives details of the contents.

Supply of Goods and Services Act 1982

Businesses which supply services such as maintaining and repairing goods must carry out their work with a reasonable degree of skill, using materials of suitable quality. A faulty or damaged car should be repaired with parts that have been manufactured for that make and model. Firms also have a legal duty to take reasonable care of any products in their possession and must complete services and repairs within a reasonable period of time, bearing in mind the amount of work involved in each instance.

Trade Descriptions Act 1968

Concerns must not falsely describe, make false statements or provide misleading information about their goods and services. Both written and verbal descriptions must be truthful and accurate. Hence, 'hand-made' items must have been made by hand, not by machine. 'Made in Cornwall' means that the product must have been produced from that county, rather than Taiwan. '24 hour photo processing' should produce photographs ready for collection within 24 hours, not 48 or 72 hours.

Prices Act 1974

Under the terms of this Act, 'orders' may be issued by the Government as and when necessary to protect customers from vague or misleading price claims made by traders. An example of such an order is the Price Marking (Bargain Offers) Order 1979 which prohibits traders from making claims such as 'Worth £100, Our Price £60' and 'Reduced by 50 per cent', in relation to other, unspecified traders and prices. Genuine bargains – few and far between in business – must be linked to the seller's previous prices or to manufacturers' suggested prices.

Consumer Act 1987

This Act is concerned mainly with product prices and safety, so far as they relate to customers. Businesses must not mislead customers about the prices of their products and services. In particular, they should not make false comparisons with their previous prices or with manufacturers' recommended prices. What often happens is that a firm will advertise an item with a sign such as 'Was £50, now only £25' when the previous price was actually £35 – clearly, an offence.

The second part of the Act deals with safety and makes it an offence to possess, offer, agree to or actually supply dangerous goods to customers.

Unsolicited Goods and Services Act 1971

Customers are under no legal obligation whatsoever to pay for products and services which were not ordered. Businesses which send out goods hoping that they will be purchased – an activity known as *inertia selling* – break the law if they forward an invoice, demand payment or threaten legal action regarding these unsolicited items. Goods that remain uncollected for six months become the property of the recipient. This six month period can be shortened to just 30 days if the customer writes to the business requesting collection within that shorter period.

Consumer Credit Act 1974

This law is designed to protect those consumers who purchase goods on credit terms. It demands that those businesses which provide finance are licensed and approved, that the true rate of interest paid by customers – the annual percentage rate or APR as it is better known – is well publicized and that the usual consumer protection laws such as the Sale of Goods Act and so on are equally applicable to those items purchased 'on tick' as they are to ones which have been bought outright, for cash.

Those businesses which break these consumer protection laws may suffer many consequences. They could be sued for a refund, damages and costs by customers. Negative, word of mouth comments may be made to friends, colleagues and other, prospective customers. Adverse media coverage in the press or on television could cause further problems and help to destroy their trade. Sensible firms adhere to the law, so far as they can.

9.4 Competition policies and laws

Competition policy in the UK as elsewhere is concerned with maintaining competition in pursuit of that perfect market where there are many sellers and buyers and prices remain competitive. There are various areas of particular concern, namely monopolies, mergers and takeovers, anti-competitive practices and resale price maintenance. Competition policies are backed up by a framework of laws, such as the Fair Trading Act 1973, Restrictive Trade Practices 1976, Resale Prices Act 1976 and the Competition Act 1980.

Monopolies

A monopoly can be described as a market in which one form provides 25 per cent or more of a particular product or service or where two or more suppliers work together to restrict or eliminate competition from other businesses. Monopolies may be prohibited if they are considered to be operating against 'the public interest'. Similarly, those mergers and takeovers which create or perhaps worsen a monopoly situation might not be allowed to proceed because of these consequences.

Anti-competitive practices

There are numerous practices employed by a firm or by several businesses acting together to prevent outsiders entering the marketplace. These are some of the more common practices, any of which may be prohibited if they are deemed to be against the public interest:

1   *Restrictive trade agreements*

Sellers within the same market – typically an oligopoly or monopoly – may enter into agreements with each other to limit supplies or fix prices or terms and conditions of sale to their own rather than their buyers' advantage.

2   *Aggregated rebates*

These rebates – or 'overriding discounts' as they are also known – are given to buyers by sellers on total purchases over a period of time rather than on single, one-off purchases. If this practice is carried out by a leading firm with regard to the distribution of its goods then it may effectively deprive would-be competitors of potential distribution outlets.

3   *Exclusive dealing*

This exists when a supplier contracts distributors to sell only its goods rather than those of its rivals as well. In return for such a commitment, a supplier will reward sole distributors in various ways, such as with preferential services, and discounts.

4   *Full line forcing*

Here, a seller persuades distributors to carry not only its key products but other ones too – even its full range on some occasions. As an example, a pet-shop owner wishing to buy a manufacturer's popular dog food may also have to purchase its cat food or whatever too.

5   *Tie-in sales*

Similar to full line forcing, tie-in sales involve a seller persuading distributors to buy the products required and related goods and services. For example, a distributor of photocopiers, fax machines and other office equipment may be obliged to purchase stationery for these items from the seller.

6   *Withdrawal of supplies*

Aggregated rebates, exclusive dealing and so on are some of the ways in which sellers can exert pressure on distributors, and limit its rivals' activities in the marketplace. Not surprisingly, the ultimate weapon used by sellers against its distributors is to threaten to withdraw its supplies to them.

Resale price maintenance

Normally, suppliers are not allowed to stipulate the resale prices of its goods when they are sold by distributors unless it is able to prove that such 'resale price maintenance' is in the public interest. Clearly, this is difficult to do, as 'RPM' almost definitely is not in the interests of customers.

Fair Trading Act 1973

This mould-breaking Act set up the regulatory body known as the Office of Fair Trading and gave it powers to oversee all aspects of competition policy from monopolies, mergers and takeovers, through restrictive trade practices to resale price maintenance. It also supervises all aspects of consumer protection, covering areas such as the sale of goods, trade descriptions and weights and measures.

Restrictive Trade Practices Act 1976

This all-important Act forbids the operation of anti-competitive (or restrictive trade) practices unless they are exempted by the Office of Fair Trading. To be exempt, any parties involved with these practices must prove that they have benefits for the public, rather than simply being self-protecting. Furthermore, it must be proved that the benefits of these practices exceed the drawbacks – no easy task.

Resale Prices Act 1976

Like the Restrictive Trade Practices Act of the same year, this Act makes the operation of resale price maintenance illegal unless it is granted exemption by the Office of Fair Trading. To obtain this, suppliers have to prove that RPM does not only offer benefits for the public, but that these exceed the drawbacks. Again, they are unlikely to be able to prove this.

Competition Act 1980

This Act developed from the Fair Trading Act 1973, and enabled the Office of Fair Trading to look into the activities of any individual business or person which might be behaving in an anti-competitive manner. Previously, only the actions of a whole trade or industry could be investigated by this body. The type of activity which comes under scrutiny most often is price cutting by larger concerns to force a smaller but growing firm out of business, perhaps in an oligopoly marketplace.

9.5   Regulatory bodies and activities

Several regulatory bodies exist to monitor and uphold the various consumer protection and competition policies and laws in the UK, coordinating their activities to protect customers and competitors, and to bring businesses into line, as and when required. The key ones include the following.

The Office of Fair Trading

The OFT as it is often called has a general responsibility to protect consumers' interest and it does this in a variety of ways such as by overseeing consumer credit and taking action against those businesses which describe goods in a misleading manner, and so on. It is also responsible for administering competition policies and laws, which it does by monitoring markets and business activities and investigating information and complaints received with regard to anti-competitive behaviour. Sometimes, the Office refers cases to the Monopolies and Mergers Commission and/or the Restrictive Practices Court for a fuller investigation.

The Monopolies and Mergers Commission

The MMC's role is to investigate and report on anti-competitive practices referred to it by the Office of Fair Trading, and on cases of existing and/or potential monopoly situations. It has to decide whether these various cases are in the public interest, or not. Having reached a decision, it can make recommendations such as cutting prices, prohibiting a merger of two companies or whatever. The Office of Fair Trading then considers these recommendations and implements them or not, as appropriate.

The Restrictive Practices Court

The role of the RPC, as it is sometimes referred to, is to study and consequently to report on cases of restrictive trade agreements and resale price maintenance passed over to it by the Office of Fair Trading. As with the MMC, the Restrictive Practices Court has to decide whether or not these are in the public interest, and it will then make recommendations on the basis of its findings.

Local authorities

The majority of consumer protection laws in the UK are enforced by local authorities, through their 'trading standards' or 'consumer protection' departments. As often as not, these departments and their officers act in an advisory and supportive role rather than a strictly censoring one. They pacify dissatisfied and unhappy consumers, persuade rogue businesses to fall into line and pass on information about unfair trade practices to the Office of Fair Trading for it to take action, if necessary. Prosecuting offending firms is almost always seen as a last resort. Nevertheless, they do take action via the courts as and when required which can lead to fines, compensation payments to customers and even imprisonment in some instances.

Representative associations

It is important to be aware that many trades and industries regulate and control themselves through voluntary agreements known as 'codes of practice' which are drawn up by representative bodies and adhered to by their members. An example of a code of practice which defines and sets the trading standards expected of its members is given in Figure 9.1. These codes are not enforced by law although those members who breach them may face expulsion from the appropriate trade or industry body. This can sometimes act as a significant deterrent for those firms that might lose trade as a consequence of this loss of status.

9.6   Rapid revision

Answers	Questions
–	1 What are the practices of the marketplace?
1 Many would say they are the practices of the jungle – kill, or be killed!	2 What is a business transaction?
2 It is a legally binding and enforceable agreement between a business and its customer.	3 What should a business transaction consist of to be a legal and valid contract?
3 (a) Intention; (b) an offer; (c) an acceptance; (d) consideration; (e) capacity; (f) genuineness.	4 What are the main consumer protection laws in the UK?
4 There are many and include, (a) Sale of Goods Act; (b) Weights and Measures Act; (c) Supply of Goods and Services Act; (d) Trade Descriptions Act; (e) Prices Act; (f) Consumer Act; (g) Unsolicited Goods and Services Act; (h) Consumer Credit Act.	5 What may happen to firms which break these consumer protection laws?
5 They could (a) be sued for a refund, damages and costs; (b) hear negative comments being made to other customers; (c) receive adverse coverage in the media.	6 What major areas of concern are covered by competition policies in the UK?

Association of Exhibition Organisers: Code of Practice

1   Integrity
Statements made by Members with respect to any exhibition will be accurate and correct and will not seek to mislead.

2   Attendance
Members undertake to record (and publish) attendance by visitors accurately and to issue attendance figures to exhibitors on request. Members also undertake to obtain the Audit Bureau of Circulation certification of attendance figures for each show and to file them with the Association within 14 days of publication.

3   Promotion
Direct expenditure (i.e. excluding related company overheads) on all forms of promotion and the costs of features, conferences, contests or similar attractions to the exhibition will be at least 10% of the net stand space revenue of the exhibition. Contributions to sponsoring associations are to be excluded from the calculation.

4   Promotional literature
Undertakings or promises made by Members in all literature shall be adhered to. In the event of necessary changes notification will be given to actual or potential exhibitors. A copy of each exhibition prospectus shall be lodged with the Association (within 14 days of publication).

5   Insurance
Members will carry a minimum of £500 000 insurance cover in respect of public liability.

6   Contractors
In appointing official contractors for an exhibition, members will choose companies who, to the best of their knowledge, have sufficient capacity and experience to perform their duties satisfactorily. They will encourage contractors to adhere to uniform and reasonable charges and will endeavour to protect exhibitors against overcharging or bad service. They will ensure that contractors adhere to the provisions of the Health and Safety at Work Act.

7   Services
Members will cause to be provided recognized services including general security, experienced organizing and attendant staff, general cleaning, rubbish removal and where appropriate, press and foreign visitor facilities in accordance with the nature of the exhibition. During the build-up, open and breakdown periods of an exhibition, exhibitors shall have access to at least one responsible executive of the organizers at all times during normal working hours during those periods.

8   Tenancies
Members will provide reasonable periods for installation and dismantling of their exhibitions, dependent on availability of halls and on the nature of each exhibition. These times will be made known to prospective exhibitors before they enter into an agreement to participate.

(continued)

Figure 9.1   A code of practice

9   International exhibitions
Members may include the word 'International' in the title of an exhibition only if it is anticipated that at least 20% of stand space will be occupied by foreign exhibits; or at least 20% of promotional expenditure is devoted to promoting overseas visitors' attendance.

10   Cancellation
In the event of cancellation or lengthy deferment of an exhibition through any circumstances within the Organizer's control, he will abide by the Association's policy to refund stand rentals received from exhibitors. If the exhibition contains specialized sections which are cancelled, the exhibiting companies contracted specifically for the sections concerned must be advised immediately, and given the option to withdraw from the exhibition without loss of stand rentals.

11   Authority
In all matters concerning compliance or breach of this Code of Practice, a decision will be taken by the Council of the Association. Members undertake to furnish any information or documentation which the Council may require for this purpose within a period stipulated by the Council. Failing settlement of a dispute by the Council, the issue may be referred to arbitration.

Figure 9.1   (continued)

6 (a) Monopolies, mergers and takeovers; (b) anti-competitive practices; (c) resale price maintenance.

7   What are the most common anti-competitive practices?

---

7   (a) Restrictive trade agreements; (b) aggregated rebates; (c) exclusive dealing; (d) full line forcing; (e) tie-in sales; (f) withdrawal of supplies.

8   What is resale price maintenance?

---

8   It is a situation whereby suppliers stipulate the resale prices of their goods when they are sold by their distributors.

9   What are the leading competition laws in the UK?

---

9   In particular, (a) Fair Trading Act; (b) Restrictive Trade Practices Act (c) Resale Prices Act; (d) Competition Act.

10   What could happen to businesses which act in an anti-competitive manner?

---

10   Their activities will be prohibited by the regulatory bodies in this held.

11   Who are the regulatory bodies in this area?

---

11 (a) The Office of Fair Trading;
(b) the Monopolies and Mergers
Commission; (c) the Restrictive
Practices Court; (d) local
authorities; (e) representative
bodies.

12 What is a code of practice?

12 It is a voluntary agreement
drawn up by a representative
association which defines and sets
the standards expected of its
members.

13 Go over the questions again
until you know all of the answers.
Then move on to the next section.

Part Four
The Local and National Environment

10
The State

10.1 What is the State?

The State is a commonplace but rather vague phrase which confuses many people who are familiar with the expression but are not totally sure what it actually means. Perhaps the simplest definition is that it is 'the administrative system which governs a community'. In the UK, the State could be said to comprise Parliament which is 'the legislature' responsible for passing laws, central government, its departments and agencies and local government which are 'the executive' responsible for implementing acts of parliament and the civil and criminal courts which are 'the judiciary' that deals with any disputes arising from the making and implementation of laws.

10.2 The legislature

Parliament – consisting of the House of Commons and the House of Lords – has the key role of passing legislation. It is sensible to have a clear but concise knowledge of the lower house and the upper house as they are sometimes known as well as a straightforward understanding of the passage of legislation and some of the ways in which Parliament delegates its legislative powers to other organizations and individuals.

The House of Commons

The House of Commons comprises 650 Members of Parliament (MPs) who belong to political organizations such as the Conservative, Labour, and Liberal Democratic parties. A general election is held at least once every five years whereby electors, generally speaking everyone over 18, in each of the 650 constituencies (or geographical areas) are given the opportunity to elect one person from a range of candidates to represent them in the House. The candidate with the most votes wins in what is sometimes referred to as a 'first past the post' system. Most voters make their choice on the basis of a candidate's political party and its perceived characteristics and policies rather than the candidate personally. Clearly, the political party with the majority of MPs can pursue its policies by voting through legislation to support them, as appropriate.

The House of Lords

This upper or 'second' chamber is an unelected body consisting of approximately 1100 hereditary and life peers, some of whom have been elevated from the House of Commons by the Monarch after a lengthy spell of service there. The House also comprises Lords Spiritual who are Bishops and Archbishops of the Anglican Church and Lords of Appeal in Ordinary who are lawyers who sit as a final court of appeal within the judicial system. The Lords acts as a check and a brake on the Commons within the Parliamentary system. With its mix of older, wiser politicians, it looks at legislation initiated by the lower house and can insist that it is revised or withdrawn – albeit usually on a temporary basis – if it appears to be ill-conceived or too extreme.

The passage of legislation

A *bill* is the name given to a law during its passage through the two Houses of Parliament and on to the Monarch for royal assent upon which it becomes a *statute* or *Act of Parliament*. Two types of bill can be readily identified. Public Bills are those which affect the public as a whole. They are normally sponsored by the government – in effect, the political party with the majority of MPs – as a way of pursuing its economic and other policies, or by individual members of Parliament and/or the House of Lords on a personal crusade. These public bills are sometimes called government bills and private members bills respectively. Private bills, not to be confused with private members bills, are those which affect a limited number of organizations and individuals perhaps in a particular region. They are sponsored by outside bodies such as a local authority.

Although the passage of legislation can be as short as two days in emergency circumstances, it is usually a long, drawn out process, typically taking nearly a year, or sometimes longer in controversial instances. A government bill will follow a similar passage to other bills (Figure 10.1). Typically, the process will commence with calls for changes, perhaps from the public, newspapers and television in response to an obvious anomoly or unfairness in the existing law.

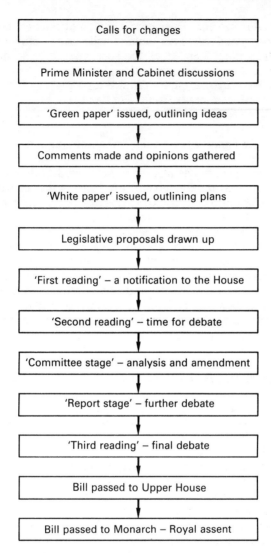

Figure 10.1 The passage of a government bill

The Prime Minister and his or her Cabinet – in essence the leader of the ruling party and his or her team of colleagues – may then discuss the situation among themselves and subsequently seek the views of informed and interested parties via the issuing of a *green paper*. This is a document which simply outlines the government's ideas which should generate comments from friend and foe alike!

Once information and opinions have been gathered together and reviewed, the government's policy will be settled and announced through a *white paper*. This is a document that outlines what is going to appear in legislation. Legislative proposals are then drafted by the government's legal experts and the bill is passed to the Commons to begin its formal procedure through the House (although it can start in the Lords and may do in some instances, usually when the bill is concerned with a non-controversial matter).

This formal procedure commences with a *first reading* – simply a notification of the bill to the House. Next, there is a *second reading* whereby the principles of the bill are debated by the House. In the following *committee stage*, a cross section of about 20 to 40 MPs look at and discuss the bill in depth, and propose amendments, if appropriate. The bill then goes to the *report stage*, whereby it is passed back to the House in its revised form. A *third reading* is the final opportunity for debate within the House before the bill is sent to the Lords to go through the same process again there. Eventually, the bill is passed to the Monarch for royal assent which in practice is a formality nowadays – the last time a bill was rejected by a Monarch was in 1707!

Delegated legislation

Parliament delegates some of its legislative powers to other organizations and individuals, and for a variety of reasons. It only has sufficient time to pass approximately 60 to 70 bills each year and the need for legislation exceeds its capabilities. Delegating to others also permits a greater degree of flexibility to enable archaic and/or unsuccessful laws to be changed swiftly and to meet developing circumstances and to draw on local and specialized knowledge and expertise to produce better, more relevant laws at a local level, or ones which are more suited to a specific industrial sector.

Delegated legislative powers are most often passed to government ministers and local authorities – both of whom form part of the executive – although other bodies may be involved too. As an example, certain professional associations are able to make rules concerning the standards of conduct expected of their members. The Law Society provides the legal framework in which member solicitors work. Possibly the best way of viewing delegated legislation is to bear in mind that Parliament passes an act which provides a broad legal outline, but leaves the 'i's to be dotted and the 't's to be crossed by other bodies.

10.3 The executive

The executive might be said to comprise central government, its departments and agencies and local government, all of which are responsible for implementing legislation. Clearly, there is some (often very considerable) overlap between the legislature and the executive as central governments, its departments and agencies and local government can all initiate legislation and in some instances can legislate themselves via the powers delegated to them by Parliament. In theory, the legislature and the executive are separate and distinct, but in practice the edges are very blurred.

Central government

The leader of the political party with the majority of seats in the House of Commons is asked by the Monarch to form a ministry, or government. The Prime Minister (PM) or First Lord of the Treasury as he or she is now called chooses individuals from the House of Commons and (occasionally) the House of Lords to join his or her Cabinet, or committee of ministers, and to fill other, less important ministerial posts. The PM and the Cabinet are the heart and mind of central government, making decisions and exercising power.

The Prime Minister has significant personal powers as a consequence of the position. He or she decides the size and make-up of the Cabinet, appointing and dismissing ministers as he or she sees fit, and chooses what will be discussed in Cabinet. By chairing Cabinet meetings, he or she is also able to lead and control discussions.

As important, the PM can ask the Monarch to dissolve Parliament at any stage, thus enabling the resulting general election to be held at a time which is most advantageous to his or her political party. Nevertheless, there are constraints on the Prime Minister. Most notably, he or she is simply one person and in practice must have the continuing support of his or her Cabinet and party to retain the leadership and prime ministerial position.

In reality, the PM will share responsibility for making, amending and executing policies with Cabinet colleagues. Although its size and make-up depends upon the Prime Minister's wishes, it will usually consist of the PM and the Chancellor of the Exchequer, Foreign Secretary, Home Secretary, Minister of Defence and Lord Chancellor representing the old, well established ministries. Other members

Prime Minister, First Lord of the Treasury and Minister for the Civil Service
  The Rt. Hon. John Major, MP
Lord High Chancellor
  The Lord Mackay of Clashfern, PC
Secretary of State for Foreign and Commonwealth Affairs
  The Rt. Hon. Douglas Hurd, CBE, MP
Chancellor of the Exchequer
  The Rt. Hon. Kenneth Clarke, QC, MP
Secretary of State for the Home Department
  The Rt. Hon. Michael Howard, QC, MP
President of the Board of Trade and Secretary of State for Trade and Industry
  The Rt. Hon. Michael Heseltine, MP
Secretary of State for Transport
  The Rt. Hon. John MacGregor, OBE, MP
Secretary of State for Defence
  The Rt. Hon. Malcolm Rifkind, QC, MP
Lord Privy Seal and Leader of the House of Lords
  The Lord Wakeham, PC
Lord President of the Council and Leader of the House of Commons
  The Rt. Hon. Antony Newton, OBE, MP
Secretary of State for National Heritage
  The Rt. Hon. Peter Brooke, MP
Secretary of State for the Environment
  The Rt. Hon. John Gummer, MP
Secretary of State for Employment
  The Rt. Hon. David Hunt, MBE, MP
Secretary of State for Social Security
  The Rt. Hon. Peter Lilley, MP
Chancellor of the Duchy of Lancaster and Minister of Public Service and Science
  The Rt. Hon. William Waldegrave, MP
Secretary of State for Scotland
  The Rt. Hon. Ian Lang, MP
Secretary of State for Northern Ireland
  The Rt. Hon. Sir Patrick Mayhew, QC, MP
Secretary of State for Education
  The Rt. Hon. John Patten, MP
Secretary of State for Health
  The Rt. Hon. Virginia Bottomley, MP
Minister of Agriculture, Fisheries and Food
  The Rt. Hon. Gillian Shephard, MP
Chief Secretary to the Treasury
  The Rt. Hon. Michael Portillo, MP
Secretary of State for Wales
  The Rt. Hon. John Redwood, MP

Figure 10.2   The Cabinet, July 1993

would include the ministers for Health, Social Security, Education, Environment, Transport, Scotland, Wales and Northern Ireland. Figure 10.2 shows the Cabinet posts and members as at July 1993.

Government departments

Various government departments comprise what is occasionally known as the central administration or more popularly Whitehall as this is where they are based in London. A government department may be defined as 'an area of government activity which is (usually) divided up by function, theme or geography'. As examples, the Department of Employment, the Department of the Environment and the Northern Ireland Office fit into these categories respectively. As always, there are exceptions though. For example, the 'law and order' activity is shared between the Home Office which is responsible for general law and order and the Lord Chancellor's department which is responsible for the judicial system of civil and criminal courts.

Each department is headed by a Minister (or Secretary of State as some of them are occasionally called), who creates and sees through policies, makes decisions in the field and takes overall responsibility for the department, answering to Cabinet, Parliament, the media and the public. As an illustration of the overlapping nature of the legislature and the executive, it is interesting to note that these ministers are members of the legislature in their role as MPs and members of the executive as heads of government departments.

The minister is aided by a permanent, politically neutral staff of civil servants who carry out the minister's wishes, albeit usually after some consultation and advice, and who attend to the administrative workload of the department. Over 750 000 people comprise the civil service and can be grouped into the following (very) broad categories:

1 The administrative class

These top civil servants are responsible for advising ministers on policy formulation, and for supervising the work areas of their particular department.

2 The executive class

Those officials who fall into this category organize the general activities of their department, making sure that they are carried out in accordance with agreed policies.

3   *The clerical class*

Here at the lower level are the various, miscellaneous civil servants who do the dogsbody work – typists, secretaries, messengers and the like. Younger recruits may start here, and work their way upwards.

4 · *The specialist class*

Those in this group include specialized advisers, inspectors and technicians who provide expert, hands-on advice across a wide range of areas.

Government agencies

Many government departments are large and unwieldy, assuming responsibilities for a whole host of areas. To take just one simple example, the Department of the Environment covers local government, planning, land use, housing and conservation – all broad and diverse activities. Hence, numerous quasi-autonomous non-governmental organizations (quangos for short) have been established to supervise and control certain activities on behalf of the government. There are approximately 2500 of these almost (quasi-) self-governing bodies – including the Monopolies and Mergers Commission and the Office of Fair Trading – which have an arm's length relationship with the government, albeit being ultimately answerable to it.

Local government

Obviously, it is not practical for central government in London to implement legislation on a localized basis. What happens in practice is that central government establishes a broad framework of laws and policies and allows local authorities to implement them and take additional steps which are required in their particular area. At present, there is a three tier system of local government with different councils carrying out particular duties, or sharing them between themselves as appropriate.

1   *County councils*

These are first tier authorities – 39 in England, eight in Wales and nine regional councils in Scotland – which cover wide geographical areas, such as Norfolk and Suffolk in East Anglia. Some services are

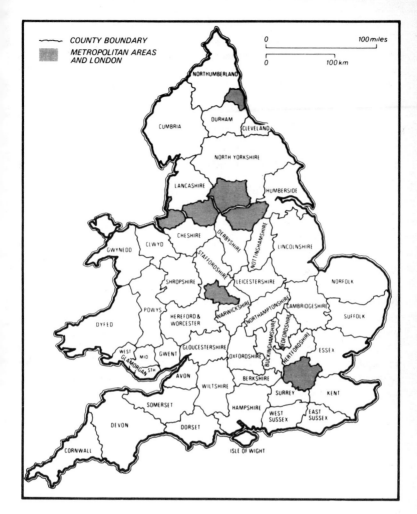

Figure 10.3 County councils. (Note: Local government was reorganized in 1974 and included a tier of metropolitan areas. These were subsequently abolished with their powers being passed to district councils)

provided exclusively by a county council, most notably education, highways, police and fire services, while others are shared with second tier authorities. Figure 10.3 shows the county councils across the country, while Figure 10.4 illustrates the types of service which they may provide.

- Town planning and development
- Public transport
- Traffic
- Highways
- Street lighting
- Road safety
- Parking
- Social services
- Education
- Youth employment
- Recreation
- Libraries
- Swimming pools
- Parks
- Open spaces
- Police
- Fire
- Consumer protection
- Refuse disposal

Figure 10.4   Typical county council services

2   District councils

These second tier authorities, of which there are 296 in England, 37 in Wales and 53 in Scotland, occupy smaller geographical areas within county council regions. Again, some services are normally supplied exclusively by these councils – housing, planning and refuse collection amongst them – while others are divided up between the top two types of council. Figures 10.5 and 10.6 highlight district councils within a county council region and their usual activities.

3   Parish councils

Set up by the District Councils to cater for highly localized needs and to provide residents with a voice, these 11 000 or so lower or third tier authorities deal with modest matters such as the upkeep of village greens and the allocation of allotments. They are relatively inconsequential in relation to county and district councils.

In many respects, a council can be likened to the House of Commons, and perhaps a government department too. Like MPs, councillors are elected by local voters usually for a four-year period and the political party with the majority of councillors is able to push through its policies, albeit within the framework set by central government. Much of the workload is discharged by committees – for

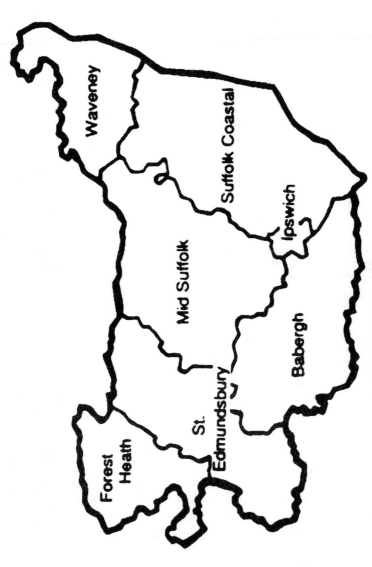

Figure 10.5 District councils in Suffolk County Council

> - Local planning and development
> - Building regulations
> - Housing
> - Clean air
> - Street lighting
> - Off-street parking
> - Country parks
> - Open spaces
> - Footpaths
> - Bridleways
> - Markets
> - Fairs
> - Local licensing
> - Allotments
> - Cemeteries
> - Crematoria
> - Refuse collection

Figure 10.6   Typical district council services

education, housing, social services and so on – which reflect the political mix of councillors. Like civil servants, officers form a group of politically neutral, professional staff which carry out the day-to-day administrative duties of the council.

10.4   The judiciary

The judiciary comprises county, high and civil appeal courts as well as magistrates, crown and criminal appeal courts. The role of these courts is to deal with civil and criminal matters and it is important to know the key differences between these two types of case. Civil cases are usually initiated by one aggrieved person or business against another, perhaps regarding the custody of children or an unpaid bill. The courts decide the rights and wrongs, with the remedy in the form of restitution or recompense. The children may have to be handed back to the other parent, and the bill paid, plus costs. Criminal cases are normally initiated by the police, possibly regarding theft or assault, with the courts seeking to punish the offender, perhaps via a fine or imprisonment.

County courts

County courts might best be described as 'local courts dealing with relatively minor civil matters and disputes arising in the vicinity'. These would include landlord and tenant disagreements, unpaid bills, individual bankruptcies, dissolution of partnerships and the winding up of small companies. The country is divided up into districts which are subdivided into 54 circuits. Each circuit has one or more circuit judges attached to it. These are drawn from a list of barristers with at least 10 years' experience. There are 400 or more county courts in England and Wales over which some 350 or so judges preside, disposing of cases on their own. Much of the general administrative workload and duties of the courts are handled by a Registrar who is a solicitor of at least seven years' standing. Registrars handle very minor cases too, where sums of £500 or less are involved.

High courts

The High Court of Justice is located in London, and has jurisdiction over more serious civil matters and disputes. It is split into three divisions, each handling different issues. Eighty or so judges cover the three divisions, dealing with cases alone.

1 The Queen's Bench division

This is the biggest and most significant of the three divisions, and handles matters not allocated to the other two, Chancery and Family, divisions. Typically, it might deal with contractual disputes between landlords and tenants, buyers and sellers and the like.

2 The Chancery division

The jurisdiction of the smallest of the three divisions is over various specialist matters, such as partnership and company law, mortgages, taxation and the administration of the estates of deceased persons.

3 The Family division

As the name suggests, this division is concerned with family law and disputes with regard to divorce, property settlements, custody of children and so on.

Civil appeal courts

In some circumstances, those parties who are dissatisfied with the judgements of county and high courts can take the matter further – to the civil appeal courts, as follows:

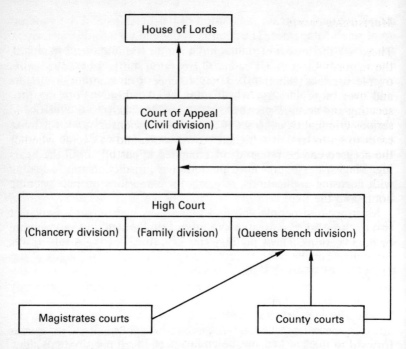

Figure 10.7 The civil courts

1 *The Court of Appeal (civil division)*

Appeals from the county court and high court on questions of fact and/or law will be referred to the Court of Appeal, which is headed by the Master of the Rolls and 18 Lords Justices of the Appeal. Three judges will preside over an individual appeal, usually studying records of the previous trial rather than re-hearing evidence. They have the power to confirm, amend or overthrow the earlier decision, and in certain cases can order a retrial.

2 *The House of Lords (Judicial Committee)*

The highest court of appeal in the land, this is headed by the Lord Chancellor – the head of the English Legal system – and the Lords of Appeal in Ordinary or Law Lords to use the more common title given to them. Cases referred to the House from the Court of Appeal are heard by five judges, and a judgement reached.

The civil court structure is summarized in Figure 10.7.

Magistrates courts

These are the lowest of the criminal courts, although they deal with the majority of criminal cases. Magistrates courts have jurisdiction over less serious (summary) criminal offences such as motoring matters and over more serious, hybrid offences like theft if both the prosecuting and accused parties agree to it. They also assess evidence in serious criminal cases to see if there are sufficient grounds for these cases to go to trial at a higher, crown court, and to decide whether the accused can be released or remanded in custody until the hearing. Magistrates courts have limited civil jurisdiction too – dealing with licensing applications, requests for extensions on pub opening hours and the like.

Most accused people will find themselves in front of a bench of two or three lay magistrates – ordinary people with no legal training or qualifications. These lay magistrates, justices of the peace or JPs for short, must be over 21 and under 65, live within 15 miles of the court, be of good character and have performed services for the community. They need no knowledge of the law as they can rely heavily on the legal advice of the clerk to the court who is a solicitor. Prospective magistrates are recommended for appointment by an advisory committee who interview and assess applicants and put names forward to the Lord Chancellor to make the final decision. An alternative to a bench of lay magistrates is a stipendiary who is a salaried, professional lawyer who works as a magistrate on a full-time basis.

Crown courts

Located in most major towns and cities, crown courts are responsible for trying serious criminal (indictable) offences which are grouped into four categories according to their seriousness, from theft through to murder. Three types of judge preside over crown court cases from part-time recorders who are barristers or solicitors with at least 10 years' experience through circuit judges to high court judges, who are the most senior and experienced, and who handle the serious cases. The judge's role in a crown court case is to ensure a fair trial, with a jury comprising 12 members of the public hearing the evidence and reaching a verdict, and the judge fixing a sentence, as appropriate.

Criminal appeal courts

Appeals made on questions of law from magistrates courts may be referred to the Queen's Bench Division of the High Court. Those

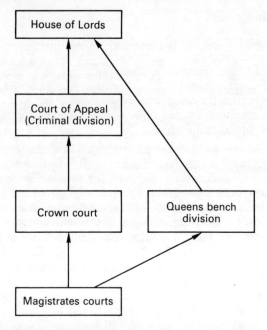

Figure 10.8 The criminal courts

appeals relating to questions of fact can be taken to the Crown Court. Any appeals from the Crown Court will go to the following criminal appeal courts:

1 *The Court of Appeal (criminal division)*

As with civil cases, three of the Lords Justices of Appeal will preside over an appeal, reviewing the records of the trial and consequently confirming, adjusting or questioning the decision, and ordering a retrial, if they believe this is relevant.

2 *The House of Lords (Judicial Committee)*

Similarly, five Law Lords will hear cases in this highest court of appeal, and reach judgement in due course.

The criminal court structure is summarized in Figure 10.8.

Tribunals

Numerous tribunals have been set up over the years to look into and resolve certain legal matters, perhaps regarding state benefits entitlements and unfair dismissal claims. With their specialists in the field and wide discretionary powers, they are usually able to handle some cases better than the courts, and often quicker and at a lower cost for those involved too. Various types of tribunal exist and can be divided into these broad categories:

1 *Administrative tribunals*

These have been established by Acts of Parliament to handle assorted administrative disputes. For example, social security tribunals hear disputes concerning individual entitlements to state benefits, such as unemployment benefit and income support.

2 *Industrial tribunals*

These have been set up by employment legislation and given the responsibility of dealing with employment disputes such as unfair dismissal, equal pay, sex or racial discrimination, and the like.

3 *Domestic tribunals*

Distinct from administrative and industrial tribunals, these have been established by professional bodies to discipline members for poor performance, misconduct, or whatever. Doctors, dentists and other professionals may have to answer to these tribunals.

10.5 Rapid revision

Answers	Questions
–	1 What is the State?
1 It is the administrative system which governs a community.	2 What does the State consist of?
2 It consists of (a) the legislature; (b) the executive; (c) the judiciary.	3 What are their respective roles?
3 (a) To pass laws; (b) to implement laws; (c) to deal with disputes arising from the passing and implementation of laws.	4 What is the legislature in the UK?

4 Parliament, comprising the House of Commons and the House of Lords.

5 What is the House of Commons?

---

5 It is an elected body of 650 Members of Parliament, or MPs.

6 Who elects MPs to the House of Commons?

---

6 Generally speaking, everyone over 18 in each of the 650 constituencies across the country.

7 What is the House of Lords?

---

7 It is an unelected body of approximately 1100 hereditary and life peers, some of whom have been elevated from the Commons by the Monarch.

8 Who else sits in the House of Lords?

---

8 Lords Spiritual, Bishops and Archbishops of the Anglican Church, Lords of Appeal in Ordinary, lawyers who sit as a final court of appeal in the judicial system.

9 What is a bill?

---

9 It is the name given to a law during its passage through Parliament and on to the Monarch for royal assent, upon which it becomes a statute or Act of Parliament.

10 What are the two main types of bill?

---

10 (a) Public bills, which affect the public as a whole; (b) private bills, which affect a limited number of organizations and individuals, or a particular region.

11 Who usually initiates these bills?

---

11 Respectively (a) the government and individual members of Parliament and the House of Lords; (b) outside bodies, such as local authorities.

12 What are the informal stages of the passage of a bill?

---

12 In brief (a) calls for changes; (b) cabinet discussions; (c) green paper issued; (d) opinions gathered; (e) white paper issued; (f) legislature proposals drawn up.

13 What are the formal stages of the passage of a bill?

13 In summary (a) first reading; (b) second reading; (c) committee stage; (d) report stage; (e) third reading; (f) to other House; (g) to the Monarch.

14 Who has received delegated legislative powers from Parliament?

---

14 Numerous organizations and individuals, notably (a) government ministers; (b) local authorities; (c) certain professional bodies.

15 What is the executive in the UK?

---

15 (a) Central government; (b) government departments; (c) government agencies; (d) local government.

16 How might the Prime Minister and his or her Cabinet be described?

---

16 As the heart and mind of central government, making decisions and exercising power.

17 What exactly is a government department?

---

17 It is an area of government activity which is divided up by function, theme or geography.

18 Who heads a government department, and staffs it?

---

18 A minister and civil servants, comprising (a) the administrative class; (b) the executive class; (c) the clerical class; (d) the specialist class.

19 What is a quango?

---

19 It is a quasi-autonomous non-governmental organization which supervises and controls certain activities for the government.

20 What are the three tiers of local government?

---

20 (a) Country councils; (b) district councils; (c) parish councils.

21 What do they do?

---

21 They implement the broad framework of laws and policies set by central government and take additional steps on their own, as relevant to their areas.

22 What is the judiciary in the UK?

---

22 It comprises county, high and civil appeal courts as well as magistrates, crown and criminal appeal courts.

23 What are the two main types of case dealt with by the judiciary?

---

23   (a) Civil cases; (b) criminal cases.

24   What are county courts?

24   Local courts dealing with minor civil matters and disputes arising in the vicinity.

25   What are the three divisions of the high court?

25   (a) Queen's bench division; (b) Chancery division; (c) Family division.

26   What are the civil appeal courts?

26   (a) The Court of Appeal (civil division); (b) The House of Lords (judicial committee).

27   What are magistrates courts?

27   The lowest of the criminal courts handling less serious criminal offences.

28   Where do more serious criminal offences go to?

28   Crown Courts, located in most towns and cities.

29   What are the criminal appeal courts?

29   (a) The Court of Appeal (criminal division); (b) The House of Lords (judicial committee).

30   What are the three main types of tribunal?

30   (a) Administrative tribunals;
(b) industrial tribunals;
(c) domestic tribunals.

31   Go over the questions again until you know all of the answers. Then move on to the next section.

11
The economy

11.1 What is the economy?

Perhaps the simplest definition of an 'economy' is to state that it is
'a system for producing goods and services and distributing them
throughout the community'. Within this broad ranging description,
three main types of economy can be readily identified.

Planned economies

In a 'planned' or 'centrally planned' economy, the production and
distribution of products and services are (predominantly) owned and
controlled by the State, in the form of central government, its departments and agencies and local government. In essence, the State
owns the resources and decides how they should be allocated, what
and how much ought to be produced, how they should be distributed
and the ways in which any profits ought to be used – all for the
benefit of the people, and with a view to creating a fair and equal
society. 'Command' and 'controlled' economies are other names for
planned economies.

Clearly, a planned economy has both advantages and disadvantages. In its favour, the State can make decisions which are right for
the community, mindful of people rather than just profit. Prices can
be kept to a minimum – so the theory goes – as the State is not
seeking to make a profit but simply to break even, unlike businesses
which are trying to make as much money as possible. Against it, the
State may misjudge what the people want which can lead to gluts and
shortages.

State ownership and control also stifle private enterprise and
competition – there is no incentive to work hard, to create, to compete, and customers are left with limited choice and (probably) higher
prices than in a more competitive environment.

Market economies

At the other extreme, 'market (free enterprise) economies' are those in which goods and services are produced and distributed (mainly) by businesses and private individuals, rather than the State. Resources are privately owned and businesses and individuals are free to use them however they wish to produce whatever goods and services they want, which will usually be those which generate satisfactory or the most profit. Customers can spend their money on whatever they like. Hence, this economy, also known as a 'capitalist' or 'laissez-faire economy', is subject to the (considerable) market forces of demand and supply.

There are several benefits which can be associated with market economies, most notably the efficient use of resources, freedom of choice for sellers and buyers and increased competition which normally leads to a wider range and better quality of products and services. However, there are drawbacks too. As examples, businesses will produce what suits them rather than society, and will charge as much as they can to maximize or at least maintain profit. Often, larger businesses will work together to squeeze out rivals and to set artificially high prices, not to the consumers' benefit at all.

Mixed economies

In practice, most economies are a mix of a planned and a market economy with the production and distribution of products and services being shared between the State and private enterprise. The UK is a good example of a mixed economy – approximately 40 per cent of (essential) goods and services such as education and health are provided by the State, with the remaining 60 per cent or thereabouts being derived from businesses and private individuals. Hopefully, mixed economies benefit from the advantages of planned and market economies, but manage to eliminate the disadvantages.

Obviously, the economy is a key part of the backdrop of the business environment. With this in mind, it is sensible to have a clear and concise knowledge of the make-up and amount of the national income of the UK economy, along with the economic objectives of the government, the economic problems that it faces and the economic policies which are pursued. This will then provide a better understanding of the UK's mixed economy.

11.2   The national income

The national income may be described as 'the total income generated by a country's economic activities over a given period of time,

	£ millions
Agriculture, forestry, fishing	9,309
Mining and quarrying	9,842
Manufacturing	114,698
Electricity, gas, water supply	13,717
Construction	32,002
Wholesale and retail trade	72,549
Transport, communication	41,613
Financial intermediation	121,704
Public administration, defence, social security	36,605
Education, health, social work	52,509
Other services	32,892
Discrepancies, adjustments	−22,846
Gross domestic product	514,594
Net property income from abroad	5,777
Gross national product	520,371
(Less) Capital consumption	−63,984
National income	456,387

Figure 11.1   The national income 1992, by output

usually one year'. National income accounts provide a breakdown of the overall production of the economy and the numerous sectors within it, and help the government to formulate appropriate economic and other policies. Working out the national income per head of population also indicates the country's prosperity which can be compared with previous years and/or other countries, as relevant. Measuring national income is a huge and complex task – there are several million transactions in just one day – but can be carried out in various, (relatively) straightforward ways.

The output method

This method adds together the value of the final outputs of each area of economic activity – agriculture, forestry, fishing and so on – to produce the total output for the relevant period. This sum is known as the *gross domestic product* (GDP). Net property income from abroad – the difference between overseas branches of UK companies remitting (some of) their incomes to here, and vice versa – is then added (or deducted) to GDP to produce the *gross national product* (GNP). As the country's capital items are used to produce output, an allowance is made for depreciation – or 'capital consumption' to use the correct term – which is deducted from gross national product to leave *net national product* (NNP) or national income. Figure 11.1 gives the UK national income for 1992, calculated via this method.

	£ millions
Income from employment	341,009
Income from self-employment	58,060
Gross trading profit of companies	64,574
Gross trading surpluses of public corporations	1,813
Gross trading surpluses of other government enterprises	89
Rent	46,846
Consumption of non-trading capital	4,207
(Less) Stock appreciation	2,216
Discrepancies	212
Gross domestic product	514,594
Net property income from abroad	5,777
Gross national product	520,371
(Less) Capital consumption	63,984
National income	456,387

Figure 11.2   The national income 1992, by income

The income method

With this method of working out the national income, all of the
incomes received from producing the output of the period are added
up. These incomes – which include rent, interest, wages, salaries and
profit – ought to equal the value of the total output, or gross domestic
product. As with the earlier method, net property income is then
added or deducted (as appropriate) to reach the gross national product
from which capital consumption is deducted to give a final, national
income figure. The UK's national income for 1992 is given in Figure
11.2, as composed via the income method.

The expenditure method

This approach to measuring national income adds together all of the
expenditures on goods and services produced by the economy during
the period to give a figure for total domestic expenditure. As some
of this expenditure will be on products and services imported from
overseas and another part of it will relate to goods and services
exported abroad, it is necessary to deduct the value of imports and
add the value of exports to the total domestic expenditure to arrive
at the GDP. Once more, net property income from abroad is added
or deducted to reach the GNP and capital consumption is deducted
to give the national income figure. Figure 11.3 gives the UK's national
income for 1992, as derived from the expenditure method.

	£ millions
Consumers' expenditure	382,696
Central government consumption	82,477
Local authorities' consumption	49,901
Gross domestic fixed capital formation	92,892
Value of physical increase in stocks and work in progress	1,992
Total domestic expenditure	605,974
Exports	139,827
(Less) Imports	−149,164
Discrepancies	−472
Net property income from abroad	5,777
(Less) Taxes on expenditure	−87,679
Subsidies	6,108
Gross national product	520,371
(Less) Capital consumption	−63,984
National income	456,387

Figure 11.3 The national income 1992, by expenditure

11.3 Economic objectives

Almost all governments, regardless of their political persuasion, share the same, major economic objectives. At local and national levels, these are to ensure a high and steady level of employment, to maintain stable prices and to promote economic growth and prosperity. In international terms, a government will usually seek to achieve a balance of payments equilibrium, which is a situation whereby sales of products and services to overseas equal, or preferably exceed, purchases of goods and services from abroad, so that the country is run at a profit rather than at a loss. The balance of payments is best considered as part of the international environment.

High employment levels

In theory, a government may seek to achieve a position of full employment which may be defined as 'the utilization of all of the workforce of the country' – in essence, everyone who is available for work has a job! Thus, output is maximized so that enough goods and services are produced for the country and at a personal level those in employment and their families are relatively happy and well off. In practice, a government will probably be satisfied with a level of employment whereby unemployment – 'the non-utilization of part of the workforce of the country' – is kept at an acceptable level.

Obviously, the interpretation of what is acceptable is open to debate. Many people may regard the 1994 unemployment level of three million or thereabouts as unacceptable.

Stable prices

Theoretically, a government will usually try to maintain stable prices so that businesses and individuals pay the same for raw materials, consumer durables and the like now as they did last year and will do in a year's time. Obviously, stable prices help the economy in many ways. As examples, they enable businesses to budget, sustain good cashflows and remain competitive in the marketplace, both at home and abroad. They assist individuals too – families with young children, pensioners on fixed incomes and so on. In reality, the government will often accept a low level of inflation – 'an increase in the level of prices over a sustained period of time' – as long as it is kept to within reasonable limits. Again, the definition of a reasonable or unreasonable rate is open to discussion. The 1994 inflation rate of about two to three per cent is regarded as reasonable by many people.

Economic growth

Economic growth may be described as 'an increase in the total output of products and services in an economy over a given period of time'. Normally, it is measured in terms of an increase in gross domestic product and/or as an increase in GDP per head of population which is a reflection of changes in living standards. Only by achieving a decent rate of growth in its production capacity can an economy produce more products and services which will provide an accompanying rise in wealth and living standards. Once more, the definition of what is decent or not is open to discussion. The average economic growth of 2 per cent over the past few years is considered decent by the majority of people.

Not surprisingly, these broad and rather diverse economic objectives are not fully compatible. For example, high employment levels usually mean more money is available to spend on goods and services which increases demand and encourages businesses to raise prices. Similarly, a growing economy normally means greater prosperity which tends to lead to demands for a wider variety of goods which can boost imports from overseas that upset the balance of payments equilibrium. Hence, most governments tend to rank their objectives, placing them in an order which is most economically viable and politically acceptable.

	Unemployment %										
	1980	1981	1982	1983	1984	1985	1986	1987	1988	1989	1990
Canada	7.4	7.5	10.9	11.8	11.2	10.4	9.5	8.8	7.7	7.5	7.5
United States	7.0	7.5	9.5	9.5	7.4	7.1	6.9	6.1	5.4	5.2	5.1
Japan	2.0	2.2	2.4	2.6	2.7	2.6	2.8	2.8	2.5	2.3	2.2
Australia	6.0	5.7	7.1	9.9	8.9	8.2	8.0	8.0	7.2	6.1	6.6
Belgium	8.8	10.8	12.6	12.1	12.1	11.3	11.2	11.0	9.6	8.1	7.8
Finland	4.6	4.8	5.3	5.4	5.2	5.0	5.3	5.0	4.5	3.4	3.3
France	6.3	7.4	8.1	8.3	9.7	10.2	10.4	10.5	10.0	9.4	8.9
Germany	3.0	4.4	6.1	8.0	7.1	7.2	6.4	6.2	6.2	5.6	5.2
Italy	7.5	7.8	8.4	8.8	9.4	9.6	10.5	10.9	11.0	10.9	9.6
Netherlands	6.0	8.5	11.4	12.0	11.8	10.6	9.9	9.6	9.2	8.3	7.1
Norway	1.6	2.0	2.6	3.4	3.1	2.6	2.0	2.1	3.2	4.9	5.3
Spain	11.3	13.9	15.8	17.2	20.1	21.4	21.0	20.1	19.1	16.9	15.9
Sweden	2.0	2.5	3.1	3.5	3.1	2.8	2.7	1.9	1.6	1.4	1.3
United Kingdom	6.4	9.8	11.3	12.4	11.7	11.2	11.2	10.2	8.3	6.9	6.2

Figure 11.4 United Kingdom unemployment, by comparison

11.4 Economic problems

Mindful of the main, local and national economic objectives – high employment, stable prices, economic growth – it is sensible to be aware of some of the leading economic problems that governments have to face and tackle via their economic and other policies which will enable them to achieve (or at least work towards) these objectives. Three of the major economic problems that have to be dealt with are unemployment, inflation and low (or even non-existent) growth. Figures 11.4, 11.5 and 11.6 give some idea of the difficulties faced in these areas by UK governments in recent years.

Unemployment

Unemployment has been described, somewhat fancifully, as 'the non-utilization of part of the workforce of a country'. It is usually quoted in numerical terms, two million, three million or whatever, although viewing it as a percentage of the total workforce conveys a more realistic picture. Various types of unemployment can be identified:

1 Frictional unemployment

This refers to those people who are temporarily unemployed while they are between work. Perhaps they left one job before obtaining

	1971–1990		1971–1979		1980–1990	
	Average	Standard deviation	Average	Standard deviation	Average	Standard deviation
Inflation						
USA	6.0	2.5	6.9	2.1	5.2	2.5
Japan	5.3	5.0	9.0	5.2	2.4	2.1
W Germany	3.9	2.1	5.0	1.5	3.0	2.2
France	8.1	3.8	9.5	2.8	6.9	4.3
Italy	12.3	5.6	14.1	5.2	10.9	5.8
UK	9.7	5.5	13.1	5.4	6.9	3.8

Figure 11.5   United Kingdom inflation, by comparison

	1971–1990		1971–1979		1980–1990	
	Average	Standard deviation	Average	Standard deviation	Average	Standard deviation
Real gdp growth						
USA	2.8	2.5	3.2	2.5	2.5	2.5
Japan	4.4	1.9	4.7	2.7	4.2	1.2
W Germany	2.4	1.9	2.9	2.2	2.0	1.7
France	2.8	1.5	3.5	1.6	2.3	1.1
Italy	3.0	2.3	3.8	3.1	2.4	1.2
UK	2.2	2.2	2.4	2.5	2.1	2.1

Figure 11.6   United Kingdom gross domestic product growth, by comparison

another and are happy to be unemployed for a short period before new work commences. Frictional unemployment is generally regarded as the consequence of the natural to-ing and fro-ing that occurs in any economy as employees come and go to better, more lucrative employment. It is not viewed with any real concern, given its short-term, transient nature.

2   Seasonal unemployment

Similar to frictional unemployment albeit on a larger and often more localized scale, this occurs in those trades, industries and regions which operate on a seasonal basis, such as agriculture and tourism. Not surprisingly, those employed in these areas will find themselves temporarily (in and) out of work as the seasons pass by.

3 *Structural unemployment*

This normally arises because of the changing demand for certain products or services which adversely affects the whole structure of the industry. For example, the falling demand for ships from the Tyne led to the substantial loss of employment there. Alternatively, it can result from changes in supply. As an example, the exhaustion of coal deposits in mines in Wales led to many job losses in that area.

4 *Cyclical unemployment*

Most economies go through what is known as a *business cycle* – fluctuations in the levels of business activity according to changes in demand – and this type of unemployment will tend to reflect this *boom, slump, boom* sequence. Briefly, in a *depression*, demand is low in relation to supply capacity which results in low output levels, unsold stock and high unemployment. Moving into *recovery*, demand increases so stock levels fall and output and employment rise. In a boom, output is at full capacity, cannot meet demand and prices tend to rise. Then in *recession*, demand falls which has a similar, knock-on effect on output and employment before falling further into depression again.

Inflation

Inflation may be defined as 'an increase in price levels within an economy which is sustained over a period of time', in short, prices keep rising! It is measured in relation to a *price index* which is a weighted average of the prices of a mix of goods and services produced in the economy over a period of time. The *retail price index* (RPI) is normally used, and measures the average level of the prices of some 600 products and services commonly purchased by the general public. Each item is weighted according to its importance. A base year is chosen so that 1984 may have an index value of 100 and any subsequent price changes are then reflected in this index over time. Hence, 1994 may have an index value of 200 which indicates an average annual rate of inflation of 10 per cent over the preceding 10-year period. Two main types of inflation can be spotted:

1 *Demand pull inflation*

This type of inflation occurs when the total (or aggregate) demand for products and services within the economy exceeds their total (or aggregate) supply. In straightforward terms, what happens in practice is that demand rises and businesses respond by increasing their output of goods and services. Supply rises to meet demand, as does employment to produce the necessary output. However, if output reaches its maximum limits and part of that total demand has still not been fully satisfied then the inevitable consequence of the demand-supply-price market forces coming into play is rising prices.

2 *Cost push inflation*

An alternative, widely held view of inflation is that it arises not from the demand side of the economy 'pulling up' prices but from the supply side 'pushing up' prices instead. Quite simply, increasing costs – most notably for raw materials and wages – force businesses to put up the prices of their goods and services if they are to survive, let alone profit and grow. In effect, these added costs are passed straight on to the customer.

Low economic growth

Economic growth has been referred to as 'an increase in the total output of products and services in the economy over a period of time', and is measured in terms of gross domestic product over time, or GDP per head of population over time. There are various reasons why economic growth may be low, or even non-existent in some cases. Here are some of the main ones:

1 A failure to increase the quantity *and* quality of resources which need to be used in the maximization of output. For output to rise steadily, it is clear that firms have to invest in more and better resources, physically to produce larger quantities and to ensure that they are competitive in the marketplace, in the face of stiff competition from overseas rivals. Particular attention has to be given to enlarging the stocks and standards of physical resources such as equipment, machinery and raw materials and of human resources, both at managerial and shopfloor levels.

2 An inability to use the resource mix efficiently, to achieve high levels of *productivity* which can be defined as 'the relationship between the resources that have gone into producing output, and the levels of output'. It is normally measured in terms of physical

output per man hour. The inefficient use of resources can be seen in many ways such as the failure to introduce new production techniques, excessive stockholding in relation to current and anticipated requirements and poor work practices like employing full timers when part timers would be more cost effective.

3 Insufficient levels of demand within the economy to ensure the full utilization of resources. Put in simple terms, there are not enough people out there who want goods and services to encourage businesses to raise their output. If a firm cannot see and/or does not anticipate a growing demand for its products and services, then it is hardly likely to invest in and use the resources that are required to actually expand its production capabilities.

11.5 Economic policies

A government's economic policies may be described as 'those measures adopted by the government in order to pursue its economic objectives, overcome economic problems and successfully manage the economy'. Broadly speaking, economic policies can be divided into fiscal, monetary, prices and incomes, and industrial measures. Such a mix of wide and diverse policies should help the government to maintain high employment levels, stable prices and economic growth, in whatever order of priority has been attached to these objectives.

Fiscal policy

Fiscal policy is 'the regulation of government taxation and expenditure to control spending levels within the economy'. There are numerous ways in which the government can actively encourage or discourage spending and thus boost or deflate demand, which will in turn have knock-on effects on employment, inflation rates and economic growth. The three principal approaches are:

1 *Raise or lower direct taxes*

If the government wants to reduce spending, it can lower income and corporation tax thresholds and/or raise income and corporation tax rates so that more income and profit is taxed, and less is left over to be spent in the economy. Alternatively, the government can raise thresholds and/or lower rates if it wishes to create the opposite effect.

Initials	Definition
M0	Currency plus banks' till money and balances at the Bank of England
M1	M0 plus UK private sector short-term bank deposits
M2	M1 plus UK private sector long-term bank and building society deposits
M3	M2 plus UK public sector deposits
M3c	M3 plus UK residents' deposits in other currencies
M4	M3 plus net building societies deposits
M5	M4 plus UK private sector holdings of bills and similar items

Figure 11.7 The money supply

2 *Increase or decrease indirect taxes*

Another, potentially complementary approach is to raise VAT on products and services generally, broaden its scope to incorporate other items such as books or increase excise duties on particular goods such as petrol. Clearly, this will lead to less money being spent on such products and services. Lowering VAT, reducing its scope and so forth will have the reverse effect.

3 *Boost or cut back on government spending in the economy*

The government itself is a huge spender in the economy – on defence, law and order, health, education and so on. Basically, it can spend more or less money, as appropriate in the current circumstances.

Monetary policy

This particular policy has been referred to as 'the regulation of the money supply, credit and interest rates to encourage or discourage spending levels in the economy'. The *money supply* is simply the stocks of money in an economy, although the precise nature of these stocks is open to several interpretations, as noted in Figure 11.7. Several common approaches can be taken, under the heading of monetary policy.

1 *Issuing a special deposit call*

This involves calling upon banks to place a proportion of their funds on deposit at the Bank of England, the UK's leading financial institution.

These are then held so that the money supply is reduced and the banks' lending activities are duly restricted too.

2 *Issuing a directive*

Here, banks are 'requested' to keep their total lending to within a specified limit, and/or to reduce financial assistance in certain areas, such as on the purchase of new homes.

3 *Selling bonds to the public*

Bonds are financial securities that are issued for a set number of years and are repayable on maturity. They have a fixed face value and interest rate and can be bought and sold rather like shares in a public limited company. To purchase these from the government, money will be taken out of banks and other financial institutions, thus reducing the amount left in general circulation and restricting the banks' ability to provide loans and other credit facilities.

4 *Imposing hire purchase controls*

With this approach, members of the public are discouraged from buying goods 'on tick', and thus encouraged to pay with ready cash instead. Typical controls might be to raise the amount of deposit required on purchases and/or to reduce the credit period allowed.

Obviously, these four, commonplace methods are all designed to discourage spending in the economy, which should have the effect of reducing demand, and so on. Clearly, adopting the opposite approaches – releasing banks' money held on special deposit, buying bonds and the like – will have the reverse effect of raising demand, and so forth.

Prices and incomes policy

A prices and incomes policy involves 'voluntary and/or statutory controls on prices and incomes to limit or reduce inflation in the economy'. As implied by this definition, there are two main ways of approaching such a policy:

1 Establishing voluntary guidelines for price and wage rises. Here, the government simply asks businesses to keep price and wage

increases to within certain limits. Not unexpectedly, such a method has met with mixed success whenever it has been adopted.

2 Demanding that price and wage rises are kept inside statutory limits – or else! With this approach, the government might insist on a prices and wages freeze for perhaps one year, followed by no more than a two to three per cent increase per year for each of the following two years, or whatever. Fines for non-compliance could be introduced, with offenders pursued vigorously.

Industrial policy

This is concerned with 'improving the efficiency and competitiveness of industry within the United Kingdom'. Clearly, the more efficient and competitive industry is, the more likely it is to employ people, make good use of its resources and increase its output – all of which benefits the economy as a whole. Industrial policy can really be sub-divided into various measures:

1 Regional measures

The government tries to regenerate areas of industrial decline by encouraging new firms and industries to locate and invest in these areas. It tends to provide financial inducements such as cash grants, tax and rent reliefs to businesses moving there and follows this up by investing in local amenities, road and rail networks and the like, to increase the attractiveness of the localities.

2 National measures

All sorts of measures are available on a national basis. For example, new small businesses can take advantage of the *enterprise allowance scheme* whereby cash is made available to those people who come off the unemployment register to become self-employed. Similarly, the government's *loan guarantee scheme* will help them to raise money from a bank, by guaranteeing the bulk of the repayment of the loan on their behalf if they fail to make a success of the business.

3 Competition measures

The government promotes greater domestic competition by monitoring mergers and takeovers, restrictive trade agreements, resale prices and anti-competitive practices through the Office of Fair Trading and the Monopolies and Mergers Commission to ensure every business is given a fair chance to succeed. It stimulates competition abroad by providing advice and guidance on exporting via the Department of Trade and Industry.

11.6 Rapid revision

Answers	Questions
	1 What is an economy?
1 It is a system for producing goods and services and distributing them throughout the community.	2 What are the three main types of economy?
2 (a) Planned economies; (b) market economies; (c) mixed economies.	3 What is a planned economy?
3 It is an economy in which the production and distribution of products and services are controlled by the State.	4 What is a market economy?
4 It is one in which goods and services are produced and distributed by businesses and private individuals, rather than the State.	5 What is a mixed economy?
5 It is a mix between a planned and a market economy with the production and distribution of products and services being shared by the State and private enterprise.	6 What is the national income?
6 It is the total income generated by a country's economic activities over a given period of time, usually one year.	7 What do the national income accounts show?
7 They show the overall production of the economy and the sectors within it, and provide an indication of the country's prosperity.	8 What are three main ways of calculating the national income?

8 (a) The output method; (b) the income method; (c) the expenditure method.	9 What is gross domestic product, or GDP?
9 It is the total output for the period.	10 What is gross national product, or GNP?
10 It is the total output for the period, plus or minus net property income from abroad.	11 What are the the major economic objectives of most governments?
11 (a) High and steady level of employment; (b) stable prices; (c) economic growth; (d) balance of payments equilibrium.	12 What is a high and steady level of employment?
12 This is open to interpretation – most governments will be satisfied with a modest level of unemployment which is considered socially acceptable.	13 What are stable prices?
13 They are prices which are the same now as they were last year and will be next year. Most governments will be happy with slight increases.	14 What is economic growth?
14 It is an increase in the total output of products and services in an economy over a given period of time.	15 How is economic growth measured?
15 It is measured in terms of gross domestic product and/or gross domestic product per head of population.	16 What are the major economic problems faced by governments?
16 (a) Unemployment; (b) inflation; (c) low economic growth.	17 What is unemployment?
17 It is the non-utilization of part of the workforce of a country.	18 What are the main types of unemployment?
18 (a) Frictional unemployment; (b) seasonal unemployment; (c) structural unemployment; (d) cyclical unemployment.	19 What is inflation?

19   It is an increase in price levels within an economy which is sustained over a period of time.

20   What are the main forms of inflation?

---

20 (a) Demand pull inflation; (b) cost push inflation.

21   What are the major causes of low or non-existent economic growth?

---

21   (a) A failure to increase the quantity and quality of resources; (b) an inability to use the resource mix efficiently; (c) insufficient levels of demand in the economy.

22   What are economic policies?

---

22   They are those measures which are adopted in order to pursue economic objectives, overcome economic problems and successfully manage the economy.

23   What are the main types of economic policy?

---

23   (a) Fiscal policy; (b) monetary policy; (c) prices and incomes policy; (d) industrial policy.

24   What is fiscal policy?

---

24   It is the regulation of government taxation and expenditure to control spending levels within the economy.

25   What might fiscal policy involve?

---

25   (a) Raising or lowering direct taxes; (b) increasing or decreasing indirect taxes; (c) boosting or cutting government spending.

26   What is monetary policy?

---

26   It is the regulation of the money supply, credit and interest rates, to encourage or discourage spending levels in the economy.

27   What might monetary policy involve?

---

27   (a) Issuing a special deposit call; (b) issuing a directive; (c) selling bonds to the public; (d) imposing hire purchase controls.

28   What is a prices and incomes policy?

---

28   It involves voluntary or statutory controls on prices and incomes to limit or reduce inflation in the economy.

29   What is industrial policy?

29   It is concerned with improving the efficiency and competitiveness of industry.

30   What might industrial policy involve?

---

30   (a) Regional measures; (b) national measures; (c) competition measures.

31   Go over the questions again until you know all of the answers. Then move on to the next section.

12
The population

12.1 What is the population?

Quite simply, 'the population' may be defined as 'the total number of people living in a given area at a particular time'. More specifically, the population can be regarded in various ways, such as in terms of its size, age and sex structure, birth and death rates, emigration and immigration as well as its occupational and geographical distribution. The population is of key significance to all businesses – most notably as a source of human resources and as markets for goods and services – and along with the State and the economy forms part of the backdrop of the local and national environment in which they operate.

12.2 The size and structure of the population

The size of the UK population has grown over the past 100 years, from approximately 38 million in 1900 to some 59 million in 1994. Although the growth rate has been slowing steadily, the total is expected to exceed 60 million in or around 2011. Figure 12.1 shows how the population has expanded since 1951 and is expected to grow through to 2025. More striking is the changing structure of the population, both in terms of age and sex. Figure 12.2 illustrates the ways in which the age structure has developed from 1951 and is anticipated to develop up to 2025. Figure 12.3 looks at the sex structure in 1993 and how it is expected to differ in 30 years.

By looking at Figures 12.1, 12.2 and 12.3, it can be seen that the UK has a growing but ageing population. It is sensible to have some idea of the reasons why this is happening, and the knock-on effects of such changes, particularly upon businesses. The size and structure of the population are mainly influenced by three key factors.

Births

The number of births within the population – usually viewed in terms of *birth rate* which is 'the number of live births per 1000 of the

	In millions
1951	50.3
1961	52.8
1971	55.9
1981	56.4
1986	56.8
1991	57.5
1996	58.5
2001	59.2
2006	59.6
2011	60.0
2025	61.1

Figure 12.1   The UK population, 1951–2025

	–16	16–39	40–64	65–79	80+	Total
1951	{	28.9 }	15.9	4.8	0.7	50.3
1961	13.1	16.6	16.9	5.2	1.0	52.8
1971	14.3	17.5	16.7	6.1	1.3	55.9
1981	12.5	19.7	15.7	6.9	1.6	56.4
1986	11.7	20.6	15.8	6.8	1.8	56.7
1991	11.7	20.2	16.5	6.9	2.2	57.5
1996	12.5	19.8	17.0	6.8	2.4	58.5
2001	12.8	19.2	18.0	6.7	2.5	59.2
2006	12.6	18.4	19.4	6.6	2.6	59.6
2011	12.1	18.1	20.2	7.0	2.7	60.1
2025	12.1	18.6	19.0	8.5	2.9	61.1

Figure 12.2   The age structure (in millions) of the UK population, 1951–2025

	–16	16–39	40–64	65–79	80+	Total
1993 Males	5.9	10.3	8.1	3.0	0.6	27.9
1993 Females	5.6	10.1	8.2	3.9	1.4	29.3
2025 Males	6.2	9.5	9.5	3.9	1.1	30.2
2025 Females	5.9	9.1	9.5	4.6	1.8	30.9

Figure 12.3   The sex structure (in millions) of the UK population, 1993 and 2025

	Births (in thousands)	Birth rate (births per 1000)
1961	944	17.9
1971	902	16.1
1981	731	13.0
1991	826	14.4

Figure 12.4 UK births and birth rates, 1961–1991

population each year' – is the biggest influence on the size and make-up of the population. Quite simply, if the birth rate rises then all things being equal, the population increases too, and vice versa. Looking at the UK from a long-term perspective from 1900 to 1994, the birth rate has fallen dramatically from about 29 to 13 per 1000. This can be attributed to many reasons such as the emancipation and careers of women, better family planning methods and a trend towards smaller families. Two is considered the norm, and perhaps even socially acceptable nowadays, whereas six, eight or even 10 children families were not uncommon earlier in the century. Figure 12.4 lists the UK's births and birth rates from 1951 to 2025.

Changing birth rates have long-term effects; indeed, they last a lifetime! For example, UK births peaked at 1 015 000 in 1964 and troughed at 657 000 in 1977, and this huge difference will be felt for many years. At the start, the State needed to provide substantial health care resources – hospitals, midwives, health visitors – in the 1960s, but far less in the 1970s. Similarly, businesses had a huge babywear and nursery goods market in the mid-1960s but not in the late-1970s. Moving on, the State had to supply educational resources – schools, teachers, textbooks in the 1970s, but not so many in the 1980s. Firms had a huge choice of school-leavers to select from in the 1980s but not in the 1990s, and so forth. A limited number of social and economic needs are given in Figure 12.5 to suggest the changes which occur as the 1964 and 1977 babies grow up, and age.

Deaths

Not surprisingly, death is the second largest influence on the population's size and composition – all things being equal, more deaths will reduce the population, and vice versa. Once again, death is normally regarded in terms of *death rate* which is 'the number of deaths per 1000 of the population each year'. Viewing the UK over the past 100 years, the death rate can be seen to have dropped considerably from around 16 per 1000 in 1901 to about 12 per 1000 in 1994. There are numerous reasons which can be readily identified for this, the most important of which are medical advances and better facilities,

Age	Social and economic needs
0–1	Maternity services, preventive medicine, health visiting
1–5	Day-care facilities, nursery education
5–16	School education
16–21	Further and higher education, training facilities, employment
16–45 (female)	Maternity services
16–65	Employment, transport, housing
60/65+	Retirement pensions
75+	Retirement pensions, health care, home helps, sheltered housing, retirement homes

Figure 12.5   Selected social and economic needs, by age

	Deaths (in thousands)	Death rate (deaths per thousand)
1961	322	12.6
1971	329	12.1
1981	329	12.0
1991	314	11.1

Figure 12.6   UK deaths and death rates, 1961–1991

improved living and working conditions and healthier lifestyles and diets. The UK's deaths and death rates from 1961 to 1991 are given in Figure 12.6.

Like birth rates, death rates have long-term effects and this is most noticeable in the UK where the lower death rate of recent years has resulted in a growing and older population. Living into your 80s is now fairly common, rather than unusual. As a consequence, the State has to provide retirement pensions for more and more people. Similarly, those businesses which build sheltered accommodation units and which run nursing and residential homes are operating in a bigger market as time goes by, which should be of benefit to them.

Migration

Sometimes termed *net migration*, this can be defined as 'the difference between the number of people leaving the population (or emi-

	1988–1992		
	Inflow	Outflow	Balance
Country of last or next residence			
Commonwealth countries			
Australia	25.8	37.8	−12.0
Canada	5.9	9.9	−4.0
New Zealand	12.6	6.9	5.7
African Commonwealth	12.8	6.5	6.3
Bangladesh, India, Sri Lanka	12.2	3.8	8.4
Pakistan	9.5	3.0	6.5
Caribbean	3.6	3.2	0.4
Other	17.9	16.3	1.6
Total Commonwealth	100.4	87.4	13.0
Non-Commonwealth countries			
European Community	62.5	58.3	4.2
Rest of Europe	14.2	12.0	2.2
United States of America	25.3	34.3	−9.0
Rest of America	3.0	3.5	−0.5
Republic of South Africa	8.0	6.2	1.8
Middle East	10.6	12.5	−1.9
Other	19.0	13.6	5.3
Total Non-Commonwealth	142.6	140.4	2.1

Figure 12.7 UK migration (in thousands), 1988–1992

grating) and those entering the population (or immigrating)'. Over the past 100 years, the UK's emigration and immigration figures have levelled out, or thereabouts. For example, the net impact on the UK population in 1986 was the addition of only 18 800 people – a relatively insignificant number given its population of nearly 60 000 000. The major sources of outflows and inflows are much the same – Europe, the USA and Australia. Figure 12.7 details relevant emigration and immigration figures for the UK.

12.3 The occupational distribution of the population

As the name implies, *occupational distribution* is simply a term which is sometimes used to describe 'the distribution of the working population between various occupations'. The phrase, *working population* can be regarded as meaning 'all of those individuals between the ages of 16 and 65 years who are looking for or who are available for work'. Thus, this includes those people who are currently unemployed.

This proportion of the total population, from which businesses draw their human resources, can be viewed in three main ways and in doing so, reveals broad ranging information about economic and business developments in recent years.

By status

Initially, the working population may be classified by employment status as shown in Figure 12.8 which covers the period from 1970 to 1991.

1   Employees

The number of people in employment – working for organizations and other individuals – over the 21-year period has remained constant although the overall workforce has increased during that time. Therefore, 'in real terms', to coin a popular phrase, the proportion of employees has fallen slightly.

2   The self-employed

Working for oneself has been a dream for many people for years and was turned into reality for millions, particularly through the 1980s. The government's economic policies and encouragement plus the threat of unemployment combined to create a 'carrot and stick' situation which persuaded innumerable people, well suited or not, to start their own firms, most often as sole traders.

3   The armed forces

Those numbers employed by the army, navy and airforce fell in real terms through the 1970s and 1980s and will continue to diminish throughout the 1990s with the break up of the old Soviet Union and Eastern bloc requiring a reduced military presence in that part of the world.

4   The unemployed

Clearly, unemployment has risen dramatically through the 1980s and into the 1990s to become a huge, ever present economic problem. A

	Employees	Self-employed	Armed forces	Unemployed	Training schemes	Total
1970	22.9	1.8	0.4	0.6	N/A	25.7
1980	23.0	2.0	0.3	1.5	N/A	26.8
1989	22.7	3.3	0.3	1.8	0.5	28.6
1990	22.9	3.3	0.3	1.6	0.4	28.5
1991	22.2	3.1	0.3	2.3	0.4	28.3

Figure 12.8 The UK working population (in millions), 1970–1991

	Males	Females	Total
1970	16.4	9.3	25.7
1980	16.2	10.5	26.8
1989	16.3	12.2	28.6
1990	16.3	12.2	28.5
1991	16.2	12.1	28.3

Figure 12.9   The UK working population (in millions), by sex, 1970–1991

portion of those people who are unemployed have left the register to attend training courses to provide them with new skills to apply for jobs in different trades and industries.

By sex

Naturally, the occupational distribution of the working population can be regrouped according to male or female sex, as seen in Figure 12.9. The past 20 years or so have been characterized by stagnation of the male workforce and the rapid and dramatic growth of the female labour force. The number of working women has increased for several reasons, some of which appear to be relatively trivial at first glance but are valid nonetheless. As examples, a growing sense of status and equality has encouraged more and more women to pursue careers. The trend towards smaller families shortens the period of time during which women are (more likely to be) tied to the home, giving them a longer working life and opportunity for a career. The decline of older, heavier industries and the development of newer, service industries has reduced male work opportunities and increased female work opportunities, often on a part-time basis which suits working mothers.

By sector

Whether employed or self-employed, male or female, the working population can also be reclassified in terms of the type of work that they do. There are innumerable trades and industries, but they can be gathered together into three, major categories as seen in Figure 12.10.

	Primary sector	Secondary sector	Tertiary sector
1961	6.5	46.8	46.7
1971	3.9	43.4	52.6
1981	3.2	37.4	59.4
1991	3.0	35.5	61.5

Figure 12.10 The occupational distribution of the UK workforce (by percentage) 1961–1991

1 *The primary sector*

Concerned with the extraction of raw materials such as coal and the production of food, this sector has been in gradual decline for some time. This is a common feature of most developing countries which tend to move away from primary industries into secondary and then service industries.

2 *The secondary sector*

This sector is involved with manufacturing and construction – traditional, male-dominated industries such as shipbuilding and engineering. Again, this sector can be seen to be in decline, and accounts for much unemployment.

3 *The tertiary sector*

Also known as the *service sector*, industries such as banking, insurance and tourism have escalated rapidly in recent years, and account for much of the growth in female employment as women have traditionally done these types of jobs.

12.4 The geographical distribution of the population

If the term *occupational distribution* can be defined as 'the distribution of the working population between various occupations' then the phrase *geographical distribution* might equally well be described as 'the distribution of the population between different regions'. In geographical terms, the population of the UK is distinguished by these key features:

1   It is city based. The UK's population is an urban rather than a rural one, with about 80 per cent of the people located in and around towns and cities and only 20 per cent or thereabouts based in the countryside. Figure 12.11 shows how the bulk of the population is gathered together around London, Birmingham, Manchester, Newcastle and the like and relatively sparse in places such as Lincolnshire, Norfolk and Somerset.

2   It is densely inhabited. There are more people per square mile in the UK than there are in most other developed countries around the world. A closer examination of Figure 12.11 indicates that there are 2000 or more persons per square mile in some of the more heavily populated areas – a phenomenal figure.

3   It is unevenly distributed. A further look at Figure 12.11 and an examination of the figures given at the bottom illustrates that the population is spread unevenly across the country. As an example, the South East has nearly five times as many people as the South West.

The geographical distribution of the population is closely linked to its occupational distribution. In the 19th century, the population gathered where the work was, such as around the coal mines in Yorkshire and although heavy duty industries such as this may be dying out, generations of people have accumulated and rooted themselves in those regions. In the 20th century, the population grew around the manufacturing and construction industries in London, the West Midlands and the like. Again, generations grew up there, increasing the population. Nowadays, with the service industries, improved technology and easier communications, there is a trend for firms and individuals to locate away from heavily urbanized areas to more pleasant rural ones. For example, there is a steady drift of the population from London to East Anglia. Thus, the geographical distribution may change in the coming years (see Figure 12.12).

12.5   Rapid revision

Answers	Questions
–	1 What is the population?
1 It is the total number of people living in a given area at a particular time.	2 Why is the population of significance to businesses?

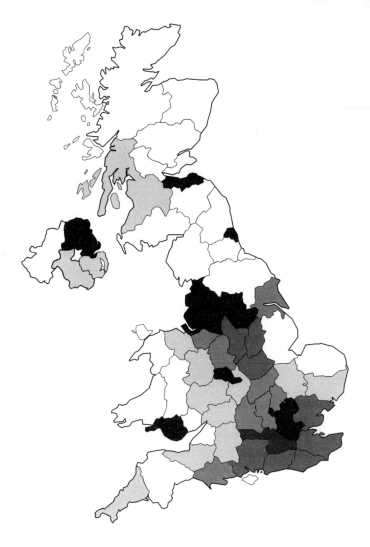

	Less than 250 persons per mile^2		750–999 persons per mile^2
	250–499 persons per mile^2		1000–1999 persons per mile^2
	500–749 persons per mile^2		2000 and over persons per mile^2

Figure 12.11 The UK population, by density

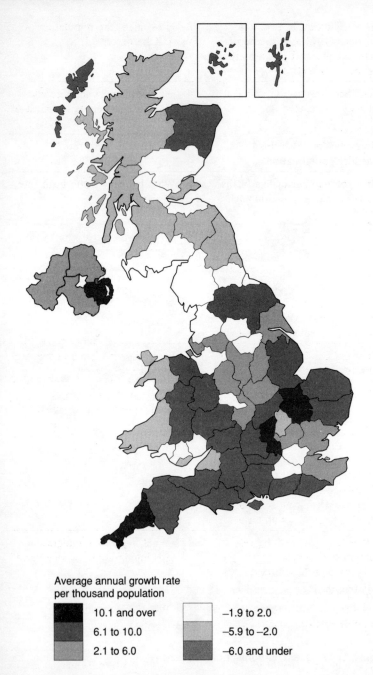

Average annual growth rate
per thousand population

■ 10.1 and over	□ −1.9 to 2.0
■ 6.1 to 10.0	▨ −5.9 to −2.0
▨ 2.1 to 6.0	■ −6.0 and under

Figure 12.12   The UK population, by change

2 It is significant in two, key ways, namely (a) as a source of human resources; (b) as a market for goods and services.

3 How might the population of the UK be described?

---

3 The best description is that it is a growing and ageing one.

4 What influences the size and structure of the population most of all?

---

4 In particular (a) births; (b) deaths; (c) migration.

5 What is the birth rate?

---

5 It is the number of live births per 1000 of the population each year.

6 What happens if the birth rate rises or falls?

---

6 All things being equal, the population increases or decreases accordingly.

7 Why has the birth rate fallen so dramatically in the UK?

---

7 Various reasons, including (a) female emancipation; (b) better family planning methods; (c) a trend towards smaller families.

8 What is the death rate?

---

8 It is the number of deaths per 1000 of the population each year.

9 What happens if the death rate increases or decreases?

---

9 Again, all things being equal, the population will fall or rise, as appropriate.

10 Why has the death rate dropped considerably in the UK?

---

10 Numerous reasons, incorporating (a) medical advances; (b) better medical facilities; (c) improved living conditions; (d) improved working conditions; (e) healthier lifestyles and diets.

11 What is migration?

---

11 It is the difference between the number of people leaving the population and those entering the population.

12 What happens if emigration exceeds immigration, or vice versa?

---

12 All things being equal, the population will decrease, or vice versa.

13 What is occupational distribution?

---

13 It is the distribution of the working population between various occupations.

14 What is the working population?

14   It is all those individuals between the ages of 16 and 65 years who are looking for or who are available for work. It includes unemployed people.

15   What are the three main ways of viewing the working population?

---

15   (a) By status; (b) by sex; (c) by sector.

16   How can the working population be divided up and seen in terms of status?

---

16   It can be divided into (a) employees; (b) the self-employed; (c) the armed forces; (d) the unemployed.

17   How has the working population of the UK changed in recent years, with regard to status?

---

17   In summary (a) employees, slightly down; (b) the self-employed, considerably up; (c) the armed forces, slightly down; (d) the unemployed, substantially up.

18   How has the working population of the UK altered in recent years, in relation to male and female employment?

---

18   In brief (a) male employment, much the same; (b) female employment, rapid and dramatic growth.

19   Why has the female working population increased so much?

---

19   Various reasons, such as (a) a growing sense of status and equality; (b) a trend towards smaller families; (c) the decline of older, heavier industries; (d) the development of newer, service industries.

20   How can the working population be classified when viewed in terms of sector?

---

20   It can be classified by (a) the primary sector; (b) the secondary sector; (c) the tertiary sector.

21   How has the working population of the UK developed in recent years, in terms of the different sectors?

---

21   In short (a) primary sector, declining; (b) secondary sector, declining; (c) tertiary sector, growing.

22   What is geographical distribution?

---

22   It is the distribution of the population between different regions.

23   What are the key features of the UK population in geographical terms?

---

23   It is (a) city based; (b) densely inhabited; (c) unevenly distributed.

24   What is the major influence on geographical distribution?

24 The occupational distribution – people go where the work is.

25 Go over the questions again until you know all of the answers. Then move on to the next section.

Part Five
The International Environment

13
The United Kingdom

13.1 How important is international trade to the UK?

International trade is of vital importance to most countries including the UK and for a variety of reasons which are best illustrated by a simple but effective example. Imagine a (typical) country with a certain mix of resources, perhaps huge quantities of some raw materials but relatively few of others, a pool of skilled human resources, equipment and machinery which is geared up to producing a particular range of products but not other ones. Like many countries, this nation wishes to be self-sufficient, providing everything that is needed and desired by its own businesses and people, with surpluses left over which can be sold to foreign countries for a profit.

As often happens, it is able to achieve this common aim in some respects. There are enough of those raw materials to satisfy everyone at home and to have sufficient amounts remaining to sell abroad. Similarly, those particular products meet the demand from domestic consumers and more besides, with additional goods being sold overseas. In other ways, the country cannot meet its objective and like the vast majority of its fellow nations needs to purchase some of the other raw materials and products required by its own firms and people (and which it cannot provide) from abroad. Hence, it will sell to and buy from other countries which are in the same, basic position as it is.

Of course, what often occurs in practice is that a country can produce some goods very well, and others extremely badly – a neighbouring country (or countries) is able to manufacture better and/or cheaper ones. Thus, it tends to concentrate on what it does best, therefore becoming even more efficient and successful as continued practice makes perfect (or as near as possible). It it persisted in producing the other, second rate items itself, then it would simply divert resources away from those goods which can be made very well and be producing more expensive and/or inferior products which its firms and people did not really want. Clearly, it is more sensible to specialize in those goods where it has the greatest relative (or comparative) advantage, selling these and buying those in which its comparative advantage is less.

Like most countries in the world, the UK is a nation which relies heavily on international trade for its prosperity. It needs to sell products and services overseas in order to pay its way and to buy other goods and services from abroad for its home-based businesses and people to use. It is worthwhile to have a basic knowledge of the UK's exports and imports, and how they merge together to form the country's balance of payments.

13.2 UK exports

Exports can be defined and classified in three main ways. They may be described as 'products that are made in the home country and which are then transported and sold to foreign countries, thus earning foreign currencies for that home country'. These are commonly known as *visible exports* which can be seen, touched and felt – anything from wheat through bags of cement to televisions. Figure 13.1 shows the value of the UK's visible exports in recent years.

They could also refer to 'services that are provided for overseas businesses and/or individuals either in the home country and/or abroad, and which produce foreign currencies for the home country'. An example of a service supplied within the home country might be trips for tourists, whereby foreign visitors are bringing money into the country, and spending it here. Examples of services provided overseas could include banking and insurance. These various services are more usually known as *invisible exports*, because they cannot be seen. Nevertheless, they do generate enormous sums for a country. Figure 13.1 highlights the UK's invisible exports in recent years.

Often ignored or ill considered, a third category of exports is 'capital which is located abroad in the form of bank deposits or investments in shares or physical assets'. Perhaps an individual can obtain a higher rate of return from a French bank than one in the UK, a German 'aktiengesellschaft' may do rather better than the equivalent UK public limited company, and an expanding home-based firm may purchase plant and equipment in the growing Scandinavian markets. These are all *capital exports*. Figure 13.2 shows the UK's total exports in 1991.

13.3 UK imports

In many respects, imports may be described and grouped along very similar lines to exports. The first group comprises 'goods which are produced overseas and are then brought to and sold in the home

	1987	1988	1989	1990	1991
CURRENT ACCOUNT					
Visible trade					
Exports (fob)	79,153	80,346	92,154	101,718	103,413
Imports (fob)	90,735	101,826	116,837	120,527	113,703
Visible balance	−11,582	−21,480	−24,683	−18,809	−10,290
Invisibles					
Credits	79,826	87,739	107,778	115,150	116,164
Debits	72,726	82,438	104,821	113,370	112,195
Invisibles balance	7,099	5,302	2,956	1,778	3,969
of which:					
Services balance	6,745	4,397	4,039	4,581	4,990
Interest, profits and dividends balance	3,754	4,423	3,495	2,094	328
Transfers balance	−3,400	−3,518	−4,578	−4,897	−1,349
CURRENT BALANCE	−4,482	−16,179	−21,726	−17,029	−6,321
TRANSACTIONS IN EXTERNAL ASSETS AND LIABILITIES					
Investment overseas by UK residents					
Direct	−19,239	−20,944	−21,515	−9,553	−10,261
Portfolio	5,163	−11,239	−35,486	−15,844	−30,908
Total UK investment overseas	−14,076	−32,183	−57,001	−25,397	−41,169
Investment in the UK by overseas residents					
Direct	9,449	12,006	18,567	18,634	12,045
Portfolio	19,535	15,564	14,603	5,276	16,627
Total overseas investment in UK	28,984	27,570	33,170	23,910	28,672
Foreign currency lending abroad by UK banks	−45,867	−15,064	−25,689	−37,440	27,394
Foreign currency borrowing abroad by UK banks	43,566	20,447	32,338	34,992	−14,802
Net foreign currency transactions of UK banks	−2,301	5,383	6,649	−2,448	12,592
Sterling lending abroad by UK banks	−4,633	−4,626	−2,923	−3,800	4,837
Sterling borrowing and deposit liabilities abroad					
of UK banks	8,867	13,641	12,401	12,620	−9,222
Net sterling transactions of UK banks	4,234	9,015	9,478	8,820	−4,385
Deposits with and lending to banks abroad by					
UK non-bank private sector	−4,914	−4,025	−9,334	−8,280	−3,580
Borrowing from banks abroad by:					
UK non-bank private sector	2,075	3,973	8,017	10,006	13,032
Public corporations	−166	−253	−1,726	−127	−49
General government	104	−10	529	−363	−65
Official reserves (additions to −, drawings on +)	−12,012	−2,761	5,440	−79	−2,662
Other external assets of:					
UK non-bank private sector and public					
corporations	93	1,070	1,468	−3,479	−4,707
General government	−796	−887	−873	−1,025	−894
Other external liabilities of:					
UK non-bank private sector and public					
corporations	1,382	1,664	21,191	8,272	10,710
General government	1,725	842	2,252	1,281	−2,246
NET TRANSACTIONS IN ASSETS AND LIABILITIES	4,334	9,396	19,259	11,091	5,249
BALANCING ITEM	148	6,783	2,467	5,938	1,072

*Assets: increase −/decrease +
 Liabilities: increase +/decrease −

Figure 13.1 UK balance of payments, 1987–1991

country, consequently leading to an outflow of foreign currencies from that country'. These are tangible, solid items like cars and washing machines, and are normally referred to as *visible imports*. The UK's visible imports in recent years can be seen in Figure 13.1.

A second, and equally important, grouping can be defined as 'services which are supplied to domestic firms and/or people by foreign

	£ million
	£ million

TOTAL UK EXPORTS — 104,877.0

Food and live animals chiefly for food — 4,715.8
Live animals chiefly for food — 288.4
Meat and meat preparations — 672.6
Dairy products and birds' eggs — 451.9
Fish, crustaceans and molluscs, and preparations thereof — 574.4
Cereals and cereal preparations — 1,102.8
Vegetables and fruit — 298.5
Sugar, sugar preparations and honey — 247.5
Coffee, tea, cocoa, spices and manufactures thereof — 465.2
Feeding-stuff for animals (not including unmilled cereals) — 302.6
Miscellaneous edible products and preparations — 311.7

Beverages and tobacco — 3,031.8
Beverages — 2,251.7
Tobacco and tobacco manufactures — 780.3

Crude materials, inedible, except fuels — 1,919.7
Hides, skins and furskins, raw — 135.1
Oil seeds and oleaginous fruit — 52.6
Crude rubber (including synthetic and reclaimed) — 198.1
Cork and wood — 27.9
Pulp and waste paper — 38.8
Textile fibres (other than wool tops) and their wastes (not manufactured into yarn or fabric) — 466.2
Crude fertilizers and crude minerals (excluding coal, petroleum and precious stones) — 365.5
Metalliferous ores and metal scrap — 526.9
Crude animal and vegetable materials — 108.5

Mineral fuels, lubricants and related materials — 7,169.0
Petroleum, petroleum products and related materials — 6,814.1
Coal, coke, gas and electric current — 355.0

Animal and vegetable oils, fats and waxes — 95.9

Total manufactured goods — 86,137.2

Chemicals and related products — 13,788.6
Organic chemicals — 3,468.4
Inorganic chemicals — 1,000.6
Dyeing, tanning and colouring materials — 1,216.4
Medicinal and pharmaceutical products — 2,556.1
Essential oils and perfume materials; toilet, polishing and cleansing materials — 1,298.4
Fertilizers, manufactured — 103.2
Plastics in primary forms — 1,332.9
Plastics in non-primary forms — 786.9
Chemical materials — 2,025.7

Manufactured goods classified chiefly by material — 15,581.1
Leather, leather manufactures, nes, and dressed furskins — 258.0
Rubber manufactures, nes — 887.9
Cork and wood manufactures (excluding furniture) — 116.4
Paper, paperboard, and articles of paper pulp, of paper or of paperboard — 1,623.8
Textile yarn, fabrics, made-up articles, nes, and related products — 2,349.0
Non-metallic mineral manufactures, nes — 3,177.1
Iron and steel — 3,011.3
Non-ferrous metals — 1,975.2
Manufactures of metal, nes — 2,182.4

Machinery and transport equipment — 43,627.1
Power generating machinery and equipment — 5,073.1
Machinery specialized for particular industries — 3,922.1
Metalworking machinery — 812.5
General industrial machinery and equipment, nes, and machine parts, nes — 4,520.6
Office machines and automatic data processing equipment — 6,590.9
Telecommunications and sound recording and reproducing apparatus and equipment — 2,942.8
Electrical machinery, apparatus and appliances, nes, and electrical parts thereof (including non-electrical counterparts, nes, of electrical household type equipment) — 5,709.7
Road vehicles (including air cushion vehicles) — 8,555.4
Other transport equipment — 5,500.2

Miscellaneous manufactured articles — 13,140.4
Sanitary, plumbing, heating and lighting fixtures and fittings, nes — 267.3
Furniture and parts thereof — 564.2
Travel goods, handbags and similar containers — 72.4
Articles of apparel and clothing accessories — 1,920.1
Footwear — 314.8
Professional, scientific and controlling instruments and apparatus, nes — 2,992.7
Photographic apparatus, equipment and supplies and optical goods, nes, watches and clocks — 1,266.1
Miscellaneous manufactured articles, nes — 5,742.9

Commodities and transactions not classified elsewhere — 1,807.6

* provisional
nes not elsewhere specified

Figure 13.2   UK total exports, 1991

bodies either in the domestic country or abroad, and which result in outgoings of foreign currencies from that domestic country'. If a UK-based person goes on an overseas holiday, he or she is effectively receiving a service from a foreign country and taking money out of the home country. Accordingly, if an insurance company in Europe provides insurance cover for a UK business in exchange for premiums, this service falls into the same category too. Such services are called *invisible imports*. Figure 13.1 shows the value of the UK's invisible imports in recent years.

The third group consists of 'capital that is placed within the home country by foreign organizations and individuals, and invested in the shape of bank deposits, shares or physical assets'. Quite obviously, if foreign bodies can see ways of making more money in the UK than elsewhere then they are going to locate or spend their capital in this country, rather than abroad. These are *capital imports* and contribute much to the wealth of a country. Figure 13.3 details the UK's total imports for 1991.

13.4 The balance of payments

The balance of payments of a country is simply a balance sheet which represents the monies that have flowed into and out of that country over a period of time. It summarizes all of the financial transactions made by individuals, organizations and the government, from the family spending money on a foreign holiday through the manufacturer exporting or importing goods to the government providing aid for less developed countries. By definition, the balance of payments must balance, although it is made up of various accounts which may be in surplus or in deficit. Figure 13.1 shows the balance of payments statements for the UK in recent years. Component parts which are as follows.

The current account

This account records all payments for goods and services and can be subdivided into *visible trade* and *invisible trade* accounts. Not surprisingly, the visible trade account deals with tangible goods such as motor cars. Deducting imports from exports leaves the visible balance or *balance of trade*, in popular jargon. When visible imports exceed visible exports, the deficit is commonly referred to as *the trade gap*. The invisible trade account concerns itself with the sales and purchases of invisible services, such as banking, insurance and tourism. The sum of the visible and invisible balances is the *current account*

	£ million		£ million
		Manufactured goods classified chiefly by material	20,519.9
TOTAL UK IMPORTS	118,786.0	Leather, leather manufactures, nes, and dressed furskins	185.9
Food and live animals chiefly for food	10,389.3	Rubber manufactures, nes	872.2
Live animals chiefly for food	203.3	Cork and wood manufactures (excluding furniture)	821.2
Meat and meat preparations	1,845.0	Paper, paperboard, and articles of paper pulp, of paper or of paperboard	3,868.4
Dairy products and birds' eggs	871.0		
Fish, crustaceans and molluscs, and preparations thereof	978.5	Textile yarn, fabrics, made-up articles, nes, and related products	3,738.0
Cereals and cereal preparations	818.5	Non-metallic mineral manufactures, nes	3,332.9
Vegetables and fruit	3,002.6	Iron and steel	2,620.2
Sugar, sugar preparations and honey	681.2	Non-ferrous metals	2,557.9
Coffee, tea, cocoa, spices and manufactures thereof	869.7	Manufactures of metal, nes	2,523.1
Feeding-stuff for animals (not including unmilled cereals)	619.1	*Machinery and transport equipment*	43,101.6
Miscellaneous edible products and preparations	500.4	Power generating machinery and equipment	3,345.5
		Machinery specialized for particular industries	3,005.6
Beverages and tobacco	1,936.1	Metalworking machinery	860.7
Beverages	1,464.8	General industrial machinery and equipment, nes, and machine parts, nes	4,202.8
Tobacco and tobacco manufactures	471.3		
Crude materials, inedible, except fuels	4,678.3	Office machines and automatic data processing equipment	7,586.5
Hides, skins and furskins, raw	68.8	Telecommunications, sound recording and reproducing apparatus and equipment	3,351.2
Oil seeds and oleaginous fruit	224.0		
Crude rubber (including synthetic and reclaimed)	223.6	Electrical machinery, apparatus and appliances, nes, and electrical parts thereof (including non-electrical counterparts, nes, of electrical household type equipment)	7,078.4
Cork and wood	1,043.7		
Pulp and waste paper	608.0		
Textile fibres (other than wool tops) and their wastes (not manufactured into yarn or fabric)	452.6	Road vehicles (including air cushion vehicles)	10,227.2
		Other transport equipment	3,443.7
Crude fertilizers and crude minerals (excluding coal, petroleum and precious stones)	284.8	*Miscellaneous manufactured articles*	17,559.3
		Sanitary, plumbing, heating and lighting fixtures and fittings, nes	368.3
Metalliferous ores and metal scrap	1,232.7	Furniture and parts thereof	1,004.7
Crude animal and vegetable materials	540.1	Travel goods, handbags and similar containers	285.1
Mineral fuels, lubricants and related materials	7,510.7	Articles of apparel and clothing accessories	4,128.5
Petroleum, petroleum products and related materials	5,773.6	Footwear	1,169.0
Coal, coke, gas and electric current	1,737.1	Professional, scientific and controlling instruments and apparatus, nes	2,525.1
Animal and vegetable oils, fats and waxes	387.5	Photographic apparatus, equipment and supplies and optical goods, nes, watches and clocks	1,565.5
Total manufactured goods	92,159.4	Miscellaneous manufactured articles, nes	6,513.3
Chemicals and related products	10,978.6		
Organic chemicals	2,618.4	*Commodities and transactions not classified elsewhere*	1,724.7
Inorganic chemicals	1,033.5		
Dyeing, tanning and colouring materials	620.9		
Medicinal and pharmaceutical products	1,371.2		
Essential oils and perfume materials; toilet, polishing and cleansing materials	798.1		
Fertilizers, manufactured	283.0		
Plastics in primary forms	2,053.1		
Plastics in non-primary forms	976.6		
Chemical materials	1,223.7		

* provisional
nes not elsewhere specified

Figure 13.3   UK total imports, 1991

balance which may be in surplus or in deficit – only by extreme coincidence will they cancel each other out, leaving a zero balance.

The capital account

Known more formally as the *Investment and Capital Flows Account*, this sets out all investment and capital transfers into and out of a country. These transfers include government loans and borrowings plus individuals' and organizations' investments abroad, perhaps on plant, equipment and machinery. The account also incorporates the inflow and outflow of speculative capital (or *hot money*) whereby governments, organizations and individuals transfer monies into and out of a country, trying to maximize their returns from the varying rates of interest available in different countries.

The balancing item

An allowance has to be made for any errors or omissions that occur when inflows and outflows are recorded, and this allowance is noted down as a *balancing item*. Quite simply, mistakes are made from time to time – perhaps by traders who might record the wrong prices or by the government which collates the huge mass of figures and puts them into order.

Official financing

If the balance of payments shows an overall deficit, this means that the country has spent more than it has received – not a good sign! Such overspending has to be financed in some way. Hence, the country has to either draw on any foreign currency reserves which may have accrued during surplus years or it must borrow from international organizations which provide finance for such eventualities. Should there be an overall surplus in the balance of payments, the country can either increase its foreign currency reserves or pay back any debts that may have been incurred during earlier, deficit years.

Balancing the books

Naturally, the government of a country will try to maintain a balance of payments equilibrium, or at least attempt to avoid year-on-year deficits which cannot be tolerated on a continuing basis – eventually its foreign currency reserves will be used up and its borrowings curtailed. A government can endeavour to 'balance the books' in various ways, including these most popular ones:

1 *Reducing its overseas aid and expenditure*

This is perhaps the obvious remedy to overspending, or at the very least a significant contributory factor towards improving matters. Such an approach was possible for the UK in the late 1980s and early 1990s when the changing situation in Eastern Europe enabled the country to reduce its military expenditure in that part of the world.

2 *Encouraging exports*

The government may be able to encourage businesses to export goods and services, perhaps by persuading banks and other financial institutions to finance their activities at preferential rates, by offering grants for would-be exporters to assess potential markets and by providing tax relief on overseas investment.

3 *Devaluing the home currency*

Dropping the value of the home currency so that £1 can be exchanged for $1 instead of perhaps $2 previously is a drastic step which consequently makes exports cheaper and more attractive to foreign buyers, while simultaneously making imports more costly and less appealing to home-based purchasers.

4 *Discouraging imports*

The government may dissuade businesses from importing goods and services, possibly by introducing import controls such as *tariffs* and *quotas*. Tariffs are taxes that are charged on particular or all imports, thus making them more expensive and unattractive in the domestic marketplace. Of course, home producers need to be sufficiently competitive to undercut the overpriced imports otherwise sales will continue relatively unabated, and at the home consumers' expense.

Quotas are restrictions on the number of (certain types of) goods that can be brought into a country over a particular period of time. *Statutory quotas* are imposed by the government whereas *voluntary quotas* are agreed informally by and between relevant organizations. As an example of a voluntary quota, an agreement exists between Japanese car manufacturers and those countries which comprise the European Union whereby Japan's car imports into Europe are limited to agreed levels.

Supporters of import controls claim they are beneficial, helping to protect domestic producers and ensuring that they survive and prosper and people within those industries remain in employment. Opponents believe that they simply protect inefficient businesses whose resources would be used better elsewhere and that home consumers suffer through unnecessarily restricted choice and higher prices. Also, other countries may respond unfavourably to import restrictions, perhaps by introducing reciprocal tariffs and quotas in retaliation.

13.5 Rapid revision

Answers	Questions
–	1 How important is international trade, and why?
1 It is very important. A country needs to sell goods overseas to pay its way and must buy other goods which it cannot provide (or cannot provide well) for its businesses and people.	2 What are the three main types of export?
2 (a) Visible exports; (b) invisible exports; (c) capital exports.	3 What are visible exports?
3 They are products that are made in the home country and which are then transported and sold to foreign countries, thus earning foreign currencies for that home country.	4 What are invisible exports?
4 They are services that are provided for overseas businesses and/or individuals either in the home country and/or abroad, and which provide foreign currencies for the home country.	5 What are capital exports?

5   They take the form of capital located abroad in the shape of bank deposits or investments in shares or physical assets.

6   What are the three key types of import?

---

6   (a) Visible imports; (b) invisible imports; (c) capital imports.

7   What are visible imports?

---

7   They are goods which are produced overseas and are then brought to and sold in the home country, consequently leading to an outflow of foreign currencies from that country.

8   What are invisible imports?

---

8   They are services which are supplied to domestic firms and/or people by foreign bodies either in the domestic country or abroad, and which result in outgoings of foreign currencies from that domestic country.

9   What are capital imports?

---

9   They are capital placed within the home country by foreign organizations and individuals, and invested in the shape of bank deposits, shares or physical assets.

10   What is a balance of payments statement?

---

10   It is a balance sheet which summarizes the monies that have flowed into and out of a country over a period of time.

11   What are the component parts of a balance of payments statement?

---

11   (a) The current account; (b) the capital account; (c) the balancing item; (d) official financing.

12   What is the balance of trade?

---

12   It is another name for the visible trade balance, reached by deducting visible imports from visible exports.

13   What is the trade gap?

---

13   It is popular jargon for the visible trade deficit when visible imports exceed visible exports.

14   What is the current account balance?

---

14   It is the sum of the visible and invisible balances in the current account.

15   What are the main ways of balancing the books of a country?

15 (a) Reducing overseas aid and expenditure; (b) encouraging exports; (c) devaluing the home currency; (d) discouraging imports.

16 Go over the questions again until you know all of the answers. Then move on to the next section.

14
Europe

14.1 Who's who in Europe

Nowadays, many UK businesses trade as much in Europe as they do
in their own country – indeed, most of them are beginning to regard
the continent as little more than an extended home market, full of
opportunities for growth and expansion. The European Union (EU),
the Single Market, the European Monetary System, the European
Free Trade Association, the European Economic Area Agreement
and numerous other international organizations and agreements are
all of primary concern to the domestic firms trading in the 1990s, and
beyond.

14.2 The European Union

The EU is a group of 12 countries working together for political
cooperation and economic success and is bound by three international treaties, namely the European Coal and Steel Community
Treaty signed in Paris in 1951 and the European Economic Community and European Atomic Energy Community treaties signed
in Rome in 1957 by France, Belgium, Germany, Italy, Luxembourg
and the Netherlands. This original group of six was joined by the
UK, Ireland and Denmark in 1973, Greece in 1981 and Portugal and
Spain in 1986. The three treaties have since been amended and
updated in various ways by the Single European Act of 1987 and the
Maastricht Treaty of 1991, to make the European Union what it is
today. There are four key institutions, based mainly in Belgium and
Luxembourg.

The Commission

The Commission proposes policies and legislation, supervises the day-
to-day running of policies and makes sure that member states comply

with EU rules and regulations. It consists of 17 members appointed by Union governments and each member state has at least one national sitting on the Commission. The UK has two. Of the 17 Commissioners – best likened to a board of directors albeit without absolute authority – one is President, six are Vice-Presidents and the remaining 10 are Members of the Commission. Commissioners are normally appointed for a four-year term. Those appointed in 1992 are listed in Figure 14.1.

Each Commissioner is responsible for particular areas of Union policy, and formulates policies within these areas which are then discussed by all of the Commissioners who decide on the exact nature of the finalized proposals. Decisions are reached by majority verdict. Every Commissioner has a Cabinet of six or more administrators plus secretarial support. Usually, Cabinet staff are the same nationality as their Commissioner. Inter-Cabinet committees (Chefs de Cabinet or Chefs) exist to identify those issues on which the Commissioner should focus at weekly meetings and to handle lesser matters, subject to formal approval by the Commissioner.

Most of the European Commission's personnel – administrators, translators, secretaries, messengers, drivers and the like – are referred to as 'the Services' in order to distinguish them from the Commissioners and their Cabinets. These Services are responsible for all of the technical preparation of EU legislation as well as its implementation – dogsbody duties, in short! The Services are staffed mostly by career officials recruited from across the 12 member states, and currently total approximately 12 000 in number.

The Council

The Council is the EU's decision-making body, adopting legislation on the basis of proposals made by the Commission. Council meetings are attended by the relevant ministers from the member states who have a set number of votes based on the relative populations of their countries. The respective votes are given in Figure 14.2. Most measures are subject to majority voting although unanimous agreement is required on politically sensitive issues such as taxation and employee's rights. Representatives of the Commission are also present at Council meetings and participate in discussions but do not vote. Council legislation can take several forms, as follows:

1 Regulations. These are directly applicable to all member states and have a binding legal effect on them. If there is a conflict between a regulation and an existing national law, the regulation takes priority.

President of the Commission

Jacques Delors

Secretariat General
Forward Studies Unit
Inspectorate General
Legal Service
Monetary affairs
Spokesmen's service

Members of the Commission

Henning Christophersen
(Denmark)

Economic and financial affairs
Monetary affairs (in agreement
with President Delors)
Credit and investments
Statistical Office

Manuel Marin
(Spain)

Cooperation and development
Economic cooperation relations
with the countries of the Southern
Mediterranean, Middle East,
Near East, Latin America and Asia
European Emergency Humanitarian
Aid Office

Martin Bangemann
(Germany)

Industrial affairs
Information and
telecommunications technology

Leon Brittan (UK)

External economic affairs (North
America, Japan, China, CIS,
Europe including Central and
Eastern Europe)
Commercial policy

Abel Matutes
(Spain)

Energy
Transport

Peter Schmidhuber
(Germany)

Budget
Financial control
Anti-fraud
Cohesion funds: coordination and
management

Christiane Scrivener
(France)

Customs and indirect taxation
Direct taxation
Consumer policy

Bruce Millan
(UK)

Regional policy
Committee of the Regions

Karel van Miert
(Belgium)

Competition policy
Personnel and Administration

Hans van den Broek
(Netherlands)

External political relations

Enlargement negotiations

(continued)

Figure 14.1   EU Commissioners, 1992

Joao Pinheiro (Portugal)	Relations with European Parliament Relations with Member States on transparency, communications and information Culture and audio-visual
Padraig Flynn (Ireland)	Social affairs and employment Relations with the Economic and Social Committee Questions linked to migration and interior/justice affairs
Antonio Ruberti (Italy)	Science, research and development Joint Research Centre Human resources, education, training and youth
Rene Steichen (Luxembourg)	Agriculture and rural development
Yannis Paleokrassas (Greece)	Environment, nuclear safety and civil protection Fisheries policy
Raniero Vanni d'Archirafi (Italy)	Institutional questions Internal market Financial services Enterprise policy: small and medium-sized enterprises

Figure 14.1 (*continued*)

Member states	Number of votes
United Kingdom	10
Germany	10
France	10
Italy	10
Spain	8
Belgium	5
Greece	5
Netherlands	5
Portugal	5
Denmark	3
Ireland	3
Luxembourg	2

Figure 14.2 EU Council votes

2   Directives, or instructions. Again these are binding on member states in that a particular result must be achieved within a certain timespan although the method of achieving that result is left to the individual State to select.
3   Decisions. These are specific to particular parties and are binding on those involved, whether individuals, companies or member states.
4   Opinions, or recommendations. These have no binding force although it may be wise for the relevant parties to take note of them!

Over a period of time, various specialist Councils have evolved in order to deal with particular areas of policy. The main ones are concerned with agriculture, finance, industry, research, labour and social affairs. In addition to ordinary and specialist Council meetings, a European Council, often referred to as the European Summit, has been established at head of government level, whereby these leaders meet on a regular, bi-annual basis to discuss broad ranging areas of policy.

The Parliament

The European Parliament is a directly elected body, consisting of 518 members, of which 81 are from the UK. Members of the European Parliament (MEPs) are elected for a period of five years at a time, 1989 to 1994, 1994 to 1999 and so on. Parliament's formal opinion is required on most proposals before they can be adopted by the Council. Usually, proposals are subject to a cooperation procedure whereby Parliament gives an initial opinion as and when the Commission makes a proposal and follows this with a final opinion once the Council has reached an 'in-principle' decision.

The Court of Justice

The European Court of Justice (ECJ) rules on the interpretation and application of EU laws. It has 13 judges, incorporating one from each member state. The Court's judgements are binding in each Union country and under the terms of the various EU treaties take precedence over each individual State's national laws. A Court of First Instance has been attached to the ECJ to relieve it of some of its substantial workload.

Other bodies

Several other institutions exist within the Union, in particular:

1 *The Economic and Social Committee*

Based in Brussels, this is an advisory body of 189 members comprising representatives of employers, trade unions and other interested groups such as consumers; 24 members are from the UK. The Committee has to be consulted by the Commission on any economic and social proposals before they are made, and by the Council prior to becoming law.

2 *The Court of Auditors*

With its headquarters in Luxembourg, the role of this Court is to audit the Union's revenues and expenditure – a substantial and complex task.

3 *The European Investment Bank*

Also based in Luxembourg, the EIB forwards funds to finance investment projects which are designed to contribute to the balanced development of the Union.

14.3 The Single Market

The *Single Market* and *1992* are simply shorthand expressions which refer to an agreement made by EU heads of government in 1985 whereby trade barriers within the Union would be removed by the end of 1992. The aim was to create 'an area without internal frontiers in which the free movement of goods, persons, services and capital is ensured'. Hence, it would be as easy to trade with businesses and individuals in the rest of the Union as it is between those in the same member state. The heads of government considered that this goal had been achieved by the time of the Edinburgh Summit in December 1992, stating that the 1985 programme was complete in all essential respects.

The Common Market, as it can also be called, has these key features which were developed successfully by the European Union during the period 1985 to 1992 (and continued thereafter) through a mixture of regulations, directives, decisions and recommendations, totalling more than 1000 in all across the whole gamut of trades and industries.

The free movement of goods and services

Member states are not allowed to maintain restrictions (or measures which have the equivalent effect) on products or services from fellow member states. Measures that have been prohibited include discriminating between home-produced and foreign items in any way, setting onerous technical standards and testing procedures, establishing burdensome labelling requirements, having unequal taxation regimes, and fixing over-rigid pricing or profit margin controls. There are a few exceptions to the general principle of the free movement of goods and services though. Governments are permitted to restrict their flow on the grounds of public morality, safety and the protection of the health and/or lives of humans, animals and/or plants.

The free movement of persons

Nationals of member states now have the right to to go another member state to look for and take up work, provided that they comply with the laws or regulations on employment and have a valid passport or national identity card. Once there, they are entitled to receive the same treatment as those nationals of the host country with regard to pay, working conditions, training, tax, social security and the like. Their immediate family may also join them, and enjoy the same entitlements. The right to employment may be limited on occasions, on the grounds of public health, security or policy as appropriate.

The free movement of capital

The free movement of capital within the European Union is recognized as being an essential complement to the free movement of products, services and people – businesses and individuals ought to be able to invest wherever they wish, at home or overseas. Hence, exchange controls which have previously restricted the availability of foreign currencies to those wishing to invest overseas have been removed (with the exception of Greece which is expected to comply in 1994).

As a consequence of the ongoing single market programme and the many changes it has brought about, the European Union is now by far the UK's largest export market, and its importance is growing all the time. In 1972, the 11 other countries which are members took 34 per cent of UK exports. This rose to 44 per cent in 1982 and is currently at 57 per cent, and rising. Other member states now account for a total of 52 per cent of all UK imports which compares with 34 per cent back in 1972.

14.4 The European Monetary System

The European Monetary System (EMS) was established by the European Union in 1979, with the aim of promoting monetary stability throughout Europe. Its four main features, which have yet to be wholly successful or even embraced in some instances, are as follows.

The exchange rate mechanism

The idea of the exchange rate mechanism (ERM) was that those EU members which participated in it, hopefully all of them, agreed to keep their currencies within 2.25 per cent of central rates against the other currencies operating in the system, thus providing financial stability in the European marketplace. As an example, the French franc (Ff) had a central rate of Ff 3.3539/DM1 in relation to the German deutschmark (DM) (which meant that someone in France could exchange 3.3539 francs for one deutschmark, and vice versa). Thus, the French franc had to be kept between Ff 3.2792/DM1 and Ff 3.4503/DM1 – 2.25 per cent above or below that central rate.

In theory, when upper or lower limits were approached, ERM members would intervene to stop the currency breaching the limits, by buying the weaker currency (or currencies) and selling the stronger one (or ones), as appropriate. Their willingness to do this would act as a brake on any further changes. As a last resort, a re-alignment could take place, whereby a currency could be formally revalued or devalued if agreed by all members. In practice, members proved to be unwilling to intervene as expected, which led to over a dozen re-alignments and an agreement in August 1993 to widen the band within which ERM currencies could fluctuate to 15 per cent – to all intents and purposes bringing the exchange rate mechanism to an end, in all but name.

The European Currency Unit

The European Currency Unit (ECU) is a composite currency, comprising a basket of currencies, namely pre-set amounts of all of the

German Mark	0.6242
Dutch Guilder	0.2198
Belgian Franc	3.301
Luxembourg Franc	0.13
Danish Krone	0.1976
French Franc	1.332
Irish Punt	0.008552
Italian Lira	151.8
UK Pound	0.08784
Greek Drachma	1.44
Spanish Peseta	6.885
Portugese Escudo	1.393

Figure 14.3   The ECU basket of currencies, 1989

currencies within the European Union. The relative quantity of each currency is a rough reflection of the economic weights of the respective countries. It is reviewed and revised if necessary every five years – 1989, 1994 and so on. The ECU basket of 1989 is shown in Figure 14.3. This (theoretical) European Currency Unit has several functions. It can be used as a unit of account as it is often easier to quote the rates of each currency against the ECU. It also serves as the basis of a divergence indicator intended to spot currencies causing tension in the ERM before formal intervention activities are triggered off. It can be used as a means of payment to settle debts.

Credit facilities

The EMS provides various credit facilities for member states. A very short-term financing facility (VSTF) exists whereby credit is automatically made available in unlimited quantities in order to fund intervention in foreign exchange markets to keep currencies within the exchange rate mechanism limits. Most borrowings have to be repaid within three months although limited amounts may be retained for up to a further six months. Short-term monetary support can be given for a nine-month period for countries with balance of payment problems. Medium-term finance may be available for longer periods, in exceptional circumstances.

Economic and monetary union

The European Monetary System also seeks to achieve full economic and monetary union between member states, effectively creating a United States of Europe. Following a request from heads of governments in 1989, the Delors Committee identified three stages of progress towards such a union. First, there must be closer cooperation between governments when formulating economic and monetary policies, and all countries should join the ERM. Second, a decision-making body made up of representatives of member states ought to be established to formulate a binding monetary policy for the whole Community. Third, all currencies should be irrevocably locked together and eventually replaced by a single European currency. Clearly, these steps remain some way off at the present time.

14.5 The European Free Trade Association

Established in 1959, the European Free Trade Association (EFTA) is an arrangement whereby its members – Austria, Iceland, Finland, Switzerland, Norway, Sweden and Liechtenstein – have eliminated tariff and other trade barriers among themselves, but remain free to set individual tariffs and the like against other, non-member countries. In many ways, EFTA is similar to the EU although the Union is usually regarded as a customs union rather than just a free trade area because it applies common (rather than individual) external tariffs against non-members. The countries of EFTA together form the EU's biggest trading partner.

Austria

Austria has a German-speaking population of 7.5 million, and its currency is the schilling. Main categories of UK exports are office equipment and machinery, chemicals and related products and road vehicles. Major UK imports include paper products, textiles and clothing.

Iceland

Iceland has a population of only 0.25 million people. Its language is (almost unlearnable) Icelandic, and its currency is the Icelandic krona. UK exports incorporate machinery and transport equipment, miscellaneous manufactured items, chemicals and associated products, UK imports are mainly fish and fish preparations, non-ferrous preparations, animal feed, iron and steel.

Finland

The Finnish population of 5.0 million speak either Finnish or Swedish. The currency is the Finnish markka. UK exports include office machinery, fertilizers, electrical machinery, vehicles, textiles and chemicals. UK imports incorporate paper products, iron and steel, office equipment and general industrial machinery.

Switzerland

The Swiss population of 6.5 million people has three main languages – German, French and Italian. Their currency is the Swiss Franc. The major categories of UK exports are office machinery and equipment, electrical machinery, road vehicles, iron and steel and non-ferrous metals, telecommunications and organic chemicals. The leading categories of UK imports are electrical machinery, textile yarns, organic chemicals and pharmaceuticals.

Norway

Norway has a population of some 4.2 million. The language is Norwegian and its currency is the Norwegian krone. UK exports include machinery and transport equipment, supplies to the offshore industry, minerals, fuels, lubricants and manufactured goods. UK imports incorporate petroleum and related products, gas, non-ferrous metals, iron and steel, specialized machinery and transport equipment.

Sweden

Sweden has a population of approximately 8.5 million, Swedish-speaking people. Their currency is the Swedish krona. Major UK exports are petroleum, electrical machinery, office machinery and equipment, general manufactured goods and industrial machinery. Key UK imports are paper products, road vehicles, cork and wood, iron and steel, and general industrial machinery.

Liechtenstein

The tiny principality of Liechtenstein has a German-speaking population of just 27 500 and shares its currency with Switzerland. Like its neighbour, the main categories of UK exports and imports are the same – office machinery and electrical machinery respectively, and so on.

14.6   The European Economic Area Agreement

The aim of the European Economic Area (EEA) Agreement is to strengthen trade and economic relations between the European Union and the European Free Trade Association. It was signed in May 1992 and is now in the process of being ratified, thus extending and establishing the world's largest single market across 19 countries, 375 million people, and accounting for 46 per cent of world trade. The EEA agreement has the following main features.

Freedom of movement

The free movement of goods, services, capital and persons will apply throughout the EEA. In particular:

1 *Goods*

Various tariffs and quotas on a range of products have been abolished or are gradually being phased out over a period of time. Other barriers to trade such as differing product standards and taxes on incoming goods have been or are being eliminated too, with standardized technical and safety regulations being set across the EEA and the use of discriminating taxation being banned. Steps are also being taken to simplify trading procedures between the EU and EFTA and to reduce the necessary formalities so far as possible.

2 *Services*

The ability to provide services freely across boundaries has often been hindered by local rules and regulations which made it difficult to compete effectively. Under the terms of this agreement, any business (or individual) established in an EEA country will be free to provide professional, commercial or industrial services throughout the region under the same conditions as in the European Union. Thus, UK firms can compete on a more equal footing with domestic suppliers.

3 *Capital*

Restrictions on the movement of capital belonging to EEA companies and individuals are in the process of being removed. Countries within the EEA must not restrict investment or retain investment rules which prohibit, limit or discriminate against investment from outside that country. Clearly, this encourages UK firms to invest overseas, and for foreign businesses to invest here.

4 Persons

The EEA agreement gives all EU and EFTA nationals the right to work throughout the EEA on the same terms and conditions as local workers, to stay in that country to work and to remain there afterwards, subject to certain status conditions. Hence, it makes it easier for UK nationals to live and work abroad in EFTA countries and for UK companies to employ EFTA nationals.

Right of establishment

The agreement introduces the right of establishment for all EEA nationals throughout the area. This simply means that EEA firms and individuals can establish themselves for business purposes anywhere within the EEA on the same terms and conditions as domestic concerns, wholly free of restrictions that do not apply to those home-based ventures. Therefore, UK companies which see advantages in setting up operations in EFTA countries rather than exporting to them from the UK will be free to do so without unfair restrictions being applied.

Competitive trading conditions

A significant achievement of the EEA agreement is the development of common rules and regulations on competition and state aid throughout the area to ensure that equal trading conditions apply on a universal basis. By and large, EU competition laws are being extended across the EEA, with responsibilities for administering them being shared between the EU and EFTA, as appropriate. The creation of a level playing field across the area enables businesses to compete on the same terms and allows consumers to gain from the increased choice and lower prices which competition brings.

Closer cooperation

In addition to extending the Single Market to EFTA, the agreement seeks to increase political cooperation between the two parties, dialogue on economic and monetary policies and the collaboration and exchange of information on such matters of mutual interest as research and technology, consumer protection, small and medium sized enterprises and the environment.

Financial mechanism

The EEA Financial Mechanism, or the EFTA Cohesion Fund as it will also be called, is simply a fund which will be set up by the EFTA countries to help the less favoured regions of the EU, most notably the Republic of Ireland, Northern Ireland, Greece, Portugal and parts of Spain. Its aim will be to finance projects in these regions whether carried out by public authorities or public and private companies, although priority is given to those which are involved with education, training, transport and the environment, and special consideration is given to applications from small and medium sized firms.

New EEA institutions

To ensure that the EEA agreement is implemented and run correctly, various new institutions will be set up, namely:

1   *The EEA Council*

This will comprise ministers from the EU and EFTA member states, plus representatives from the European Commission. It provides political direction for the EEA, making its decisions by consensus of the two parties.

2   *The EEA Joint Committee*

Made up of EU and EFTA officials, this will be the main EFTA forum and will be responsible for the day-to-day administration of the agreement. In particular, it will ensure that the EU and EFTA comply with the agreement and the two areas adopt a comparable approach to their interpretation of the agreement. Also it will decide which new EU measures should apply to the EEA and will resolve any disputes between the two sides.

3   *The EFTA Surveillance Authority*

The ESA which will be set up by EFTA will be responsible for making sure that the agreement is complied with by the EFTA countries. It will have similar powers within EFTA to those exercised by the European Commission within the EU. Not surprisingly, the two authorities will work closely together to maintain a common approach as far as they can.

4 *The EFTA Court*

This will be set up by the EFTA countries and will consist of seven EFTA judges, with one from each of the member states, and will consider EEA issues, actions regarding breaches of the agreement as revealed by EFTA surveillance procedures and appeals against ESA decisions.

5 *The EEA Joint Parliamentary Committee*

Consisting of members of the European Parliament and EFTA parliamentarians, this committee will exist to promote mutual understanding between the EU and EFTA, via dialogue and debate. It will not have any legislative powers.

6 *The EEA Consultative Committee*

This committee will comprise members of the EU's Economic and Social Committee and the equivalent EFTA consultative committee. It will examine economic and social issues and will try to promote better cooperation on these matters between the EU and EFTA.

14.7 Other international organizations and agreements

Not surprisingly, these are other organizations and agreements in Europe and across the world stage which are of some relevance to the UK and its businesses and people. These are some of the leading ones.

Group of 7

G7 is a group of countries which work together to promote steady exchange rates between their currencies, thus providing greater monetary stability and trading conditions for each other. The finance ministers of the UK, France, Germany, Italy, USA, Canada and Japan meet on a regular basis to set informal limits on exchange rate fluctuations between their respective currencies.

General Agreement on Tariffs and Trade

GATT is an agreement signed by 170 or so countries world-wide which seeks to promote international trade. It is based on four overriding principles which signatories are expected to pursue. When import controls are imposed they should be in the shape of tariffs rather than quotas. Members should work together to reduce tariffs between themselves. All members ought to receive the same treatment in respect of import controls – every member is a most favoured nation. There should be ongoing consultations between members on matters relating to trade restrictions.

International Monetary Fund

The IMF is financed by and acts as a banker to approximately 150 member countries, including most of the leading western nations. It seeks to promote the expansion of international trade, while maintaining balance of payments equilibrium for individual countries. To achieve this, the Fund has helped to keep steady exchange rates between currencies and also provides borrowing facilities for those nations facing balance of payments problems.

Organization for Economic Cooperation and Development

OECD has a membership made up of the economically advanced countries in the world. Its main role is to provide a forum for debate between trade and finance ministers of member countries, enabling them to discuss economic issues with a view to promoting international trade and economic growth. The organization is also responsible for coordinating aid packages to less developed countries, which will typically take the form of (soft) loans on generous terms and conditions, as well as the provision of skilled personnel and up-to-date technologies to help assist in the development of economies.

United Nations

The UN aims to maintain world peace, and to advance social harmony and economic development across the globe. Comprising most of the world's nations, it operates numerous satellite agencies which strive to further these aims through a mix of advice, information and practical guidance. Most notably, the International Labour Office tries to improve working and social conditions throughout the world, the Food and Agriculture Organization attempts to raise agricultural efficiency and nutritional standards in developing countries and the Conference on Trade and Development seeks to secure economic aid for developing countries and negotiates tariff and quota reductions on goods sold by them to developed nations.

International Bank for Reconstruction and Development

The purpose of the World Bank, as it is known in more popular jargon, is to help countries to develop by providing them with economic aid in the shape of loans and some technical assistance. Funded mainly by developed nations, the Bank finances a whole host of projects in under-developed countries such as the establishment of schools, hospitals, roads and new trades and industries.

14.8 Rapid revision

Answers	Questions
–	1 What are the main organizations and agreements in Europe, of relevance to the UK's businesses and people?
1 (a) The European Union; (b) the Single Market; (c) the European Monetary System; (d) the European Free Trade Association; (e) the European Economic Area Agreement.	2 What is the European Union, and who are its members?
2 It is a group of 12 countries working together for political cooperation and economic success. The countries are France, Belgium, Germany, Italy, Luxembourg, Ireland, Denmark, Greece, Portugal, Spain, the Netherlands and the UK.	3 What are the four key institutions of the European Union?
3 (a) The Commission; (b) the Council; (c) the Parliament; (d) the Court of Justice.	4 What does the Commission do?
4 It proposes policies and legislation, supervises the day-to-day running of policies and makes sure that member states comply with rules and regulations.	5 What does the Council do?
5 It makes decisions, adopting legislation on the basis of proposals made by the Commission.	6 What are the main forms of Council legislation?

6 (a) Regulations; (b) directives; (c) decisions; (d) opinions.

7 What does the Parliament do?

7 It gives opinions on Commission proposals before the Council makes decisions.

8 What does the Court of Justice do?

8 It rules on the interpretation and application of EU laws.

9 What other bodies exist within the European Union?

9 (a) The Economic and Social Committee; (b) the Court of Auditors; (c) the European Investment Bank.

10 What is the Single Market?

10 It is an area without internal frontiers in which the free movement of goods, persons, services and capital is ensured.

11 What are the key features of the Single Market?

11 (a) The free movement of products and services; (b) the free movement of persons; (c) the free movement of capital.

12 What are the major features of the European Monetary System?

12 (a) The Exchange Rate Mechanism; (b) the European Currency Unit; (c) Credit facilities; (d) Economic and Monetary Union.

13 What is the European Free Trade Association?

13 It is an arrangement whereby its members eliminate trade barriers among themselves, but are free to set individual barriers against non-member countries.

14 What is the main difference between the EU and EFTA?

14 The EU is a customs union which applies common barriers against non-members, EFTA is a free trade area which applies individual barriers against outsiders.

15 What countries belong to the European Free Trade Association?

15 (a) Austria; (b) Iceland; (c) Finland; (d) Switzerland; (e) Norway; (f) Sweden; (g) Liechtenstein.

16 What is the European Economic Area Agreement?

16   It is an agreement between the EU and EFTA which seeks to strengthen trade and economic relations between the two groups of countries.

17   What are the leading features of the Agreement?

17   (a) Freedom of movement; (b) the right of establishment; (c) competitive trading conditions; (d) closer cooperation; (e) a financial mechanism, or fund.

18   What new institutions will be set up as a result of the Agreement?

18   (a) The EEA Council; (b) the EEA Joint Committee; (c) the EFTA Surveillance Authority; (d) the EFTA Court; (e) the EEA Joint Parliamentary Committee; (f) the EEA Consultative Committee.

19   What other international organizations and agreements are of some relevance to the UK's firms and peoples?

19   (a) Group of 7; (b) General Agreement on Tariffs and Trade; (c) International Monetary Fund; (d) Organization for Economic Cooperation and Development; (e) United Nations; (f) International Bank for Reconstruction and Development.

20   Go over the questions again until you know all of the answers. Then move on to the next section.

15
Trading overseas

15.1 Why trade overseas?

The decision to export or to import is not an easy one for a home-based business to make – trading with a firm in Brussels, Stuttgart or wherever can never be quite as straightforward as dealing with one in London or Bradford, whatever the Single Market has done to remove trade barriers and related obstacles. A domestic concern needs to consider the reasons for trading abroad, contemplate the drawbacks and assess itself to see if it has what it takes to be a success in the international arena. Only then should it proceed any further with its plans, if at all.

Reasons for trading abroad

A business may initially think about exporting or importing for all sorts of reasons. These can be listed separately although in practice the firm will probably take account of several of them. The following are some of the more influential:

1 *Price*

A concern might contemplate exporting its products if it can see that they would be significantly cheaper than those already on sale in a foreign market, thus enabling it to build a customer base there. Similarly, a firm may choose to import goods such as raw materials from abroad because they are less expensive than those offered by domestic producers.

2 *Other attributes*

Many products are exported or imported because they have better or simply different qualities to those currently sold in the marketplace.

Sales may be determined as much by personal preferences for alternative characteristics as by price. Sometimes, goods are exported or imported just because they can be delivered more quickly than those produced by rivals.

3   Demand

The demand for certain products and services may be higher in one market than in another. Gaining extra sales abroad is obviously an attractive proposition for a home-based firm if the domestic marketplace is stagnant or even contracting.

4   Supply

Various goods such as raw materials and foodstuffs are in short supply or even non-existent in some countries, making it essential or desirable that these are brought in for businesses and people. Equally, a country may have an insufficient number of manufacturers of certain products and the only option available is to import if domestic users and consumers are to be satisfied.

5   Survival, profit and growth

The bottom line reason for any form of trade is to survive, profit and grow. More markets means more customers, sales, profits and so on. By trading abroad, a firm reduces its dependence on just one market and the possible impact of any changes in that marketplace which may affect it, for better or for worse.

Drawbacks of trading overseas

Despite the simplifying changes brought about by the Single Market and other developments, there are still some drawbacks involved with foreign trade which a business needs to be aware of and able to overcome. In particular, it must face these universal problems:

1   Unfamiliarity

A home-based firm does not possess a hands-on, detailed understanding of a foreign market and its concerns and people, and the formal and informal rules and procedures which govern trading practices within them. As an example, bribes are an accepted business tactic in some countries but a gross insult in others. However well established a firm becomes in a foreign market, it can never truly match the knowledge and understanding possessed by local concerns.

2 *Lack of contact*

Less closely involved on a day-to-day basis with distant markets, a business will often find it difficult to stay in touch with key changes and developments. Hence, it may miss out on opportunities which a closer involvement would have revealed, and fail to spot impending disasters such as the introduction of better products from rivals which may go unnoticed until it is too late.

3 *Extra demands*

A move into overseas markets inevitably increases the demands and stresses on a firm and its personnel – seeking information, choosing the correct selling method, signing contracts, handling different documents, chasing payments and the like all take up staff time and energies. Changing priorities within the business organization may create pressures too, and limit its ability to stay abreast of and adapt to developments in the home marketplace.

4 *Additional regulations*

In some markets, businesses will have to contend with tariffs and quotas which may make goods less competitively priced and/or limit the volume of trade. Even in those markets where barriers do not usually exist, unofficial ones tend to arise. Typically, products sold across the Single Market should all be of the same, minimum standards but customers in various countries will still expect more from these products than those in other countries and firms need to be flexible enough to satisfy them.

5 *Exchange rate fluctuations*

Some countries fix the value of their currency against another so that 100 units of their currency can always be exchanged for 200 units or whatever of another country's currency. Others allow it to move freely according to demand and supply, so that 100 units can be changed for 200 units on one day, 100 or 300 on the following one.

These are what are commonly known as 'fixed' and 'floating' exchange rates respectively.

Clearly, floating, and therefore fluctuating, exchange rates pose difficulties for firms. Imagine a business signs a contract to supply goods for a price which is set in a foreign currency. When converted to the domestic currency, the price received is favourable. However, if the exchange rate alters between signature and payment, which will inevitably happen, the firm may discover that it has entered into an unprofitable deal. Even if it makes more money, it will now be very aware of the vagaries and risks involved.

6 *Slow payers*

The curse of each and every business, payments from overseas firms may be even slower than those from home-based concerns which places additional stresses on cash flows. Also, there is an increased risk of non-payment and chasing debtors via foreign courts is even less appealing than pursuing this course of action through domestic ones.

7 *Lack of commitment*

Sometimes, exporters and importers find that their other halves are not as committed to trading as they are. A typical example of what often happens is when an exporter enters a foreign market because the home one is in a slump and then decides to pull out suddenly when the domestic market improves, thus leaving the importer high and dry.

Making the choice

Aware of the reasons for trading overseas and conscious of some of the main drawbacks involved, a business then needs to assess itself to see whether it would be a suitable exporter or importer, as appropriate. The successful exporter or importer needs to have the following, key ingredients:

1 *Substantial financial resources*

Clearly, it is imperative that any firm planning to expand into overseas trade is financially sound, and has access to additional funds as and when required. For example, a business intending to export may need to purchase additional raw materials, increase production levels, pay more overtime and incur a host of other expenses before receiving any orders, let alone payments. Such a 'speculate to accumulate' approach can only be pursued from a sound financial base.

2 Quality human resources

Just as important are a firm's human resources, in terms of both types and numbers. As a simple example, if the business employs sales representatives to generate orders, these people must be fluent in the appropriate language and conversant with local customs. Similarly, the right number must be employed – there is little point in having six representatives in the UK and only two in France, as that country is nearly three times the size of this one.

3 Satisfactory product capability and flexibility

A business needs to have the capacity to cope physically with all of the extra orders resulting from its move into trading abroad, while maintaining speed and quality standards at the same time. Also, it has to be flexible enough to be able to produce variations of its goods for different customers and markets.

4 A well-developed strategy

Quite simply, the firm needs to know what it is doing and where it is going if it is to succeed. Linked to this is the necessity to have a firm commitment to this course of action, and to see it through.

Once a business has considered the reasons why it should export or import, has contemplated the drawbacks and thought about itself, it should be ready to decide whether it will proceed, or not. If it concludes that it is worthwhile to go on, it will then need to seek information and advice and look at different selling methods before finding out about the ins and outs of contracts, documents and getting paid.

15.2 Seeking information

Innumerable organizations exist which provide information, advice and guidance for businesses planning to export to or import from Europe, or elsewhere in the world. The key ones can be grouped into the following, broad categories.

Government departments

These departments and other government bodies should be the first port of call for would-be exporters and importers.

1   Department of Trade and Industry

The DTI's *Business in Europe* offers a unified approach to the wide ranging services of the Department. Services include factual information on Single Market legislation, advice and active assistance on overcoming illegal trade barriers, help with documentation and technical standards, free and reasonably priced publications on major issues and access to experienced, successful exporters and importers. This is *the* place to go for complete advice and guidance.

2   Customs and Excise

This department has set up a network of Single Market Liaison Officers (SMLOs) to advise on the changes and developments which the Single Market has and will bring about in the fields of VAT, customs, excise and trade statistics.

3   Local authorities

These can provide valuable advice on the implementation and enforcement of many Single Market measures. For example, their trading standards departments are able to offer free assistance to UK businesses on European and national legislative requirements for products, including technical standards.

Professional advisers

Many firms fail to realize that their usual professional advisers may be a valuable source of advice on Europe and beyond.

1   Banks

All of the major high street banks have international or export departments which are able to give advice and provide various services to their customers. For example, Lloyds offers a brochure *Europe, Your New Home Market* plus services such as money transmission, credit management, foreign currency exchange and specialist advisory services for concerns entering Europe for the first time.

2 *Solicitors*

The Law Society of England and Wales offers a business referral scheme called 'Solicitors in the Single Market' which comprises a list of 950 or more practices which can provide advice on Single Market issues. The list details the languages spoken in each firm and its contacts with lawyers in other member states. The Law Society of Northern Ireland and the Law Society of Scotland have comparable services.

3 *Consultants*

The Institute of Management Consultants (IMC) operates a free introductory service for businesses wishing to liaise with a management consultant with Single Market knowledge and expertise. The British Consultants Bureau (BCB) and the Management Consultancies Association (MCA) also offer services of a similar nature.

4 *Educational establishments*

Many educational establishments such as colleges and universities offer consultancy and/or advisory services on Single Market matters. Language courses may also be available to businesses via some establishments.

Representative bodies

A prospective exporter or importer can join a whole host of different types of representative body, and benefit from their specific guidance.

1 *Professional organizations*

The majority of these can provide across the board advice on a wide range of export and import matters. As an example, the Confederation of British Industry with its membership of 250 000 or so companies publishes a quarterly, loose leaf briefing pack *Europe sans frontières* and offers advice on subjects as diverse as export methods, contracts and documents, and being paid.

2   *Trade associations*

Similarly, most of these bodies offer detailed advice relating to thei particular trade or industry, most notably on differing product an technical standards. Some of them also sponsor members who wis to participate in exhibitions in foreign countries.

3   *Local business groups*

Chambers of commerce often have international links and are thu able to provide hands-on guidance. Some even have export develop ment advisers to help firms to maximize their potential in oversea trade. Export clubs are informal associations of local exporters wh meet regularly to discuss export matters and to advise each other a a consequence of their experiences.

Specialist organizations

Not surprisingly, various special bodies have been established to dea specifically with exporting and importing issues:

1   *European Business Foundation*

This is a non-profit-making foundation which provides a wide range of services to companies. These include monitoring and advising on EU developments, supplying intelligence and commenting on new EU initiatives, organizing conferences on new and proposed legislation and undertaking research based on individual company requirements.

2   *Technical Help to Exporters*

THE provides exporters with information and advice on technical requirements which affect their products in overseas markets. Services include free technical enquiries as well as translations of foreign standards and laws, publications covering the technical aspects of exporting, technical research, and consultancy and updating services.

3   *Simpler Trade Procedures Board*

SITPRO is the UK's trade facilitation body aiming to simplify international trade for exporters so far as possible. It provides a comprehensive range of export products and services – export documents, documentation software systems, export guides, training seminars and material, advice and consultancy.

4 Language Excellence Centres

LX Centres as they are commonly known exist to help firms strengthen their business performance via a range of language training and consultancy services. These include translating and interpreting and trade briefings. Two other bodies – the Institute of Linguists and the Institute of Translation and Interpreting – provide similar services.

5 European Commission Offices

The EC has four offices in the UK which act as signposts for businesses looking for sources of European information. European Commission papers and legislation are stocked in their libraries.

15.3 Selling overseas

There are various ways for a firm to sell its goods and services into an overseas market. Probably the most common ones are as follows.

Direct selling

Quite simply, a firm's sales representatives can travel abroad to France, Germany or wherever to meet prospective customers at exhibitions and in their shops, offices, factories and homes, dealing with them in the same way that they would handle customers in the domestic marketplace. Of course, there are advantages – the establishment of close relationships, face-to-face negotiations and two-way communications. Nevertheless, there are disadvantages too. It takes an enormous amount of preparatory work, time and travelling to make and build up a contacts list. The exporter's representatives must be ready at all times to visit at short notice to sort out problems as and when they occur – sometimes easier said than done!

Via an export house

An export house acts in one or more of three different ways, namely:

1   *As an export merchant*

Here, the house buys goods from the business and then sells them on to its overseas contacts or customers, at a profit. To all intents and purposes, the firm is trading with a domestic customer and in the normal manner. This may be the easiest and most satisfactory method for the business but there is always the nagging doubt that the export house is making a substantial profit at the concern's expense.

2   *As an export agent*

With this approach, the export house acts as the firm's export department – it promotes sales abroad, deals with contracts, documents and other formalities at home and overseas and may sometimes provide after sales service for foreign buyers as well.

3   *As a confirming house*

Here, the house obtains orders for goods and services from overseas businesses and then seeks a supplier in the home country which can fulfil that order. In effect, it acts as a go-between, paying the domestic firm, collecting or receiving the completed order and forwarding it on, and chasing the customer for payment.

Through an overseas agent

By far the most common method of selling overseas is via an agent (or agents) in the appropriate country (or countries) which will arrange sales on behalf of a firm and then earn commission on these sales. Many agents take full control of and responsibility for all aspects of sales promotion, from advertising through to after sales service. Clearly, it can be advantageous for an exporter to have someone on the spot who speaks the language (both literally and metaphorically!) to sell to end users, and to assist with any problems that subsequently arise.

Most exporting firms will obtain a shortlist of overseas agents via the Department of Trade and Industry which uses the commercial departments of British embassies to find suitable representatives. Banks and chambers of commerce are also helpful, using their international links in much the same way. Usually, an exporter will meet several agents face to face on their own territories and will want to receive positive answers to several questions before appointing one. Typical questions would include: Does the agent have

- The names and addresses of the two parties
- A description of the products covered by the agreement
- A definition of the territory covered by the agreement
- Details of the agent's duties to the client
- Details of the client's duties to the agent
- The date of commencement of the agreement
- A description of each side's responsibilities (with regard to such matters as advertising, deliveries and collecting payments)
- Details of the performance levels to be achieved by the agent
- Details of the rate of commission to be paid (the basis of its calculation, how and when paid)
- Details of any other payments which the agent may be entitled to (perhaps relating to sales made via other sources)
- The terms and conditions for terminating the agreement, and any compensation that may need to be paid
- Details of any arbitration arrangements in the event of a dispute
- The date of the conclusion of the agreement

Figure 15.1   Agency agreement checklist

sufficient resources and expertise to market our products properly, advertising, selling them and providing after sales service? Is it fully experienced in this field? What other firms and products does it deal with – are they complementary or in competition? Does it have a good status and credit report from the DTI?

Once appointed, and it is invariably a long and careful selection process drawing on the advice and guidance of many bodies such as the DTI, the chosen agent will be protected by law, and cannot be dismissed easily as and when the firm wishes. Thus, it is essential that an agreement is drawn up outlining various duties, terms and conditions and equally important that it is checked thoroughly by an experienced solicitor to ensure it is fair and complies with EU and national laws. Figure 15.1 gives a checklist of points that should be included in an agency agreement.

Naturally, it is vital that the client–agent relationship is nurtured on an ongoing basis if it is to be a success. It is sensible for a firm to discuss its plans with the agent, and to benefit from its hands-on suggestions on matters such as promotional policies and pricing levels. Similarly, the business should provide the agent with up-to-date information about its products and other developments, perhaps training the agency's staff in their usage, if appropriate. Agents have many clients and those concerns that pay most attention to their agent will probably be rewarded with the greatest attention and service in return.

By becoming a multinational company

A *multinational* is simply a company which owns outlets in more than one country, often opening them in the same way that a London-based business might establish a second office or factory in Birmingham or Manchester if the developing situation makes this a financially viable option. There are several distinct benefits in having an outlet in a key foreign market, not least a closer proximity to and increased understanding of that marketplace, reduced distribution costs and the avoidance of tariffs and quotas. Numerous other advantages may exist too, such as access to greater technical know-how and expertise and lower labour costs.

However, there are various obvious drawbacks in becoming a multinational enterprise, with outlets here, there and everywhere. Investing time and money upfront on finding premises, buying equipment and machinery and hiring staff all in an unfamiliar and sometimes hostile environment is enormously risky, with no guarantee that sales and profits will reach the desired levels. Hence, such a bold and dramatic move is probably unwise in the early days of overseas trading activities but may become a possible option in later years if sales via direct selling, export houses or agents prove to be worthwhile on an ongoing basis.

15.4   Signing contracts

A firm which sells direct to overseas customers will negotiate contracts with them in the same way that it does with domestic customers. If the business works with an export house or agent, they may attend to this task, although it is advisable for the firm to stay abreast of what is being done on its behalf. Various types of contract can be recognized, grouped under the following 'incoterms' which are common expressions used in foreign trade.

Ex works

With this type of contract, the seller is responsible for no more than having the goods ready for collection at an agreed time and place – usually the factory gates! The buyer has to uplift them, and make payment there and then in most instances. The goods belong to the buyer from that point onwards, who must transport them at his or her own expense and risk of accident or loss.

Free on rail

FOR, to use the abbreviated expression, means that the selling firm is obliged to pack and deliver the goods to the nearest railway station. Free on truck (FOT) extends responsibilities to loading the items onto a train. Payment may fall due when the goods arrive at the station or on the train, which coincides with the stage at which risk of theft or damage passes to the buyer.

Free alongside ship

This is a similar arrangement to an FOR contract. Here, the seller has to transport the goods alongside a ship of the buyer's choice. Free on board (FOB) requires the items to be placed on that ship, at the seller's expense. The goods might need to be paid for when they are FAS or FOB, and it is at these points that the risks switch to the buyer.

Ex-ship

This type of contract obliges the selling firm to ship the goods to a port nominated by the buyer, which will invariably be in the buyer's home country. He or she will collect and perhaps pay for them upon their arrival at the chosen destination. During their transit, the risk of damage or loss remains with the seller.

Cost, insurance, freight

CIF, in common parlance, means that the seller has to pay for the goods to be transported to the port of shipment, plus loading and freight charges to the port of destination as well as insuring them up to this point. The buyer then pays to unload, transport and insure them to their final destination. Cost, Freight (CF) is a variation of CIF.

15.5 Handling documents

Again, a business selling direct to Europe or further afield will personally have to sort out the documents involved in exporting. If it uses an export house or agent, one of these parties may attend to matters on its behalf. The following are the main export documents which the firm may come across during its international dealings.

Bills of lading

A bill of lading performs several roles. It acts as a contract for the carriage of the goods, a deed of ownership to be transferred to the buyer and a receipt for the goods upon transfer. It will usually detail the goods along with the terms and conditions of carriage, the name of the vessel carrying them and their port of destination. A bill should be signed either by the master of the ship or by another, authorized person.

Invoices

Two types of invoices can be identified:

1   Commercial invoices

A commercial invoice issued by a business is basically the same whether the goods are sold to a customer in Cardiff, Glasgow, Milan or Paris. It will normally detail the buyer and seller, the goods including their quantities, weights and prices and the type of contract entered into, such as FOR or FAS.

2   Consular invoices

A consular invoice, quite different from a commercial one, is required for goods which are being exported to certain places in the world, such as some South American countries. It is issued in the exporter's country by the consulate of the importer's country and verifies the details of the goods being exported for the relevant authorities in that importer's country.

Certificates

Three key certificates may be recognized, as follows:

1   Certificates of origin

A certificate of origin is simply a statement by the exporter which declares where the goods have come from.

2   Certificates of value

As the name suggests, this certificate verifies the value of the goods being exported so that the correct duty can be levied on them, as appropriate.

3   Certificates of insurance

Clearly, all goods must be insured during transit – accidents and thefts do happen quite often – and this certificate will need to be checked by the shipping company.

Other documents

In addition to these most common documents, other ones may be required in some instances. A *customs declaration* is a signed statement detailing the contents of parcels and packages. A *health certificate* may be necessary for animals and drugs. A *declaration of dangerous goods* could be required for chemicals and explosives. A *weight note* details the gross weight of packages. *Export licences* and *import licences* might be needed for certain products such as antiques and military equipment and for some destinations.

15.6   Getting paid

Whether handled by the firm itself, an export house or an agent, the aims remain the same – to deal with creditworthy customers who pay up on time. There are various ways of getting paid, some of which are fairer and safer than others. In most cases, buyers and sellers will reach a compromise which satisfies both sides. Four main payment methods are popular.

Cash with order

Obviously, this is by far the best payment method for the exporter as it guarantees payment without hassles or difficulties – no money, no goods! It helps the firm's cash flow too, ensuring that it has sufficient funds to produce the desired goods. Naturally, it is the least favoured payment method so far as the buyer is concerned. At best, its cash flow will be severely restricted as there will be a delay in receiving the goods, selling them and recouping that early outlay, with profits. At worst, the goods may not even be sent, perhaps because the exporter has ceased trading in the meantime – this has and will continue to happen. Buying on a *pro-forma* basis often occurs at the beginning of a trading relationship if the buyer really wants the goods and continues until the exporter is willing to offer credit.

Open account

Once a close and trusted relationship is established between the home seller and foreign buyer, then the goods will normally be paid for by what is known as an *open account*. This operates in the same way that two home-based businesses trade, with the seller despatching goods and an invoice and the buyer subsequently paying for them within a certain time. The seller may give the buyer a credit limit enabling him or her to take a set amount of goods on tick. The pros and cons of this approach virtually reverse those for the cash with order method – this time the exporter's cash flow is weakened and his or her risks are increased, while the importer's cash flow is improved and his or her risks are reduced. Obviously, both cash with order and open account methods are open to abuse by one party or the other, so alternative methods may be preferred which are a compromise between the two approaches.

Bills for collection

This is a popular payment method which offers some security to both sides in the transaction. The exporter despatches the goods to the buyer and simultaneously sends the various shipping documents to his or her own bank which then forwards them to a bank in the importer's country. The foreign bank may be the buyer's bank or an overseas branch of the exporter's bank. Whichever it is – and the exporter may feel happier using a branch of his or her own bank – the documents await collection by the buyer.

These shipping documents will incorporate what is known as a *bill of exchange* or *draft*. This is a demand for the payment of a particular sum of money at a specified date, which may be on demand (now!) or in 30, 60 or 90 days after the bill is received by the buyer. Such bills may be called *sight bills* or *sight drafts* and *after sight bills* or *term drafts* respectively.

If the bill is not payable on demand when the documents are collected, the buyer must accept it by signing it, thus obliging him to make payment when the bill matures after 30, 60, 90 days, or whatever. Not surprisingly, sight bills are preferred by exporting businesses and tend to be accepted by their buyers as being the fairest compromise between the two extremes of cash up front and credit terms. The use of after sight bills requires some trust, which might be abused.

Documentary credits

This is probably the fairest and safest payment method of all, and is much favoured by many exporters and their buyers. At its simplest, a clause is inserted in the contract of sale which states that payment will be made by a bank. Hence, the buyer and his or her bank instructs a bank in the exporter's country to pay up on the presentation of export documents which conform precisely to the terms and conditions of that contract. That bank then issues a *letter of credit* to the exporting firm confirming this arrangement – and everyone is happy!

15.7 Rapid revision

Answers	Questions
–	1 What are the main reason for trading abroad?
1 (a) Price; (b) other attributes; (c) demand; (d) supply; (e) survival, profit and growth.	2 What are the universal drawbacks of trading overseas?
2 (a) Unfamiliarity; (b) lack of contact; (c) extra demands; (d) additional regulations; (e) exchange rate fluctuations; (f) slow payers; (g) lack of commitment.	3 What does an exporter or importer need to have to be successful?
3 (a) Substantial financial resources; (b) quality human resources; (c) satisfactory product capability and flexibility; (d) a well-developed strategy.	4 Which government departments can provide information to prospective exporters and importers?
4 (a) Department of Trade and Industry; (b) Customs and Excise; (c) Local authorities.	5 Which professional advisers are able to other advice to would-be exporters and importers?
5 Most notably (a) banks; (b) solicitors; (c) consultants; (d) educational establishments.	6 Which representative bodies are worth contacting?
6 (a) Professional organizations; (b) trade associations; (c) local business groups.	7 Which specialist organizations might be approached?

7   (a) European Business Foundation; (b) Technical Help to Exporters; (c) Simpler Trade Procedures Board; (d) Language Excellence Centres; (e) European Commission Offices.

8   What are the main ways for a firm to sell into an overseas market?

---

8   (a) Direct selling; (b) via an export house; (c) through an overseas agent; (d) by establishing a branch in that market.

9   What does an export house do?

---

9   It may act (a) as a merchant, buying and selling goods; (b) as an agent, promoting goods for a firm; (c) as a confirming house, obtaining orders and then seeking a supplier to fulfil them.

10   What does an agent do?

---

10   It arranges overseas sales on behalf of a home-based firm, and earns commission on these sales.

11   What are incoterms?

---

11   They are expressions which are commonly used in international trade.

12   What are the most common types of contract used in international trade?

---

12   (a) Ex-works; (b) free on rail; (c) free on truck; (d) free alongside ship; (e) free on board; (f) ex-ship; (g) cost, insurance, freight; (h) cost, freight.

13   What is a bill of lading?

---

13   It is a document which performs several roles: (a) as a contract for the carriage of goods; (b) as a deed of ownership to be transferred to the buyer; (c) as a receipt for the goods upon transfer.

14   What types of invoice are used in international trade?

---

14   (a) commercial invoices; (b) consular invoices.

15   What types of certificate are used in international trade?

---

15   (a) Certificates of origin; (b) certificates of value; (c) certificates of insurance.

16   What other documents might be used in international trade?

16 (a) Customs declarations;
(b) health certificates;
(c) declarations of dangerous
goods; (d) weight notes; (e) export
licences; (f) import licences.

17 What are the four main
payment methods used in
international trade?

---

17 (a) Cash with order; (b) open
account; (c) bills for collection;
(d) documentary credits.

18 Go over the questions again
until you know all of the answers.

Further reading

The business environment is a broad subject, encompassing a wide and diverse range of topics. Reading the following recommended texts will help you to develop your knowledge and understanding of some of the more important topics.

Part One   Business organizations

Anderson, Alan and Fahad, Ghalib, *Effective Entrepreneurship*, Oxford, Blackwell Publishers, 1994.

Anderson, Alan and Kyprianou, Anna, *Effective Organizational Behaviour*, Oxford, Blackwell Publishers, 1994.

Gregson, Shaun and Livesey, Frank, *Organizations and Management*, Oxford, Butterworth-Heinemann, 1993.

Keasey, Kevin and Watson, Robert, *Small Firm Management*, Oxford, Blackwell Publishers, 1993.

Lorange, Peter, *Strategic Planning and Control*, Oxford, Blackwell Publishers, 1993.

Luffman, George, Sanderson, Stuart, Lea, Edward and Kenny, Brian, *Business Policy*, Oxford, Blackwell Publishers, 1993.

Taylor, Bernard and Harrison, John, *The Manager's Casebook of Business Strategy*, Oxford, Butterworth-Heinemann, 1991.

Part Two   Business resources

Anderson, Alan, *Effective Personnel Management*, Oxford, Blackwell Publishers, 1994.

Broadbent, Michael and Cullen, John, *Managing Financial Resources*, Oxford, Butterworth-Heinemann, 1993.

Henry, Chris, *Strategic Human Resource Management*, Oxford, Butterworth-Heinemann, 1993.

Part Three   Business markets

Harrison, Barry, Smith, Charles and Davies, Brinley, *Introductory Economics*, Basingstoke, Macmillan, 1992.
Lowes, Bryan, Pass, Christopher L. and Sanderson, Stuart M., *Understanding Companies and Markets*, Oxford, Blackwell Publishers, 1994.

Part Four   The local and national environment

Bain, A. D., *The Economics of the Financial System*, Oxford, Blackwell Publishers, 1992.
Cordell, Jim, *Essential Government and Politics*, London, Collins Educational, 1992.
Reekie, W. D., Allen, D. E. and Crook, J. N., *The Economics of Modern Business*, Oxford, Blackwell Publishers, 1991.

Part Five   The international environment

Bennett, Roger, *Selling to Europe*, London, Kogan Page, 1991.
Briggs, Peter, *Principles of International Trade and Payments*, Oxford, Blackwell Publishers, 1994.
Brown, Richard, *Managing in the Single Market*, Oxford, Butterworth-Heinemann, 1993.
Ghoshal, Sumantra and Bartlett, Christopher, *Managing Across Borders*, London, Random House, 1993.
Ketelhöhn, Werner, *International Business Strategy*, Oxford, Butterworth-Heinemann, 1993.
Lynch, Richard, *European Business Strategies*, London, Kogan Page, 1990.
Moran, Robert T. and Johnson, Michael, *Robert T. Moran's Cultural Guide to Doing Business in Europe*, Oxford, Butterworth-Heinemann, 1992.
Ricks, David, *Blunders in International Business*, Oxford, Blackwell Publishers, 1993.

Useful addresses

You may wish to find out more about some of the topics which comprise the subject of the business environment. If so, the following organizations are worth contacting for further information and advice:

Part One   Business organizations

Chartered Institute of Marketing, Moor Hall, Cookham, Maidenhead, Berkshire SL6 9QH. Tel: 06285 24922.

Chartered Institute of Transport, 80 Portland Place, London WC1. Tel: 071 636 9952.

Companies House, Crown Way, Maindy, Cardiff CF4 3UZ. Tel: 0222 388588.

Co-operative Development Agency, Broadmead House, 21 Panton Street, London SW1Y 4DR. Tel: 071 839 2988.

Institute of Directors, 116 Pall Mall, London SW1Y 5ED. Tel: 071 839 1233.

Institute of Purchasing and Supply, Easton House, Easton on the Hill, Stamford, Lincolnshire PE9 3NZ. Tel: 0780 56777.

Institute of Small Businesses, 13 Golden Square, London, W1R 4AL. Tel: 071 437 4923.

Small Firms Service, Steel House, Tothill Street, London SW1H 9HF. Tel: 273 3000.

Part Two   Business resources

Advisory, Conciliation and Arbitration Services, 11–12 St James Square, London SW1Y 4LA. Tel: 071 210 3000.

Association of Investment Trust Companies, Park House, 16 Finsbury Circus, London EC2M 7JJ. Tel: 071 588 5347.

British Venture Capital Association, 1 Surrey Street, London WC2R 2PS. Tel: 071 836 5702.

Central Office of the Industrial Tribunals, 93 Ebury Bridge Road, London SW1W 8RE. Tel: 071 730 9161.

Chartered Institute of Bankers, Emmanuel House, Burgate Lane, Canterbury, Kent CT1 2XJ. Tel: 0227 762600.

Commission for Racial Equality, Elliot House, 10–12 Allington Street, London SW1E 5EH. Tel: 071 828 7022.

Equal Opportunities Commission, Overseas House, Quay Street, Manchester M3 3HN. Tel: 061 833 9244.

Institute of Administrative Management, 40 Chatsworth Parade, Petts Wood, Orpington, Kent BR5 1RW. Tel: 0689 875555.

Institute of Personnel and Development, IPD House, Camp Road, Wimbledon, London SW19 4HW. Tel: 081 946 9100.

National Association of Pension Funds, 12–18 Grosvenor Gardens, London SW1W 0DH. Tel: 071 730 0585.

Society of Pension Consultants, Ludgate House, Ludgate Circus, London EC4A 2AB. Tel: 071 353 1688.

Training Agency, Moorfoot, Sheffield, Yorkshire S1 4PW. Tel: 0742 753275.

Unit Trust Association, 65 Kingsway, London WC2B 6TD. Tel: 071 831 0898.

Part Three Business markets

Office of Fair Trading, Field House, 15–25 Bream's Buildings, London EC4A 1PR. Tel: 071 242 2858.

Monopolies and Mergers Commission, New Court, 48 Carey Street, London WC2A 2JT. Tel: 071 324 1467.

Restrictive Practices Court, Field House, 15–25 Bream's Buildings, London EC4 1PR. Tel: 071 242 2858.

Part Four The local and national environment

Central Statistical Office, Great George Street, London SW1P 3AQ. Tel: 071 233 3000.

Her Majesty's Stationery Office, 51 Nine Elms Lane, London SW8 5DR. Tel: 071 873 0011.

Part Five The international environment

British Consultants Bureau, 1–7 Artillery Row, London SW1P 1RJ. Tel: 071 222 3651.

British Exporters Association, 16 Dartmouth Street, London SW1H 9BL. Tel: 071 222 5419.

British Importers Confederation, 69 Cannon Street, London EC4N 5AB. Tel: 071 248 4444.

Confederation of British Industry, Centre Point, 103 New Oxford Street, London WC1A 1DU. Tel: 071 379 7400.

Customs and Excise, New Kings Beam House, 22 Upper Ground, London SE1 9PS. Tel: 071 620 1313.

Department of Trade and Industry, 1–19 Victoria Street, London SW1H OET. Tel: 071 215 5000.

European Business Foundation, 1 St Mary's Place, London W5 5HA. Tel: 081 579 4688.

European Commission Office, 8 Storey's Gate, London SW1P 3AT. Tel: 071 973 1992.

Institute of Export, Export House, 64 Clifton Street, London EC2A 4NB. Tel: 071 247 9812.

Institute of Freight Forwarders, Redfern House, Browells Lane, Feltham, Middlesex TW13 7EP. Tel: 081 844 2266.

Institute of Linguists, 24a Highbury Grove, London N5 2EA. Tel: 071 359 7445.

Institute of Management Consultants, 32–33 Hatton Garden, London EC1N 8DL. Tel: 071 242 2140.

Institute of Translation and Interpreting, 318a Finchley Road, London NW3 5HT. Tel: 071 794 9931.

Language Excellence Centres, PO Box 1574, Regents College, Inner Circle, Regents Park, London NW1 4NJ. Tel: 061 224 3748.

Law Society, 113 Chancery Lane, London WC2A 1PL. Tel: 071 242 1222.

Management Consultancies Association, 11 West Halkin Street, London SW1X 8JL. Tel: 071 235 3897.

Simpler Trade Procedures Board, Venture House, 29 Glasshouse Street, London W1R 5RG. Tel: 071 287 3525.

Technical Help for Exporters, Linford Wood, Milton Keynes MK14 6LE. Tel: 0908 220022.

Glossary

There will have been some words and phrases used in the text which you will wish to refer to again, perhaps to refresh your memory or to check your understanding of them. Many of the key words and expressions in the book were highlighted in italics and are repeated or expanded upon here. If you cannot find what you are looking for, you will need to study the index on pages 307 to 312.

Act of Parliament　A bill which has received royal assent and become law. Also known as a statute.

After Sight Bill　A document which demands payment of a particular sum of money from the recipient at a specified date in the future. Also called a term draft.

Articles of Association　A document which specifies the internal affairs of a company.

Authorized capital　The total value of the shares which a company is allowed to issue according to its Memorandum of Association.

Balance of trade　The difference between a country's visible exports and imports. Known more formally as the visible balance.

Balancing item　A figure recorded in a country's balance of payments statement which takes account of likely errors and omissions made when recording trade activities.

Bill　A proposed law which is in the process of being passed through Parliament.

Bill of exchange　A document which demands payment of a specified sum of money from the recipient at a paticular time. Also known as a draft.

Birth rate　The number of live births per 1000 of the population each year.

Boom　A period of time characterized by high levels of demand, business output and employment.

Business An organization which produces and/or distributes goods and/or services for profit.

Business cycle A repetitive series of fluctuations in the levels of business activity, invariably linked to demand.

Business plan A document which details the commercial and financial activities of a firm, verifying them with supporting material in appendices.

Buyers' market A market in which more goods and services are being provided by sellers than are required by buyers, so stocks remain unsold and prices drop. Clearly, this is to the buyers' advantage.

Capital exports Capital which is located abroad in the form of bank deposits or investments in shares or physical assets.

Capital imports Capital which is placed in the home country by foreign organizations or individuals and invested in bank deposits, shares or physical assets.

Cash flow The flow of monies which come into and go out of a business as sales are made and bills are paid.

Certificate of incorporation A document issued to a company by the Registrar of Companies authorizing it to commence trading.

Committee stage An advanced stage in the passage of a bill through Parliament, during which a cross section of twenty to forty MPs study proposals and suggest amendments.

Concentric diversification A situation whereby a business expands into different markets by producing similar goods and services to its existing ones.

Conglomerate A business which trades in various, unrelated areas and activities.

Constructive dismissal A situation in which an employee feels forced to resign because of his or her firm's unreasonable behaviour. To all intents and purposes it amounts to a dismissal.

Cooperatives An organization which is owned and run on a democratic basis by its workers.

Creditors Those organizations and individuals to whom a business owes money.

Current account balance The sum of the visible and invisible balances within the balance of payments statement.

Customs declaration A signed statement detailing the contents of parcels and packages being exported and imported.

De facto authority The informal capacity to exercise power, typically through respect.

De jure authority The formal right to exercise power, invariably through position.

Death rate The number of deaths per 1000 of the population each year.

Declaration of dangerous goods A statement required to export and import potentially harmful items such as explosives.

Depression A period of time characterized by low demand in relation to supply capacity, resulting in unsold stocks, low output levels and high unemployment.

Draft A document which demands payment of a specified sum of money from the recipient at a particular time. Also called a bill of exchange.

Early settlement discount A trade discount offered by a supplier to persuade a customer to settle an invoice relatively quickly. Also known as a prompt payment discount.

Enterprise Allowance Scheme A government-backed scheme whereby people signing off the unemployment register to become self-employed receive regular sums of money for a set period.

Executive An all-embracing phrase used to describe those State organizations responsible for implementing laws, namely central government, its departments and agencies and local authorities.

Expenditure variance The difference between the anticipated and actual overhead costs of a product or service.

Export licence A licence which is required by firms planning to export some types of goods and/or to certain destinations.

Factor An organization which pursues outstanding debts due to other firms, in exchange for a percentage of the monies collected.

First reading An early stage in the passage of a bill through Parliament, whereby it is announced to the House of Commons or the House of Lords, as appropriate.

Fixed capital investment The investment on assets of long-term use to a business, typically equipment and machinery.

Fully integrated A situation whereby a firm is involved in the production and distribution process from beginning to end.

Functional relationship A relationship which exists between employees working in different functional departments within the same organization.

Geographical distribution   The distribution of the population across different regions of a country.

Green Paper   A document which outlines the government's ideas with regard to a new bill.

Gross domestic product   The value of the total output of all of the economic activities of a country over a given period of time.

Gross national product   Gross domestic product plus or minus net property incomes from abroad.

Health certificate   A document which is needed to verify the good health of animals being exported and imported.

Horizontal business   A firm which specializes in a single activity within the production and distribution sequence.

Hot money   Speculative capital used by organizations and individuals trying to maximize their returns from investments.

Human resources   Managers and employees within a business, viewed as useful items rather than as people.

Import licence   A licence which is required by firms planning to import some types of goods and/or from certain countries.

Induction   The process of installing a recruit into his or her new job.

Inertia selling   A business practice whereby unrequested goods are sent to organizations and individuals in the hope that they will be purchased.

Insolvency   A situation in which a firm's liabilities exceed its assets and debts cannot be paid.

Instalment credit   A payment arrangement whereby an organization or an individual purchases an item by making an initial payment followed by a series of regular, additional payments to cover the balance, plus administration and interest charges. Better known as hire purchase, or 'HP'.

Investment appraisal   The process of assessing the costs of, and returns from, investment opportunities.

Investment capital   The finance put into a business by its owners.

Investment and capital flows account   An account within the balance of payments statement which sets out all of the investment and capital transfers into and out of a country.

Invisible exports   Services which are provided for overseas businesses and/or individuals either in the home country and/or abroad, and that produce foreign currencies for that home country.

Invisible imports Services which are supplied to domestic firms and/or people by foreign bodies either in the domestic country and/or abroad, and that result in outgoings of foreign currencies from that domestic country.

Invisible trade The trade in invisible services between home and overseas organizations and individuals.

Invitation to treat An invitation for prospective buyers to make an offer which may or may not be accepted.

Issued capital The value of the capital issued to the shareholders of a company in the form of shares.

Judiciary Those organizations and individuals responsible for dealing with disputes arising from the passing and implementation of laws, most notably civil and criminal courts.

Labour efficiency variance The difference between the estimated and actual labour costs of a product or service, attributable to more or less time being taken than expected.

Labour rate variance The difference between the anticipated and actual labour costs of a product or service, attributable to more or less wages being paid than expected.

Lateral relationship A relationship which exists between two employees working alongside each other in the same department.

Lease A contractual agreement between a landlord and a tenant of a property. 'To lease' simply means to rent.

Legislature Those organizations and individuals responsible for passing laws, most notably Parliament.

Letter of credit A letter of confirmation provided by a bank or other financial institution promising to make a payment to an organization or individual on receipt of certain documents.

Limited/Ltd Word or abbreviation which must, by law, be added to a private limited company's name to indicate that its owners have limited liability for its debts.

Limited partnership A partnership in which some partners have limited liability so that their responsibility for debts is limited to the amount of money they have invested in that partnership.

Line relationship A relationship which exists between a superior and a subordinate.

Liquidator An organization appointed by a court to take charge of an insolvent company, to collect its assets, pay off debts and distribute the remaining funds as appropriate.

Loan capital Finance provided by a bank or another financial institution.

Loan Guarantee Scheme A government-backed scheme whereby businesses or individuals without sufficient assets to offer as security can borrow money which is part-guaranteed by the government.

Loss leader A product or service sold at a loss in order to attract customers to it, or to other goods and services.

Materials price variance The difference between the estimated and actual cost of materials, attributable to higher or lower prices than expected.

Materials quantity variance The difference between the anticipated and actual cost of materials, attributable to more or less material being used than expected.

Memorandum of Association A document which specifies the relationship between a company and the outside world.

Money supply The stocks of money in an economy.

Multinational A company which owns outlets in more than one country.

Net migration The difference between the number of people leaving and entering a population.

Net national product Gross national product less an allowance for the depreciation of a country's capital items used to produce output.

Occupational distribution The distribution of the working population between various types of occupation.

Open account An account whereby goods are despatched with an invoice and are subsequently paid for by the recipient at a mutually agreed time. It operates on trust.

Ordinary share A share in a company which may entitle the holder to an appropriate dividend in a successful trading year.

Paid up capital The amount of capital which has been paid for by the shareholders of a company.

Partnership The relationship which exists between people running a business together with a view to making a profit.

Physical resources An all-embracing phrase which describes any physical item used within an organization.

Preference share A share in a company which entitles the holder to a guaranteed dividend each year.

Price discrimination   A pricing policy whereby a firm varies its prices for the same goods and services in different markets.

Price index   A weighted average of the prices of a mix of products and services produced in the economy over a given period of time.

Primary business   A business which is involved in extracting raw materials from above or below the ground.

Private limited company   A business owned by shareholders and managed by a board of directors. Shareholders and directors are often one and the same in this type of company.

Pro forma invoice   An invoice which must be paid before goods are despatched or made available for collection.

Productivity   The relationship between the resources that have gone into producing output and the resulting levels of output.

Prompt payment discount   A trade discount offered by a supplier to persuade a customer to settle an invoice fairly promptly. Also referred to as an early settlement discount.

Public limited company/plc   A business owned by shareholders and managed by a board of directors appointed by them.

Pure diversification   A situation whereby a firm grows into alternative markets by producing goods and services which are wholly different to those in its existing range.

Quota   A restriction on the types and/or numbers of goods which can be brought into a country over a given period of time.

Recession   A period of time characterized by falling demand, output and employment.

Recovery   A period of time characterized by increasing demand, output and employment.

Regional Enterprise grant   A grant given to a business locating in a neglected area of the country.

Report stage   An advanced stage in the procedure of a bill whereby it is passed back in revised form from the committee of MPs to the House of Commons or the House of Lords for further debate.

Reserve capital   The unpaid capital of a company which can only be called up when that company is to cease trading and has to settle debts.

Retail Price Index   A weighted average of the prices of some 600 products and services commonly used by the general public over a given period of time.

Sales price variance   The difference between the budgeted and actual value of sales attributable to higher or lower selling prices than expected.

Sales volume variance   The difference between the estimated and actual value of sales attributable to a higher or lower volume of sales than expected.

Second reading   An early stage in the passage of a bill whereby its principles are debated in the House of Commons or the House of Lords.

Secondary firm   A business which is involved in manufacturing and/or processing products.

Secured loan   A loan against which a borrower has provided assets as security in case of non repayment.

Sellers' market   A market in which more goods and services are required by buyers than are being provided by sellers, so buyers compete against each other and prices rise. Obviously, this is to the sellers' benefit.

Share capital   Finance put into a company by its owners in return for shares.

Shareholder   A part owner of a private or public limited company who enjoys limited liability for its debts.

Sight bill/draft   A document which demands immediate payment of a specified sum of money from the recipient.

Single Market/1992   An agreement made by European Union heads of government in 1985 whereby trade barriers within the Union would be removed by the end of 1992.

Slump   A period of time characterized by low levels of demand, output and employment.

Sole trader   An individual who owns and controls his or her own business. Also known as a sole proprietor.

Staff management   An all-purpose term used to describe those activities associated with handling employees, from induction through disciplining and motivating to dismissal.

Staff relationship   A relationship which exists between a manager and an employee who answers to him or her alone. That employee does not have a line relationship with other employees in the organization.

Statute   A bill which has become law after receiving royal assent. Also called an Act of Parliament.

Statutory quota A formal and binding quota imposed by government.

Tariff A tax charged on some or all imports to make them more expensive and unattractive in the home market.

Term draft A document which demands payment of a specified sum of money from the recipient at a particular date in the future. Also known as an after sight bill.

Tertiary firm A business which is involved in supplying services to its customers.

Third reading A stage in the passage of a bill whereby the House of Commons or the House of Lords has the final opportunity to debate that bill.

Trade gap The deficit between a country's visible imports and exports.

Ultra vires A situation whereby a company acts outside of its legal powers.

Unit A part of an investment fund controlled by a unit trust.

Unit holder The owner of units of an investment fund.

Unlimited liability A situation whereby an individual cannot limit his or her liability to debts only to his or her business assets. He or she is personally and fully responsible for debts.

Unpaid capital The proportion of the capital not yet paid to a company by its shareholders.

Unsecured loan A loan which is provided without the need for any security.

Variance analysis The process of comparing the differences between the budgeted and actual results of a firm's activities.

Vertical firm A business which combines two or more related activities within the production and distribution chain.

Visible export Products made in the home country and transported and sold to foreign countries, thus earning foreign currencies for that home country.

Visible import Goods which are produced overseas and then brought to, and sold in, the domestic country, consequently leading to an outflow of foreign currencies from that country.

Visible trade The trade in visible products between home and overseas organizations and individuals.

Volume variance   The difference between the estimated and actual volume produced, sold or whatever.

Voluntary quota   A quota agreed informally by and between various organizations.

Weight note   A document which details the gross weight of packages.

White Paper   A document which outlines government policy with regard to prospective legislation.

Working capital investment   The investment on assets of short-term use to business, typically raw materials, component parts and finished goods for resale.

Working population   The total number of people between the ages of sixteen and sixty-five who are looking, or available, for work.

Index

An index should help you to find your way around a book. Too short, and you are left flicking from page to page trying to spot a particular word, phrase or topic. Too long, and you spend all your time going from one reference to another to find a relevant one. Hopefully, this index strikes a balance by incorporating the key words and references you are most likely to need and find useful.